Jeff Davis's Own

COLORADO

KANSAS

Ft. Atkinson

⚔ Fight on Crooked Creek

NEW

OKLAHOMA

Canadian R.

Antelope Hills

Camp Radziminski ⋈

•Wichita Village
⋈ Ft. Arbuckle

MEXICO Llano Estacado

Red R.

Camp Cooper ⋈ Ft. Belknap
Double Mountain ⋀ ■ •Jacksboro
Comanche ▦ Brazos • Dallas
Reserve Reserve

Trinity R.

Big Spring• Ft. Chadbourne

⋈ Camp Colorado

■ Site of
Parker's Fort

Horse Head
Crossing Approximate line
of frontier →
settlements in 1860

TEXAS

Traditional
Comanche war
trail to Mexico

⋈Ft. Mason

Brazos R.

Devil's R.

Camp Hudson Fredricksburg •Austin

Rio Grande ⋈Camp Verde

Colorado R.

Ft. Clarke •San Antonio

⋈Ft. Inge

⋈ Ft. Merrill

MEXICO

GULF
OF
MEXICO

⋈ Ft. McIntosh

Comanche Country
and Adjacent
Territory in 1860

Laredo•

Ringgold Barracks •Rio Grande City Arroyo Colorado
Edinburg• •Brownsville
Reynosa• Matamoros

© 2000 by D. L. McElhannon

Jeff Davis's Own

Cavalry, Comanches, and the Battle for the Texas Frontier

James R. Arnold

John Wiley & Sons, Inc.

New York • Chichester • Weinheim • Brisbane • Singapore • Toronto

Published by John Wiley & Sons, Inc.
Published simultaneously in Canada.

This publication is designed to provide accurate and authoritative information in regard to the subject matter covered. It is sold with the understanding that the publisher is not engaged in rendering professional services. If professional advice or other expert assistance is required, the services of a competent professional person should be sought.

Library of Congress Cataloging-in-Publication Data

Arnold, James R.
    Jeff Davis's own : cavalry, comanches, and the battle for the Texas frontier / James R. Arnold.
       p. cm.
    Includes bibliographical references and index.
    ISBN 0-471-33364-6 (cloth : alk. paper)
    1. United States. Army. Cavalry, 2nd—History. 2. Indians of North America—Wars—1815–1875. 3. Indians of North America—Wars—Texas. I. Title.

UA31 2nd .A75   2000
357'.183'097309034—dc21   00-021316

Contents

Acknowledgments

I GRATEFULLY WISH to thank Jon Bigler for his research at the Library of Congress; Grace McCrowell at the Rockbridge Regional Library, who diligently helped track down obscure sources and whose effort was indispensable; John Slonaker for helping guide me around the holdings at the Military History Institute, Carlisle, Penn. It was a pleasure renewing acquaintances with the research staff at the National Archives. Mike Musick was particularly helpful at pointing me in the right direction. The librarians and staff at the University of Virginia, Virginia Military Institute, and Washington and Lee University extended every courtesy, for which I am especially appreciative. I am delighted to work again with Hana Lane at John Wiley & Sons: no writer could ask for a more supportive editor. Also at Wiley, Michael Thompson performed many helpful chores to keep this project on track. Chuck Antony completed a valuable copyedit. Benjamin Hamilton coordinated our production efforts with efficiency and good cheer. José Almaguer designed the cover. After eighteen or so books, one runs out of ways to express thanks anew, so I simply say thank you again to my soul mate, Roberta.

Prologue

Comanche Moon

AFTER A LONG ABSENCE, Elder Daniel Parker returned from his mission to scout the Southwest. He reported to the members of his Pilgrim Predestination Baptist Church that he had found their new home. They were true believers: his command was theirs to obey. The following year, 1833, he led a wagon train carrying the pilgrims and their scant possessions on the long trek from Illinois to Austin's colony, in Texas.

An advance party led by John Parker reached the chosen ground, some eighty miles west of old Fort Houston, in December. Parker and his sons began immediately clearing brush and felling trees to build, first, a structure of critical importance, more important even than a place of worship: they built a stockade fort. The Parkers' chosen ground was in the middle of Indian country. Although the Pilgrim Predestination Baptist Church believed in spreading the gospel to the far corners of the world, when one of those corners lay in the middle of prime hunting land frequented by exceptionally warlike Indians, defense had first claim on labor and resources.

By the spring of 1834, thirty-one church members lived within the stockade. They were among the first white settlers to penetrate this wilderness. Their nearest neighbors were five buffalo hunters who homesteaded two miles to the north. But these men used their two crude cabins as a hunting camp and were seldom there. The closest sizable white settlement lay a three-day ride east. Because they were so isolated and because they knew that they lived in a dangerous country, the inhabitants of Parker's Fort maintained a rigorous security. During the daylight hours of that first spring, they cleared the nearby land for planting. At night they retired behind the palisades and closed and barred the main gate.

Life was good. The men easily supplied the tables with fresh game by hunting the nearby thickets. Everyone toiled in the fields, and their efforts began to bear fruit. Better still, there was little contact with Indians and no trouble whatsoever. Seasons passed in peace and prosperity. The settlers praised God for their good fortune, extended their labors to fields farther from the fort, and grew careless about routine safeguards. They took to leaving the main gate open; it required a hard effort to swing it closed at night, and this with tired muscles sore from tilling the soil. It was annoying, too, to heave it open again first thing in the morning before beginning chores. Annoying and unnecessary, so they stopped doing it. For convenience they also cut additional gates through the fort's walls, and they left them all open and un-guarded.

They had little notion of events outside their enclave, about Texas's armed insurrection against Mexico. In the spring of 1836, while most of Texas reeled in the aftermath of the death of Travis, Crockett, and Bowie at the Alamo, their thoughts cen-tered on spring planting. For Tom Plummer, L. D. Nixon, and James Parker, a fine May morning began like any other. They carried their hoes and mattocks out the main gate just as the sun rose above the trees, and set out for the distant fields. Behind them wisps of smoke rose from chimneys as their women began the day's first meal. The animals called for the morning feed. Children stirred. One adventuresome lad ran gaily through the gate. Suddenly, his screams shattered the quiet, signaling to everyone that this day was not like the others.

Parker's Fort's undefended blockhouse, adjacent to the gate Benjamin Parker closed in a futile effort to thwart raiding Indians in the spring of 1836. The fort is a modern reconstruction. (The Texas Collection, Baylor University)

Just beyond the gate stood a large band of Comanche and Kiowa warriors. They had emerged silently out of the nearby thicket and now stood gazing toward the fort as if assessing the defenses. The frightened settlers peered through the spaces between the logs at the line of mounted men. Their quick count soon exceeded a hundred. The settlers well knew that they were defenseless; their handful of rifles was in the possession of hunters who had departed before dawn. Someone noticed that an Indian had tied a white flag to the point of his lance. Maybe the Indians wanted to parley.

John's son Benjamin Parker was the first to react. He bravely left his cabin and walked to the main gate. He managed to close and bar it. Still the Indians remained motionless. Benjamin walked out another gate and approached the warriors. Using signs and a few words, he asked them what they wanted. A young warrior replied that the band was hungry and that they also wanted instructions to the nearest water hole. Benjamin Parker nodded and returned to the fort to relay the intelligence to his father.

The patriarch of the colony, Elder John Parker, must have wondered why the Indians were asking about the availability of water. To approach the fort they must have crossed the nearby Navasota River bottom. Perhaps hope or faith clouded his judgment; probably he could conceive of no alternative. He loaded Benjamin's arms with food and sent him out to buy off the warriors. Benjamin dutifully went outside again. Mastering his fear, he handed the gifts to an Indian. He hastily began walking back toward the stockade. The noise of galloping hooves was the last sound he heard. Several Comanches drove their barbed lances clean through his body. Inside Parker's Fort, the settlers watched in openmouthed horror. The air filled with war cries issuing from hundreds of throats. No one could mistake the cry of impending doom. Scores of Indians charged toward the fort. Panic-stricken women and children began running to their cabins, the homes that had been their sanctuary for three years. Behind them a surging wave of Indians poured into the stockade. At first contact, down went John Parker and his son Silas, both bludgeoned to death with war clubs. Samuel Frost and his young boy Robert died nearby. The ensuing thirty minutes witnessed bloody massacre.

Having killed all adult males, the Indians began an orgy of raping and looting. Then they collected the surviving women and children. Mrs. Silas Parker watched a warrior seize her nine-year-old daughter, Cynthia Ann, as well as Cynthia's younger brother, John. The Indians added the children to a small group of select individuals. Among the chosen was John Parker's daughter Rachel Plummer; young, fit, and four months pregnant, Rachel and her son, James, joined the prisoners. The killers herded their captives out the gate.

Her husband had heard the war cries and came running. Plummer and his two companions watched helplessly from a nearby thicket. Three unarmed men could do nothing against such odds. The last sight Plummer had of his wife and child was of them struggling on foot, trying to keep pace with the mounted Indians, threatened and cuffed if they lagged.

For six days the Indians harried their barefoot prisoners through thicket and over scrub desert. Torn and bleeding, they staggered on. Their first food came after two days, when the warriors contemptuously tossed a dead polecat into their midst. Two days later they provided a second skunk along with a few land turtles. It was only the beginning of a terrible ordeal.

No one endured a worse fate than Rachel Plummer. She traveled with her captors as they pursued their nomadic life. She lived on the margins, despised by most men and women alike because she was white, valued only for the work she could do. Six months after her capture she managed to bear a child, her second son. Although banished to the cold and snows outside the tepee whenever the baby cried, she managed to nurture it along for some five months. Then one day a group of young warriors seized the baby from her arms and began to strangle it. Plummer fought to save her son. The warriors knocked her to the ground. Someone tossed the baby into the air and let him plummet to the ground. After repeated tosses they handed the apparently lifeless body back to his mother. When the baby uttered a weak cry, they angrily took him again. They tied him to a lariat and threw him repeatedly into a stand of nearby cacti, dragging him back to his mother torn and bleeding. Finally they tied the lariat to a saddle and rode around in a triumphant circuit until what was left was hardly recognizable as a human being.

Over time, the Comanches and Kiowas traded most of the captives of Parker's Fort to other Indians. The going rate was one mule and one horse. In turn, these Indians traded them back to the whites. Sam Houston personally redeemed one captive for $150. After six years, a band of Indians brought Tom Plummer's boy to Fort Gibson, on the edge of the Indian Territory. The army ransomed the boy. No one heard of his mother's fate until some white buffalo hunters encountered her in a Comanche camp in the foothills of the Rocky Mountains. They traded for the captive, and she, too, returned home to Texas. Destroyed in spirit and body, Rachel Plummer did not live long. But the Comanches retained a few prisoners as slaves and raised others as members of the tribe. Among this select group were Cynthia Ann and John Parker.

The ordeal experienced by the captives of Parker's Fort was entirely typical. Settlers in Texas learned to fear the full moon, the Comanche moon, the time of nocturnal brightness that brought the silent raiders to their free-range herds and isolated ranches. From the time of the Texas Republic until well after the Civil War, Indians terrorized the Texas frontier. More than any other single incident, the massacre at Parker's Fort formed the attitude of Texas settlers toward the Indians. The fact that some of the captives were freed over a prolonged period of time kept the massacre in the public eye. Then there were the rumors, stories told at a distant remove of sightings of a woman believed to be Cynthia Ann Parker, who remained alive somewhere in the Llano Estacado, the Staked Plain, far beyond the Texas frontier. Later came tales of the emergence of a particularly audacious Indian leader, of a man who seemed preternaturally able to evade the combined might of the U.S. Army and the Texas Rangers. But always there was the lunar cycle, the waxing moon, the coming of the Comanche moon.

Nearly twenty-four years after the attack on Parker's Fort, a detachment of troopers belonging to the Second United States Cavalry, operating with a group of Texas Rangers, found a blue-eyed Indian woman. She had forgotten her language, yet when she heard a familiar sequence of sounds, she pointed at herself. Against her very strongly held will, Cynthia Ann Parker was liberated. Thirty-nine years after the attack, the much-feared leader of the last band of wild Comanches rode into Fort Sill to surrender. His name was Quanah Parker.

Thereafter, the Comanche moon was feared no more.

1

"Jeff Davis's Own"

The duty of repressing hostilities among the Indian tribes, and of protect-ing frontier settlements from their depredations, is the most difficult one which the Army has now to perform; and no where has it been found more difficult than on the Western frontier of Texas.

— Secretary of War Jefferson Davis, 1853 (in Davis
to Bell, September 19, 1853, in Dunbar Rowland,
ed., *Jefferson Davis, Constitutionalist: His Letters,
Papers, and Speeches*, vol. 2)

TEXAS. Unimaginably vast. More than six times the size of Ohio, about three times the size of Great Britain, larger than France. Only recently ascended to the constellation of state stars that appeared on the national flag, much of this outsized territory was little known to white men. Bold and enterprising army officers had tried to measure Texas's ill-defined frontier and concluded that it stretched some 1,400 to 1,700 miles. To defend this frontier against Indian attack and to fight the Indians elsewhere, in 1855 Congress resolved to raise two new regiments of cavalry. For army officers facing stalled careers (the overwhelming majority in the small regular army of the 1850s), the new regiments presented a priceless opportunity for promotion. Throughout the nation they anxiously waited for a message from the War Department. Only a select handful received the coveted missive.

Their wait was merely one more challenge from an organization that seemed to delight in thwarting ambition. Indeed, the antebellum United States Army tested a man's character, revealing much. Most officers served in small frontier garrisons, where boredom and isolation reigned supreme. Their duties seldom provided zealous officers with an avenue for either intellectual or military betterment. Some became indolent, others fell to drink. Prospects for promotion were so poor—a West Point graduate could anticipate a wait of more than fifty years before becoming a colonel—that many gifted leaders resigned to pursue alternatives. The entire army had only two major generals and four brigadiers. A suspicious, parsimonious Congress established a rule of law that provided that no vacancies be filled until this number fell to one major general and two brigadiers. So men of talent, and those who believed they possessed talent, waited until either death or rare chance gave them an opportunity to ascend the lofty heights where one wore a colonel's or a general's insignia. Meanwhile, West Point cadets and graduates alike sang the old drinking song, "May the army be augmented—may promotion be less slow," and they sang it with feeling.[1] In spite of it all, Lieutenant Colonel Robert Edward Lee had stuck with it. Yet he, too, had been unable to capitalize upon his sterling reputation, a reputation gained during the glory times of the war against Mexico.

In 1847, just eight years before Congress issued the call for the new regiments, Captain Lee had served as the principal prop upon which General Winfield Scott had leaned as he plotted his advance to Mexico City. It was Lee who found a way to outflank the Mexican fortifications on the Acapulco Road, and Lee who had guided the assault column against Chapultepec. It was Lee who opened the door to the Halls of Montezuma. He had received promotion to brevet lieutenant colonel. Yet the brevet rank was largely honorific, and it could not and did not substitute for a true promotion.[2] Moreover, a man could remain at a brevet rank year after year, and so it proved for Lee. He stayed a brevet lieutenant colonel, his glory years seemingly behind him, growing older, stagnating, and failing to see any alternative.

The long hoped for message from the War Department found him at West Point, where he was immersed in his duties as superintendent of the U.S. Military Academy. It contained an appointment to the Second U.S. Cavalry. Despite all of its coveted promise, the appointment was a mixed blessing. On the one hand it offered promotion, which otherwise would be problematic. But he was already drawing pay as a colonel by brevet and he enjoyed his service at West Point. Cavalry service would require living on the frontier. It also involved a transfer from his beloved engineering service. Lee had thoroughly mastered the scientific details required of an army engineer and enjoyed a national reputation. To switch to the cavalry required, if not a leap into the unknown, then a step into unfamiliar duty because he had not studied cavalry tactics since his days as a cadet at West Point, twenty-six years earlier. In the end, he had little choice. Lee placed a high value on duty. He was also ambitious. To decline would mean permanent removal from the promotion ladder. So he abandoned the comforts of West Point and set out for regimental headquarters at Louisville, Kentucky.

In contrast, when a War Department message addressed to Brevet Second Lieutenant John Bell Hood reached Fort Jones, California, the young officer received it without equivocation. Brevet second lieutenants were a dime a dozen; the rank was a reward for surviving West Point. Hood was one of too many graduates for whom there was no permanent position. Moreover, Hood had found duty in California, "this country of gold and extravagance," expensive on a salary of $60 a month.[3] True, to make ends meet and perhaps do a bit better, he had recently invested in land on which to sow a large crop of wheat. His experienced eye—at age fifteen he had managed his father's

11

farm—anticipated that this effort would yield a fine profit in the inflated northern California market. But an appointment as second lieutenant in the Second Cavalry might illuminate his military rather than his agricultural skills, so he accepted without reservation. He trusted that his new friend and business partner, Lieutenant George Crook, could manage the harvest. After Lieutenant Philip Sheridan relieved him at Fort Jones, Hood began his return east by riding to San Francisco. Here he secured funds for his travels at the Lucas, Turner & Company bank, run by a former military man with a "piercing eye and nervous impulsive temperament," William Tecumseh Sherman. Then he set sail for New York City en route to report for duty at Jefferson Barracks, Missouri.[4] There he would receive his portion of the profits for his wheat investment, a neat $1,000 in gold.

In Texas, a young, troubled man named Charles E. Travis greeted his appointment to the cavalry with joy. Within the state, he possessed unsurpassed public recognition because he was the living embodiment of Texas's greatest legend. Charles Travis's father was the Travis of Alamo fame. Side by side with Crockett, Bowie, and the others, his father had fought a sacrificial battle to secure liberty. Charles Travis had not quite lived up to his big name. He reckoned that serving as a captain in the Second Cavalry would help him see his way toward solid achievement and renown commensurate with his birthright.

WHEN LEE, HOOD, AND TRAVIS entered the cavalry, it was a branch of the service that held an undistinguished tradition within the U.S. Army. During the American Revolution, the Continental Congress had authorized the formation of four dragoon regiments. In theory a dragoon trooper was equally capable of fighting on horse and on foot. In practice some unhappy form of compromise usually arose. Equipment suitable for mounted combat—stiff riding boots and sabers, to name two examples—made dismounted movement awkward. Training for a horse soldier sought to persuade him that no opposing line of infantry could withstand a determined cavalry charge. If this was somewhat short of the truth, it did at least instill the requisite dash and élan. Had dragoon training ended there it probably would have produced a serviceable cavalryman. But then the dragoon received infantry training, which naturally taught that a heart-of-oak line of footmen could repel any mounted attack. So, while the confused dragoon learned that he was neither fish nor fowl, he was made keenly aware of the perils associated with both mounted and dismounted combat.

Except in the southern theater late in the war, the Continental dragoons contributed little to the American war effort. In passing it is well to note that among the Continental army's mounted units was a highly capable outfit commanded by Major Henry "Light-Horse Harry" Lee, Robert's father. The Continental Congress quickly mastered the fact that maintaining a cavalry regiment was considerably more expensive than maintaining one of infantry. Troopers required special equipment such as saddles and bridles, and none of it came cheap. The purchase of suitable horses was more expensive, and worse, the equines displayed a shocking proclivity toward disabling disease and even death while not on campaign, and an inability to dodge bullets and cannonballs while in battle. The shrewd economists in Congress also observed that horses ate more than lowly foot soldiers. So to save money, until 1833 mounted units were typically recruited only in response to emergencies, and then disbanded as soon as possible.

By that year the United States was confronting an ongoing emergency against a numerous mounted foe against whom infantry could accomplish little. The Indians of the Great Plains were unsurpassed horsemen, akin to irregular light cavalry, who specialized in hit-and-run raids. To cope with them Congress authorized the First Regiment of Dragoons. A Second Dragoon Regiment followed three years later, its colonel a David E. Twiggs, who would later be district commander when the Second Cavalry went to Texas. The war with Mexico produced the Third Dragoons as well as the Mounted Rifles Regiment. Four regiments of cavalry were very few indeed for an army engaged in an invasion of Mexico and a defense of the sprawling territory west of the Mississippi. Victory over Mexico brought a heavier burden. The annexation of Texas and the settlement of the dispute with Great Britain over the Oregon Territory increased the nation's territory by two-thirds. In keeping with the lack of logic that has typified the political response to increased national responsibilities, Congress reduced the army to its lowest strength since 1838. However, since unfriendly Indians occupied most of the new territory, Congress did not disband the cavalry following the war with Mexico. Yet they were not enough to protect the white citizens who eagerly settled the new acquisitions or to guard the constant streams of wagon trains carrying emigrants to the California goldfields and to Oregon. Nowhere was this more true than in Texas.

The War Department based the defense of the Texas frontier upon a chain of forts. Scarcely had the chinking set between the forts' logs than settlers, in their lust for virgin country, moved past them. Located behind the expanding frontier, the weakly manned outposts neither kept Indian raiders from stabbing at Texans living on the frontier nor deterred them from continuing their habitual raids into Mexico. This latter behavior brought the Indian conflict into the realm of foreign policy. The war-ending agreement with Mexico, the Treaty of Guadalupe Hidalgo, compelled the United States to keep its hostile Indians out of Mexico. The American negotiators who accepted this term were blithely unaware of the magnitude of the obligation they were imposing upon the army.

14

Neither had the Comanches, the Kiowas, and their fellow spirits been consulted about the treaty, and they cared not one whit for its terms. As soon as grass emerged in the spring, from as far away as the river Platte they rode to the staging area at the Big Springs of the Colorado. From here they rode south to collect horses, prisoners, scalps, and other desirable loot from hapless Mexicans. So much Indian traffic moved along these war trails that they appeared on period maps of the region. A Texas scout describes coming across them: "Twenty-five deep worn and much used trails made a great road, which told us that this was a highway by which each year the Comanche of the North desolate Durango and Chihuahua."[5] In the decade following the treaty, 652 Mexicans were killed, wounded, or captured in the state of Nuevo León alone. Raids were so ferocious that the settlement line in northern Mexico actually receded, leaving behind a ruined, empty region termed the Desert of the Frontier.

For a brief time in the early 1850s, federal and state troops began successfully interdicting the war trails to Mexico. Several chiefs complained to the Department of the Interior's Indian agents that the troops were preventing them from going to Mexico to obtain horses and mules "as they had always done."[6] The Comanches responded in the same way the North Vietnamese would respond to American efforts to interdict passage along the Ho Chi Minh Trail in the 1960s; they made new trails, farther away from military bases. In Texas, these new invasion paths to the west and north helped prompt the government to construct a new line of frontier forts. When troops moved to western Texas to garrison these forts, the Comanches slid in behind the forts, returning to northern Texas to attack the exposed frontier. Even the area a long distance from the frontier, including ranches within twenty miles of Austin and in the region around San Antonio, became occasional targets. The army in Texas discovered, as would their successors in Vietnam one hundred or so years in the future, that its ability to provide security for civilians did not extend beyond gunshot range of its outposts.

Part of the problem was that the mix of forces assigned to defend Texas was wrong. Twenty of the twenty-eight regular companies were infantry, and they were next to useless for repelling some of the world's most expert horsemen. A Texan asked the House of Representatives if members could "conceive of anything more absurd than starting in pursuit of the flying Comanche in a wagon drawn by mules?"[7] By the mid-1850s, the Comanches had long practice at evading frontier outposts and their infantry garrisons. The army's horsemen, eight companies of Dragoons and Mounted Rifles, were spread too thin to seriously annoy Indian raiders. In the spring of 1854, a resident of Laredo described the situation to Texas governor Elisha Pease: "I do not know how you can help us. The nine companies of infantry here have not twenty horses in their stables. The rifles [Mounted Rifles] are sixty miles off, and before we can send news to them of the depredations the Indians are gone beyond pursuit . . . the Indians stole last night all the loose horses grazing around the town, and left one dead, shot with arrows, within one hundred yards of the outside houses of the town—panic prevails."[8]

A typical petition to the governor from the inhabitants of Bexar County was a woeful list of stolen stock and murdered women and children: "It is worse than idle to say the Indians are not at war. If the action of regularly organized bands from the Lipan, Comanche, Waco and Tawakoni, robbing murdering and ravishing, and carrying into captivity women and children does not constitute a State of war, we are at a loss to define the meaning of war among barbarians."[9] Although about a fourth of the entire army was already in Texas, the three-thousand-odd soldiers were unequal to demands of fighting this war.

General Winfield Scott, commanding general of the army and one of the top-flight senior leaders the nation has ever pro-

Savage, persistent Indian attacks on the Texas frontier convinced Congress to expand the army. (*Harper's Weekly*, May 1, 1858)

duced, recognized these problems. He went before Congress in 1853 to explain why the army needed to be expanded. Congress denied his request. The following year Scott tried again. Testifying before a skeptical Congress, Scott reduced the issue to something the meanest understanding could grasp. Indian raids into Texas were more destructive than at any other place in the nation. Even when the soldiers were successful, casualties were too high. The loss rate was in inverse proportion to the strength of the unit involved: small units lost or won, but suffered dearly; larger units won and suffered fewer losses. Scott concluded that considerations both of policy (the treaty obligation to keep Indians from raiding Mexico) and of humanity dictated an expansion of the army "in order that adequate protection may be afforded to our border inhabitants without a useless sacrifice of our brave detachments."[10]

As straightforward as Scott's logic may seem, at the time it fueled an acrimonious Senate debate. From the times of the Founding Fathers, most Americans had held a strong mistrust of a regular, or standing, army. American Revolutionary leaders had received classical educations complete with histories of Roman generals using their legions to undo the republic. Their fathers had family knowledge of Oliver Cromwell ordering his musketeers to expel the Long Parliament and of a subsequent Parliament declaring a Bill of Rights that charged King James II with subverting liberties by maintaining a standing army in time of peace. Consequently, they, too, believed that standing armies led to the despotism of military dictatorship. Most concluded that a democratic nation should instead depend upon its militia, citizen-soldiers summoned for duty in emergencies and then dismissed. At the end of the American Revolution, the public largely believed that a patriotic militia—sharpshooters all (though in fact they were anything but), possessing native field craft (a talent that most, except the southern frontiersmen, had long lost) and motivated by a sense of public virtue—had won freedom from the Crown. Thereafter, the justification for the existence of a regular army became a central part of the postwar political battle for control of the Revolution's legacy. Then politicians displayed their timeless ability to select the lessons they preferred from the historical record and argue their cases with great fervor.

In the 1850s many still viewed any proposed army expansion suspiciously. One of their spokesmen was Senator Sam Houston of Texas. Back in 1850 the army had added, at considerable expense, five thousand more soldiers to its roster, in large part to confront the Indians in Texas. But they had not added to the state's security. As one keen-eyed traveler who journeyed across Texas wrote, "Keeping a bull-dog to chase musquitoes [*sic*] would be no greater nonsense than the stationing of six-pounders, bayonets, and dragoons for the pursuit of these red wolves."[11] Houston observed that in the days of the Texas Republic, the expenses of the Indian war did not exceed $10,000 and the people enjoyed better protection than they currently received with the presence of numerous regulars. Now the administration proposed raising even more expensive cavalry units, and Houston had no doubt that the increased costs would not yield improved security.

The opposition camp also included Senator Thomas Benton of Missouri. He did not care for the army and abused them loudly, calling them "schoolhouse officers and pothouse soldiers."[12] He doubted that President Franklin Pierce and Secretary of War Jefferson Davis truly intended the new regiments as relief for the frontier. More likely, he thundered, the object was to provide places for West Point graduates and assorted administration friends. In fact, as Benton considered the proposition, he conceived that the administration might be playing an even deeper game. Benton was far from a pacifist—he had been one of the architects of the conquest of Mexico—but he was very much a politician and he did not care for Pierce's brand of democrat. He warned that Pierce and Davis might want the expanded army for conquest, probably all the way to the shores of Cuba. However persuasive these senators' eloquence, few could ignore the overriding fact that the federal Indian policy in Texas was a failure on all counts.

Thirty-one senators resolved to try something new and agreed to expand the army. Twenty did not. The Pierce administration found a more sympathetic House. By a two-to-one majority it passed a bill to raise two new infantry and two new cavalry regiments.[13] Thus was born the Second Cavalry.

* * *

Secretary of War Jefferson Davis evaded the rules of seniority to select personally the officers to lead the newly raised Second Cavalry. (National Archives)

SECRETARY OF WAR DAVIS prided himself on his strict adherence to the letter of the law on issues both small and large. He interpreted the bill as giving him authority to raise and maintain the new cavalry regiments as a distinct arm of the service.[14] It may have been legal nitpicking, an activity the secretary greatly enjoyed, but it also meant that he could furnish the regiments with officers selected on the basis of merit rather than seniority. If a meritorious officer happened to be a friend of the secretary's, so much the better. But first and foremost, Davis preferred military professionals who had graduated from West Point.

During the years preceding the Civil War, the entrance exam at the U.S. Military Academy was far from the intellectual challenge it later became. By law, this exam could not include subjects beyond the scope of work typically required in the nation's rural schools. A sound understanding of reading, writing, and arithmetic sufficed to pass it. Reputedly, U. S. Grant said that he never saw an algebra book until he arrived at West Point. The academy's academic course of study provided an education roughly equivalent to that of the nation's other top-notch educational institutions. It was heavy on daily recitations, whether the topic was moral philosophy or integral calculus.

In addition, cadets received military instruction that began with the basics. Classroom work in the Department of Tactics was rote learning, generally of the most numbing sort. During his first year, a cadet endured thirty-two hourlong recitations on the subject of the artillery, and fifteen apiece on infantry and cavalry. By the time he graduated, a student would have spent 540 hours reciting on the topic of the infantry. Under the supervision of the grand-sounding Department of Practical Military Engineering, a cadet spent his first year learning the duties of an ordinary private; his time from 4 P.M. until sunset was spent on the drill field. He then advanced to the duties of a corporal and participated in the "school of the company," a course designed to teach everything important about the drill and internal management of a small unit of soldiers. If the student survived to participate in the academy's more advanced classes, he received artillery instruction and learned the "school of the battalion," at that time a group half the size of a regiment. During the final year, the young man received some instruction in the science of war.

Overall, West Point emphasized French, mathematics, drawing, and engineering over the serious study of military history and leadership.[15]

Good conduct counted for much. A poor academic record, such as that earned by the man who would become the Second Cavalry's senior major, William Hardee, could partially be offset by meticulous attention to duties. In Fitzhugh Lee's case, a "good seat" (a superior riding posture) propelled him to a first-place ranking in personal horsemanship and helped him overcome certain academic and conduct deficiencies. Whether Hardee's ability to shine spotlessly when inspected or Fitzhugh Lee's peerless seat would correlate with leadership in battle was problematic, but at least graduation from West Point demonstrated persistence, and on the Texas frontier that would count for a great deal.

Twenty of the thirty-four officers who received commissions in the Second Cavalry were West Point graduates. But military service attracted some men who lacked the wherewithal to attend West Point. To ascertain whether they were worthy to serve as officers in the two new cavalry regiments, Secretary Davis ordered the existing cavalry regiments to convene boards of examination. Here young officers were tested as to their fitness for duty with the new units. Since this procedure implied that an officer qualified to serve with the Dragoons and Mounted Rifles might not be suitable for the new units, it clearly delineated both the First and Second Cavalry as elites. Ten officers who were not West Point graduates but had distinguished themselves in the Mexican War entered the Second Cavalry after passing the exam. An additional handful of civilians demonstrated the necessary qualities. Twenty-four of the original thirty-four officers had seen combat prior to joining the Second Cavalry. Nineteen had served in the Mexican War, seven of whom held brevet rank for gallant and meritorious service during that war. By casting his net wide, Davis was able to select men he perceived possessed surpassing qualities. With one notable exception, events would vindicate his choices.

By the end of March Davis had made most of his selections. Not everyone could or did accept his appointment. Irish-born John Williams had managed that rare feat of rising from the ranks of the Mounted Rifles. He passed the board of examination, received an assignment to the Second Cavalry as a second lieutenant, and was killed before joining the regiment. When William Emory declined his appointment as the regiment's junior major, a Captain Braxton Bragg received it instead. But Bragg had decided he was going to resign from the army. Consequently, he too declined. Bragg recommended that another officer in his artillery regiment receive the appointment, in spite of the fact that this man was the unit's most junior captain. Because of Bragg's endorsement, Davis's insistence on merit over seniority, and the fact that the captain possessed the two prime qualifications for service in the new regiment, by being both a competent West Point graduate and southern born, George H. Thomas secured a fabulous opportunity. In one of the many ironies of service in the antebellum army, eight years later Bragg and Thomas would be confronting each other as opposing army commanders in Tennessee.

The offer found Thomas on garrison duty at one of the army's least favored posts, Fort Yuma, Arizona Territory. Fort Yuma lay in a bottomland that seemed to concentrate the heat. Daytime temperatures in the shade reached 116 degrees. In later years Thomas would regale his subordinates with a story about a notoriously bad man who died at Fort Yuma. His behavior had been such that no one doubted where he went after his death. One night shortly after his funeral he entered the squad room looking as he did in life. A comrade called out, "Bill, what do you want?" Bill replied, "Boys, I have been to h—l and came near freezing to death, so I just asked the 'boss' for a pass for an hour to enable me to come here for my blankets."[16] The decision to escape Fort Yuma's excessive heat was not difficult for Thomas.

The man designated to command the regiment was already in Texas. There, Major Albert Sidney Johnston had been serving as army paymaster since 1849. It was anything but a distinguished position for a man whom Zach Taylor had once called "the best soldier he had ever commanded."[17] Poverty had compelled Johnston to accept the paymaster assignment, and he loathed it. Six times a year he rode a 620-mile circuit from fort to fort along the Texas frontier to deliver money to the troops. He slept on the ground, exposed to alternate cycles of heat and cold, ate poorly, and grew worn and thin. It was a cycle of unrelenting drudgery. Each time he returned to his family in Austin, his wife observed deeper signs of hard usage. She doubted he could endure.

But Johnston possessed some solid political connections through two relatives, one a congressman and the other a senator. Johnston's sister skillfully used her position as Congressman William Preston's wife to campaign on the major's behalf. She besieged General Scott with charm and skill—her influence was worth that of two or three senators, noted one observer—and wrote "pretty" letters to the secretary of war pressing Johnston's claim to promotion.[18] The Texas legislature knew and liked Johnston, and its members also threw their support behind him. Best of all, Secretary of War Davis had been Johnston's friend and admirer ever since Johnston's quick-thinking reaction to a dangerous confrontation during the Mexican War had probably saved Davis's life.

While Davis and Johnston were entering Monterrey to complete the negotiation of capitulation terms with the garrison, a mob of angry Mexican soldiers had surrounded them. With scores of muskets leveled at them from the rooftops and several cannon pointed at them from behind nearby barricades, Johnston coolly assessed the situation. He recognized a Mexican staff officer who was trying to slink off and let the mob complete its work. With Davis at his side he boldly rode up to the officer to demand an escort to Mexican army headquarters. Johnston made it quite clear what he would do if the officer declined. The implied threat succeeded and Johnston's newest best friend led them to safety. Johnston's quick perception and decisive action cemented Davis's esteem.

The only other serious candidate for the colonelcy was an enterprising Texas Ranger named Benjamin McCulloch. Like Johnston, McCulloch had influential friends. But he had never attended West Point, and this helped tip the balance in Johnston's favor. McCulloch instead received an appointment as a major in the First Cavalry. It was a high compliment. He was the only field officer selected from civilian life. The prideful McCulloch, smarting under the defeat for higher office, declined. Before his death while leading a Confederate brigade at Pea Ridge, McCulloch would acknowledge that the War Department had acted wisely when it chose Johnston ahead of him. So in 1855 Sidney Johnston, the former frontier paymaster, received a promotion to colonel and command of the Second Cavalry. Political influence helped others as well to receive posting to the new regiment. Pennsylvania-born Cornelius Van Camp enjoyed the patronage of Congressman Thaddeus Stevens. It allowed the young man to gain the coveted step to second lieutenant. For Colonel Johnston the promotion brought renown and some glory. For Van Camp it brought something distinctly different.

Sixteen of the officers who accepted appointments to the Second Cavalry became generals in the Civil War. Of the eleven who served in the Confederate Army, four became full generals, thus supplying one-half of the Confederacy's eight officers who attained that rank. Secretary of War Davis had succeeded in his aim of selecting officers who were the best to be found in the army and in civilian life. Because of his effort, and because of the subsequent prominent careers in the Confederate Army of so many of them, the Second Cavalry became known as "Jeff Davis's Own."

2

To the Staked Plain

No white person would risk settling as far in the wilderness as the lined fixed upon, if the United States troopers were not on that line to protect them.

> —Texas governor James Henderson, 1847 (in Henderson to Neighbors, December 10, 1847, in 30th Congress, 1st Session, Reports of Committees, No. 171)

___ I. Jefferson Barracks ___

Twenty-eight-year-old Second Lieutenant Richard Johnson, a future major general in the Union Army, greeted his appointment as a first lieutenant to the Second Cavalry with surprise and pleasure: "It opened up a new life for me. Under the old order of things I hardly hoped to be a captain before I was fifty years old; now it seemed almost within my grasp."[1] Not even his assignment to the less-than-glamorous duty of serving as the regimental quartermaster dampened Johnson's happiness. He well knew that although prevailing army wisdom held that a quartermaster had only two duties to perform—to make himself comfortable and to make everyone else as uncomfortable as possible—an enterprising officer could still find scope for his zeal. In this frame of mind,

Johnson bundled his family together and headed for Jefferson Barracks, Missouri.

Another officer shared Johnson's attitude, but it was leavened by a healthy bite of anxiety. Thirty-one-year-old Captain Edmund Kirby Smith possessed credentials that were at least equal to those of his fellow officers. He had served with the Dragoons along the Mexican border, and then his company was chosen to escort the boundary commission that surveyed the permanent line between the United States and Mexico. Still, he found his new posting as the unit's second most senior captain a bit intimidating. He was somewhat in awe of Colonel Sidney Johnston, whom he characterized as "a man of great talents and ability and of good common sense." Then there was the unit's lieutenant colonel. Smith had taught mathematics at West Point during the time Robert Lee was superintendent. He described Lee as "the most accomplished officer and gentleman in the army." Amid such distinguished officers, Smith was unsure of his place. A career soldier and a bachelor, he maintained an intimate correspondence with his mother back in Florida. He confided to her that "your harum scarum boy is the least deserving" star in such a constellation of talent.[2] Smith knew that Johnston was determined to make the Second Cavalry the finest in the entire army and he worried about how he could contribute.

Like the other junior officers, Smith's first duty was to recruit men to serve in the ranks. Congressional authorization of a new regiment was merely the first step. The unit would be a paper formation until its officers recruited the necessary manpower. Recruiting was an early test of their leadership, or at least of their charisma, since convincing a young man to forsake a booming economy and a beckoning frontier for the job of fighting Comanches in Texas would not be easy. They traveled to points ranging from Winchester, Virginia, south to Mobile, Alabama, and west to the Mississippi River. Once there, they found that the men who were most susceptible to their beguiling tales of the glories associated with cavalry service were single, poor, uneducated, and without any particular skills. Recent Irish immigrants provided a particularly large pool for the needed manpower. A typical batch of recruits included thirty-eight born in the United States, thirty-five Irish, thirty-one Germans, ten English, four Scots, two Canadians, one Frenchman, one Italian, and one "various."

That a man would get drunk was no bar to his enlistment. His moral character was without interest. As long as he was physically fit, the recruiting officers figured that the regiment could attend to the rest. Already-trained soldiers who had served with European armies were particularly prized. A contemporary described how a recruiting officer passed his time "in ardent endeavors to add to the United States forces as many deserters from the ranks of her majesty of England, as could persuade the recruiting sergeant they were regularly discharged, and the doctor that they were 'able bodied.'"[3] Occasionally officers could be solicitous for the recruit's well-being. A young man who volunteered for a Dragoon regiment in 1850 describes how the recruiting officer tried to discourage him: "And mark me, young man, if you take this step you will regret it only once, and that will be from the time you become acquainted with your position until you get out of it."[4] The officer added that many recruits never survived their three-year term of enlistment. Such expressions of concern depended upon the ease with which the officer was meeting his quota. More typically, the recruiting officers were more than willing to allow a man a fresh chance and to ignore whatever motives—disappointment in love, family troubles, financial disaster, escape from the law were common—prompted an enlistee. If the recruit was looking to hide himself from the world, then the Second Cavalry could oblige, thank you very much.

Except for the regimental band, recruited by Major Thomas in New York City, odds and sods from the Cavalry Depot in Carlisle, Pennsylvania, and one company from western Pennsylvania, they were signed up at places either in the South or in border states. This was in keeping with the regiment's officers and gave the unit a decidedly southern complexion. To take a group like this and convert it into a crack regiment required training and discipline. The regiment looked no further than its senior major to teach these qualities.

William J. Hardee had been a mediocre student at West Point. He graduated twenty-sixth out of forty-five and achieved this only because he avoided demerits. But in 1840 Hardee received the plum posting to the French cavalry school at Saumur. For the officer who was to teach the Second Cavalry its drill, it could not have been more fortuitous. French professionalism contrasted with the American citizen army. Moreover, French veterans of the Algerian campaigns were teaching new tactics based upon hard-earned experience fighting desert Bedouins and mountain tribesmen. This irregular warfare had shown the necessity of unorthodox approaches to novel situations. Hardee lacked the mental flexibility to appreciate this and had only partially absorbed the lessons of mobile warfare against irregular opponents. Instead, first and foremost, he saw the advantages of "intensive military instruction, rigorous discipline, and a professional attitude toward military affairs."[5] Upon his return to America, Hardee became known as an expert trainer of soldiers. He also distinguished himself during the Mexican War. Whereas that war gave many of the future officers of the Second Cavalry their opportunity to shine, Hardee's great chance came late in 1853 when the War Department chose him to prepare a new army tactics manual.

American military men regarded France as the world center of military science. Because of the Algerian experience, French

military manuals promoted rapid movement and elastic forma-
tions. Since American conditions resembled those of Algeria, it
seemed all the more reasonable to use the French manuals as
models. Working closely with Secretary of War Davis, Hardee
began by translating the French cavalry manual. He modified it
for American service and included a supplement on the Colt
revolver. By 1861, Hardee's publications would dominate American drill and training. In 1855, when Senior Major Hardee stood
before the officers and men of the Second Cavalry on the parade
ground at Jefferson Barracks to bark out his commands, he was
already renowned as "the model drill and duty officer of the
mounted service."[6]

Under Hardee's tutelage, officers and their indispensable
sergeants worked hard breaking in recruits and their horses.
Hardee enjoyed instructing soldiers, so he also conducted officers' drill. He taught them the manual of the saber and carbine
as well as tactical lessons. From reveille to tattoo the officers
were either conducting drill or receiving schooling themselves. It
was a superb opportunity for these young officers to learn from
the nation's foremost drill officer. Drill could and did instill the
habits of discipline. But officers and troopers alike were to find
that it was of little value in combat because once men were in
the midst of a running fight with Indians, each trooper generally
became his own commander.

The other duty to absorb Hardee's attention that summer
was also dear to his heart. Along with Colonel Johnston, he traveled to Washington, D.C., to join a cavalry equipment board to
select the uniform and equipment the new regiments would utilize. Jefferson Davis was the most progressive secretary of war
since this office had been established. He wanted his cavalry to
field-test numerous innovations in everything from clothing to
armaments to horse equipment. Among the novelties the cavalry
equipment board chose was the Hardee hat to replace the cus-

tomary cap. Named after its designer, it was made of black felt, trimmed with gold cord, and ornamented with a brass eagle to pin up the brim on the right side, much in the manner of a modern Australian bush hat. Ostensibly the upward fold on the right allowed a trooper to wield his saber without interference. Three black feathers denoted a field grade officer, a major or a colonel; two sufficed for a captain or a lieutenant; and the lowly enlisted man made do with but a single feather. An additional distinguishing mark for the officers was the regimental number pinned to the front of the hat. The enlisted men's hats also featured the company letters: *A* to *K*, excluding *J*, because in this era of handwritten messages, the letters *I* and *J* might be confused.

No one doubted the Hardee hat's elegance. Many doubted its utility. Although its proponents argued that it offered superior protection against the sun, company captain Albert Brackett believed that it made the troopers look ridiculous. Its style was like that worn by a well-known theatrical personality of the time, Fra Diavolo. "If the whole earth had been ransacked," Brackett wrote, "it is difficult to tell where a more ungainly piece of furniture could have been found." During their time in Texas, troopers took special delight in folding their Hardee hats into ludicrous shapes. To their chagrin they then discovered that after one or two rains the hat lost its elegance entirely, presenting a "bedraggled and wilted appearance."[7] As is often the case when combat troops are issued inadequately tested equipment, something small but significant was overlooked by the cavalry equipment board in its zeal to innovate. Even though the board members were experienced equestrians, no one thought how the Hardee hat would stay atop a trooper's head when the wind blew or he asked his horse for something faster than a walk. Even though the hats were uncomfortably warm and lacked ventilation, it is doubtful that the War Department intended troopers to cool off by losing the hat entirely. Not until 1859 would the

The designated uniform for the regiment had a martial elegance that proved thoroughly impractical. Left to right: bugler, company officer, private in fatigue uniform, corporal in full dress. (Company of Military Historians)

Quartermaster Department issue chin straps. Until then, the Second Cavalry had to make do with what later generations would call "field expedients."

The board selected a dark blue shell jacket with sleeves cut very full in the elbow to permit the arm easy movement to use revolver and saber. The pale blue trousers were reinforced at the points of contact with saddle and horse, namely on the inner leg and seat. Underneath the jacket a trooper wore a flannel shirtlike jersey; beneath the woolen trousers, long flannel drawers. Flannel was chosen because of "its conduction of heat and its superior absorption of moisture." Naturally, the army offered only one

Service in Texas quickly taught officers and men alike to adopt more serviceable clothes. (National Archives)

weight of flannel, regardless of whether a trooper was destined to serve in Texas or Utah. Commenting about this uniform, a military surgeon remarked, "The system of proportioning the clothing to the actual temperature is practised by every community except the military."[8] To reduce their stifling discomfort, troopers tried going without their flannel drawers. But the chafing of rough jersey trousers soaked with sweat from horse and man compelled even the hardiest cavalryman to submit to his drawers.

While the War Department was indifferent about the comforts of flannel drawers and woolen trousers in a Texas summer, with Jeff Davis's prodding it was keenly interested in making the two new regiments truly special. To distinguish them further, the War Department ordered that the jacket feature yellow trim instead of the orange of the Dragoons or the dark green of the Mounted Rifles. The trouser stripe was also yellow. Thus was born the Yellow Leg tradition, the association of the color yellow with the cavalry.[9] Whereas the need to wear some form of waterproof protection was the same in the 1850s as it is today, the equipment board had fewer choices regarding material. It selected a loose-fitting cape, or talma, that extended almost to the knees and was made from gutta-percha, a rubberlike gum extracted from the latex of certain Southeast Asian trees. When a true Texas norther set in, troopers wore a woolen greatcoat. Because they were expected to fight both mounted and dismounted, they wore shoes instead of riding boots. In contrast to this eminently practical decision was the decision to adorn the troopers with brass scales on their shoulders. The scales were designed to deflect saber strokes, but the Indians carried no sabers. The brass also glinted off the sun, making the trooper unnecessarily conspicuous.

Four squadrons (a squadron comprised two companies) received the same Grimsley saddle that had served for the army's other mounted regiments. Whether this was a good choice was open to debate. Captain Earl Van Dorn, who was a fine equestrian, complained that the Grimsley saddle fit poorly and rubbed the horses raw, particularly during a long march under inclement weather. Sidney Johnston dismissed this notion. He praised the saddle and said that sore-backed horses resulted from the troopers' ignorance of the proper method to adjust it. In another outburst of innovation, the equipment board also issued one squadron brass-mounted Campbell saddles with wooden stirrups. While the Campbell's brass fittings polished up splendidly for inspection, they were not quite the thing for stealthily tracking Comanches across a sunlit desert.

In conjunction with the equipment board, the War Department also foisted some experimental new weapons upon the cavalry. It gave three squadrons muzzle-loading Springfield rifled carbines, an exceedingly poor choice for mounted or dismounted skirmish combat. With this weapon a mounted trooper could fire but once since there was no chance of reloading while in the saddle. When dismounted, instead of being able to remain behind cover while reloading a breech-loading weapon, he would have to expose himself to hostile fire while ramming a bullet down the muzzle. Another squadron received what was called a movable-stock carbine, along with instructions to experiment with this item to ascertain whether it worked better with a ten- or a twelve-inch barrel. The answer would turn out to be neither, and troopers would turn in this weapon for something more conventional at first opportunity. The remaining squadron got the most appropriate weapon, breech-loading Perry carbines.

Far more useful was the issue of Colt's navy revolvers, a six-shot weapon that was to allow the troopers to dominate close combat. Yet even this was a curious decision. The .44-caliber army version of Colt's revolver was already in service on the frontier. The .36-caliber navy model offered the advantages of lighter weight—2 pounds, 6 ounces versus 4 pounds, 4 ounces—and portability, but at a significant loss in penetrating power. It also complicated ordnance inventory and ammunition supply. Perhaps an 1850s version of a weapons-procurement scandal explains this decision. At any rate, Samuel Colt knew how to grease the wheels of the government procurement machinery. After the Mexican War he had collected testimonials for his revolving pistols, including one from then Colonel Jefferson Davis. When the government subsequently ordered the so-called dragoon model for its mounted forces, Colt showed his gratitude by sending beautifully tooled presentation revolvers to important people, including soon-to-be Secretary of War Davis.

Troopers wielded a heavy dragoon saber, in 1855 already an anachronistic armament. One veteran sardonically observed that if a trooper got close enough to an Indian to use his saber, it was an even-odds proposition as to who went under first. At least the equipment board discarded the traditional white saber belt and shoulder strap in favor of a less visible black leather.[10] In a further exploration of the utility of gutta-percha, one squadron received gutta-percha pistol cases and cartridge boxes instead of the traditional leather ones.

While the regiment received a decidedly mixed bag of uniform and equipment, it had the unequaled opportunity to select magnificent horses. Sidney Johnston appointed a purchasing board composed of veteran Dragoon officers, including Hardee, Theodore O'Hara, and Charles Field. O'Hara's poetical soul—he was the nationally renowned author of the popular poem "Bivouac of the Dead"—must have soared when he learned that in the pursuit of the best horses, price was no object. In a departure from usual procurement practices, they could buy a horse without constraint as to a maximum amount. Furthermore, Secretary Davis had seen the effect of an elegant appearance upon fighting prowess. In the Mexican War his First Volunteer Rifle Regiment presented a sartorial splendor in their white duck trousers and long-sleeved red shirts. To create a similar effect in the Second Cavalry, Davis wanted each company to ride horses matched in color. The purchasing board did Davis and the regiment proud. They traveled through prime horse-breeding country in Kentucky, Indiana, and Ohio and chose only the best purebred creatures. They bought 850 horses at an average cost of $150, which was a very high sum for the time. The purchase of first-class horses would turn out to be a mixed experience. Those who endured proved superb. Many others perished in Texas's harsh environment. Company G acquired eighty-five superb Kentucky horses; after six years of rigorous campaigning, forty-four of them were still serviceable. The board also managed the feat of buying enough horses of the same color so that Company A rode grays, Companies B and E sorrels, Companies C, D, F, and I bays, Companies G and H browns, and Company K roans.

In spite of the expert eyes of the purchasing board, some wily sellers did slip some vice-ridden mounts through the selection process. After all, the frontier tradition of sharp practice had long before given the term "horse trader" a negative connotation. Inexperienced riders did not help. At Jefferson Barracks a lieutenant watched two Irish recruits try to mount an untrained, fractious horse. They succeeded only by throwing a blanket over the horse's head, backing it up to a log, and then springing onto the animal's rear. This was not quite the technique taught by the cavalry manuals.

While in Washington, Johnston received reports of a steady increase in the number of enlisted men reporting to Jefferson Barracks: April, 39; May, 221; June, 611, including 119 transferred from the Cavalry Depot; August, 765. Then he recalled the recruiting officers so they could take their place with their men, and traveled west himself to inspect the regiment. He was not pleased with what he saw. Recruiting officers had seduced enough men; Hardee, O'Hara, and Field had purchased splendid horses; but somehow the War Department could not provide the fancy new uniforms. To the officers' frustration, the clothing requisitioned in early May did not come until mid-September. When Lieutenant Colonel Lee arrived, he found a new recruit standing at muster "in a dirty, tattered shirt and pants." Lee asked him why he did not put on clean clothes and he replied he had no clean clothes. Lee asked if he could not wash and mend those he had on, and he answered he had nothing else to wear. "I then told him immediately after muster to go down to the river, wash his clothes, and sit on the bank and watch the passing steamboats till they dried, and then mend them. This morning at inspection he looked as proud as possible, stood in the position of a soldier . . . with his toes sticking through his shoes, but his skin and solitary two garments clean. He grinned very happily at my compliment."[11] For this one recruit, Lee had worked magic of the sort that would make him a beloved leader to an entire army.

Johnston took an altogether different tack, and the regiment quickly learned what constituted their colonel's notion of discipline. For a breach of conduct he ordered six men whipped and drummed out of the regiment with "shaven heads and other marks of degradation."[12] Johnston had barely begun to get the reins of his regiment in hand when the War Department ordered both him and Lee to sit on a general court-martial at Fort Leavenworth until September 24. The decision annoyed Johnston. He well knew that the birth of a new regiment was a delicate operation: "bringing form out of chaos" he called it.[13] Every officer should be present to participate. To make his concern more acute, while at Fort Leavenworth he began receiving reports that a dreaded disease had afflicted his regiment. Cholera had twice before visited Jefferson Barracks, killing generals and privates with impartiality, and now it had come again.

Americans had watched with dreadful fascination back in April 1832 when cholera killed thirteen thousand Parisians. A shipload of immigrants brought it to Quebec in June. Thereafter, it "spread along rivers, trade routes, and overland trails and raged through cities and army barracks."[14] During the next two months it killed three thousand New Yorkers. New Orleans's shallow drinking water supply condemned four thousand people in a three-week epidemic. Another outbreak, brought from Europe in 1848, spread even more rapidly along the new railroad lines.

An afflicted trooper who had drunk from the post's contaminated water supply did not have to ask to be dismissed from duty. His condition presented no choice. First came an abrupt but painless watery diarrhea. In and of itself this was not un-usual. What passed for sanitary practices on the American fron-tier frequently gave people loose bowels. But cholera-induced diarrhea purged the body, causing it to excrete three to four gal-lons of liquid in the first twenty-four hours. Convulsive vomiting followed. At this point the post surgeon knew what he con-fronted, and he also knew that there was very little he could do to check its inexorable progress. Prevailing wisdom believed that cholera spread by bad air and noxious vapors. Lying on his sweat-stained bed, the dehydrated trooper's skin became cold and withered. His face became drawn. Severe muscular cramps ensued, but it was the raging thirst that commanded attention. If the surgeon administered the treatment of choice, hot peppers in whiskey, it only increased his patient's suffering. The final stage, which could come within two days of the illness's onset, saw the sick trooper enter a deep stupor. Twenty-two cavalrymen did not emerge from this stupor and perished. The troopers' fear of this mysterious, awful disease was such that many literally fled for their lives. By the time the regiment departed for Texas, 404 troopers had deserted.

Subtracting the men dead from cholera, the deserters, and the fifteen discharged left 696 troopers who responded when the bugle blared "Boots and Saddles" before dawn on October 27, 1855, to begin the march to Texas.

—— II. "Hurrah for Texas" ——

The planned route of march was southwest from St. Louis, over the Ozarks, south down the Missouri border to Maysville, Arkansas, and then southwest again through the Indian Territory to Texas. The total distance was over seven hundred miles. The early days featured balmy Indian summer weather. Regimental officers quickly learned that if their colonel was a demanding

Colonel Albert Sidney Johnston, an officer Davis esteemed above all others, provided the regiment with an excellent leadership model. (National Archives)

officer, he was also willing to reinforce their initiative. At 6 A.M. one morning, he called at Lieutenant Johnson's wagon to issue instructions to his quartermaster. Young Johnson had anticipated his duties and departed three hours earlier to accomplish them. Recognizing that he was dealing with a zealous subordinate, thereafter Johnston gave the lieutenant the latitude to conduct his duties without close supervision. By force of example, the colonel was instructing a new generation of officers.

Riding his superb horse, Grey Eagle, Johnston found this trek far easier than his biannual paymaster tours of Texas. Not so for many of the new recruits. Their stiff new saddles tormented them. The inexperienced riders learned that the only cure for saddle soreness was to continue to ride until the body grew accustomed to it. Most of the enlisted men had no previous experience in camp life. The bugles awakened them at 4 A.M. each morning. Two hours later the column of march had formed. A picked detachment of pioneers went first. Their special duty was to remove any obstructions that might impede the wagons. At the head of the main column was a set of ambulances carrying the families of four officers. Then came the cavalry companies in alphabetical order, with Senior Captain Earl Van Dorn's Mobile Grays, comprising Alabama recruits riding gray horses, leading the way. Twenty-nine supply wagons hauled by six mules apiece followed the fighting men, carrying tents, food, tools, and very little else. The small number of wagons in proportion to the number of men made the march particularly spartan. Captain Kirby Smith complained that the War Department "has been experimenting upon us as new and picked troops" and ordering "us off on a 1,000 mile march without transportation."[15] The War Department's intent was to test the unit's mobility and save money in the process. At day's end it was particularly gratifying to bivouac for the night and enjoy the society of the handful of women who accompanied the regiment.

Since Texas was to be the unit's home for the next several years, four of the married officers took their wives, families, hired servants, and slaves. The wives of Captains James Oakes and Innis Palmer and Lieutenant Johnson joined the colonel's wife, Eliza Johnston, on the journey. Their husbands had purchased carriage ambulances outfitted with steel springs to convey the families. They featured seats and backs that could be shifted to form a sleeping bed. However, they were so fully packed that this proved to be a nearly useless feature. A feeling of belonging to a band of brothers may have pervaded the officers, but these four women strictly observed rank order. Along with everyone else they arose at reveille to prepare or direct the

The March to Texas

1 Oct. 27, 1855: depart Jefferson Barracks

2 Nov. 10: Evans pursues deserters

3 Nov. 21: Regiment passes through Jollification

4 Nov. 27: Regiment passes through Tahlequah, Cherokee Nation capital

5 Nov. 28: Regiment rests three days at Fort Gibson

6 Dec. 5: Regiment negotiates the quicksands of the Canadian River

7 Dec. 12: Champagne feast at Fort Washita

8 Dec. 15: "Hurrah for Texas"

9 Dec. 22: Severe norther immobilizes the regiment

10 Dec. 27: Arrival at Fort Belknap

11 Jan. 3, 1856: Hardee's detachment arrives to build Camp Cooper

12 Jan. 14: Johnson's six companies arrive at Fort Mason

© 2000 by D. L. McElhannon

preparation of breakfast. They entered the line of march just behind the pioneers in order of seniority, with the colonel's wife leading the way. Ten or twelve weary hours sitting bolt upright as their ambulance wagons jolted along increasingly rough roads followed. There was no break for lunch. A journey like this was a trial for even the best-willed women.

Yet it was not without compensations. Eliza Johnston was a fine sketch artist, fully capable of doing justice to the interesting flora she encountered along the way. Her word sketches, entered daily in her diary, were similarly able to depict some of the romance of cavalry life. Having completed a day's march, she drove "through the camp in the darkness with a thousand camp fires blazing around the white tents with the glimmering fire light shining upon them the soldiers standing around some bending over the Kettles cooking their suppers others seated on their blankets talking over the expected pleasures of the campaign."[16]

As a rule, bachelor officers helped their married comrades whenever possible, performing the small gallantries that made travel less tedious. They erected the wives' ten-by-ten tents that then became social centers for the horse soldiers, a visible reminder of the softer world left behind. Back in that den of iniquity, Benny Havens's saloon near West Point, cadets had composed a verse in their honor:

> To the ladies of the Army, our cups shall ever flow,
> Companions of our exile, and our shields 'gainst every woe.
> May they see their husbands generals, with double pay also,
> And join us in our choruses of Benny Havens O!![17]

As was natural at any social center, within the tents' confines the women exchanged gossip, and no story was more gripping than that involving Lieutenant Charlie Field. In the future, Field would become a renowned, audacious fighting general in the Army of Northern Virginia. On the march to Texas his fellow officers somewhat enviously celebrated his romantic audacity, while the four wives clucked about his wretched behavior. It seemed that back at Jefferson Barracks, while his seniors were off recruiting, the burly, affable Field did his own recruiting at the home of an officer belonging to a different unit. Not only had he successfully seduced this officer's wife, which was bad enough, but he was secreting her among the camp followers accompanying the march, which, to the four wives, was very bad indeed.

* * *

43

FOR THE FIRST ten days the march followed the Pacific Railroad Survey route through Missouri. A pair of second lieutenants preceded the regiment in order to arrange provisions and forage. It was easy to supplement the contract butcher's fresh beef with local purchases of fowl, fruit, and dairy products. Such regular means of procurement did not satisfy the teamsters, who began to lag behind in order to steal from nearby farmers. Each night a party of angry farmers would beset Colonel Johnston with their complaints. Around this time young Lieutenant Kenner Garrard, whose brush with glory at Gettysburg lay eight years ahead, had his career almost prematurely ended when a poisonous snake bit him. He remained behind until he recovered. Then on November 1 it began to rain. While this presented a fine test for the troopers' gutta-percha capes—they turned the rain "like Ducks feathers"—the wet weather sickened the children, killed off a cholera-weakened trooper, and reduced progress to a crawl. The government had spent a considerable sum for the cavalry horses but it had economized when purchasing the lowly draft mules. Now these too-young animals lacked the stamina to haul the wagons over the boggy sections of mountain road in southwestern Missouri. Having seen enough of army life, troopers began to desert. Johnston assigned his senior lieutenant, Nathan G. Evans, to go back and collect them.

Evans succeeded in bringing back one deserter's horse; the recruit escaped in a swamp. But Evans also succeeded in rejoining the regiment before it reached a special town in Missouri. He was a man who appreciated a good drink: he would course the battlefield of First Bull Run accompanied by an aide charged with the important duty of conveying his "barlito" of whiskey. His spirits must have soared as the column approached Jollification, Missouri. The regiment divided into teetotalers and imbibers. Whereas a man like the temperate Lieutenant Colonel Lee, recalling how demon alcohol inspired excessive demerits among West Point cadets, would write his son to warn him to avoid it—"I am sorry to say that there is great proclivity for spirit in the army in the field. It seems to be considered a substitute for every luxury"[18]—Colonel Johnston had a different attitude. He had obtained War Department permission to allow sutlers to sell whiskey to the troops. The colonel thought that whiskey would help maintain morale and fortify the inner man against fatigue and hardship. In particular, he conceived that it "would dull the keen sense of desire" that would otherwise rise among soldiers going without female company for a very long time.[19] For the sutlers, this decision was easy profit. They could replenish stocks from such places as Jollification, Missouri—the name derived from the town's distillery—and sell to a captive but eager market. How eager became apparent on the third day out, when a drunken private fell from his horse and split his skull on the ground. His subsequent death was one of two whiskey-inspired fatalities the regiment suffered during the march.

The column moved along the St. Louis–to–Fort Gibson track, the main overland artery for immigration to Texas. For more than ten years it had been so packed that travelers reported seeing hundreds of wagons a day. So it continued in the autumn of 1855, with the troopers regularly passing wagon trains heading west. The civilian wagons presented temptation for light-fingered soldiers. More trouble came when some troopers joined the teamsters to rob and pillage nearby civilians and their homes. Nightly searches and inspections found everything from stolen watches to pilfered hogs. Henceforth, dismounted troopers in chains trailed the column, compelled by Johnston's orders to walking as punishment for their crimes. South and west they tromped, heading toward the Indian Territory.

The Indian Territory was the home of the Five Civilized Tribes, Indians who had lived east of the Mississippi River until too many whites found their presence insufferable. In 1829 the

45

Georgia legislature figured out how to deal with this problem by decreeing that all of the state's Indians were to be subject to Georgia law but not protected by it. In his first State of the Union message, President Andrew Jackson asked Congress to establish an area west of the Mississippi, outside of any existing organized state or territory, for a permanent residence for the Indians. Jackson hoped the Indians would move voluntarily. If not, he was quite prepared to use force. When the Indian Removal Act of 1830 passed, the exodus began. Among the vanquished were the Creeks, once outstanding warriors, whose defeat at the battle of Horseshoe Bend drove them from their land and who were now a symbol to western Indians of their potential fate. Captain Albert Brackett observed "many a grim old warrior" watching the hated army soldiers as they traversed Creek territory.[20] On November 17 the regiment passed through the capital of the Cherokee Nation. This country reminded many of their native South. The Cherokees built large and tasteful brick homes and kept slaves to work their fields.

The column reached Fort Gibson on November 28. Here the army had established an outpost in 1824. At the time it was the U.S. Army's westernmost garrison. Nominally, its purpose had been to protect the region's Indians from one another and to prevent whites from moving onto the Indian lands. The Indians knew it best neither for its failure to prevent Indian-against-Indian conflict nor for its inability to slow white encroachment, but rather because Fort Gibson had served as the western terminus of the Indian removal route, the Trail of Tears. The cavalry enjoyed their first extended break at Fort Gibson. For three days they rested and repaired equipment while the officers and their families gorged on turkey, venison, jelly cake with fine butter, and brandied peaches.

With the weather turning colder, the march resumed. The December 4 campsite was near a village where lived a few Seminoles—a tribe driven into the deep Florida swamps, from where it had waged a fearsome guerrilla war until it, too, succumbed to the might of the United States. As the regiment passed through the Indian Territory, no one fully appreciated that when the Cherokees and other eastern tribes were settled on hunting lands formerly controlled by the Comanches, thus creating one more stress driving the Comanches to raid Texas.

As the regiment moved through the more desolate sections of the Indian Territory, the route turned difficult. Because the Canadian River was well known for its hazardous quicksands, Lieutenant Johnson and Captain William Bradfute rode ahead to select a crossing point. They found a solid bottom, rode into the water, and agreed that this was the place. The next day the regiment arrived at the river with Bradfute leading the way. Bradfute was a celebrated marksman. He was a less skilled rider. He rode to the ford, but this time his little brown horse, Bow-Legs, balked. Not to be embarrassed before the entire regiment, Bradfute viciously dug his spurs into Bow-Legs's sides. The animal plunged in, and horse and rider disappeared. Apparently they had disturbed the sand while testing the bottom the evening before. The sand then shifted, leaving a ten-foot hole. The captain and his sagacious Bow-Legs survived. That evening the regimental officers met to deliver their verdict. They shared a standing wager that if an officer was thrown from his saddle he owed the other officers a basket of champagne. Bradfute's comrades agreed that his near drowning did not constitute a fair toss from the saddle.

The crossing of the North Fork of the Canadian River was more than a symbolic passage. It marked the divide between settled country and a more wild, desolate region. The lurking wolves who gathered that night just outside the glow of the blazing campfires underscored the divide. Their yelping made one's hair stand up on end. Inexperienced recruits wondered if it was the sound of Indians whooping before an attack. The veterans assured them that it was.

It had taken most of an entire day to cross the Canadian River. Perhaps the difficulty of shifting bogged wagons while avoiding the dangerous quicksands frayed everyone's nerves, because around this time arose a squalid episode involving Second Lieutenant Robert Wood Jr. and Captain Charles E. Travis. Both officers came from families of national prominence. Bob Wood was the son of the army's assistant surgeon general and was Zach Taylor's grandson. According to Eliza Johnston, he was "a gentleman born and bred." The lieutenant presented himself before Colonel Johnston to protest that the captain had accused him of stealing $250 from him. It was a malicious, false charge, asserted Wood, probably concocted by Travis to evade the accusation that Wood was about to make. During some of their nightly card play, Travis had been caught cheating! Wood demanded a court-martial. By this time Johnston did not particularly care for the captain of H Company. Travis had an ugly disposition—Eliza labeled him "a mean fellow"—and was neither liked nor esteemed by his fellow officers.[21] However, Johnston knew that he would have to proceed with care, for in dealing with Travis he was dealing with the incarnation of Texas's greatest legend.

Travis's father had commanded the doomed defenders of the Alamo. Surrounded by Santa Anna's Mexican army, Colonel Travis sent a last letter to the outside world in which he asked a friend to "take care of my little boy." The colonel continued, "If the country should be lost, and I should perish, he will have nothing but the proud recollection that he is the son of a man who died for his country."[22] Almost twenty years later, Colonel Johnston knew that it was his turn to hold the fate of Colonel Travis's "little boy" in his hands. Still, the evidence against Travis seemed so persuasive that Johnston conceived that he had little choice. He relieved him of company command and placed him under arrest. Shamed and shunned, Travis accompanied the regiment to Texas, where he hoped for vindication.

On December 12 the regiment arrived at Fort Washita. The fort's gunners fired a thirty-gun salute to greet the unit. Artillery captain Braxton Bragg, who had not yet resigned from the army, followed this handsome gesture with an officers' banquet catered by the post sutler. Officers enjoyed the feast of venison, partridge, turkey, and hot bread with butter. Better still was the champagne—one wonders what possible vintage endured transport across frontier America—that flowed abundantly and quickly produced good cheer and a celebration of fellowship. Even thirty years later, Lieutenant Johnson fondly recalled the champagne feast, but lest the reader think the drinking improper or excessive, he hastened to add that it was not the quantity imbibed but rather the nature of champagne itself: "Sparkling wine always develops wit and good humor among gentlemen."[23]

It also promoted boasting. Lieutenant Evans claimed he owned the fastest horse. Indeed, his fellow cavalry officers knew it to be true because his mount, Bumble-Bee, was the colt of a famous racehorse. The garrison's gunners could not let such a challenge go unanswered, and so a race was proposed. The evening ended after the colonel delivered a memorable toast to the garrison and to its caterer: "Hospitality, the offspring of a noble sentiment."[24] The next day, with pounding temples, officers gathered to watch Bumble-Bee demolish the Third Artillery's champion. The following evening, when the rain finally desisted, the cavalry departed for the nearby Texas border.

By now, everyone had heard tales of this rugged, wild, proud country. They learned that any male Texan of any note has some title—Colonel, Major, Captain, Judge, or simply Esquire—and that it was dangerous to challenge that title's authenticity. The violence of the frontier would astonish some of the officers. It was what Sidney Johnston had come to expect. Drawing upon his wide experience in Texas, he related a story in which a man, after due deliberation, decided to kill his neighbor. He went to his house, rang the bell, and plunged his Bowie knife into his breast. Putting his weight behind the knife, the murderer spilled his victim's bowels on the doorstep. Subsequently he realized that he had killed the wrong man. The coroner's jury acquitted him on the grounds that the man died by an accident.[25]

Splashing across the Red River on December 14, most soldiers shared the sentiment expressed by their colonel's daughter, Maggie. As her wagon ascended the far bank, she exclaimed, "This is my country, hurrah for Texas."[26]

The column now entered the high Texas plateau, some 2,000 feet above sea level. It was a region subject to abrupt changes in the weather. It had been a balmy day with a warm southerly breeze. On the night of December 22, while Johnston was thinking about his son in distant New York City and pitying his having to live through a northern winter, the weather changed. For the first time the troopers encountered a true Texas norther. Colonel Johnston's description cannot be improved upon: "Norther! It makes me cold to write the word. I do not believe that any of the hyperborean explorers felt the cold more intensely than did my regiment. . . . Think of a northern blast, sixty miles an hour, unceasing, unrelenting (the mercury below zero, ice six inches thick), coming suddenly down on the highest tableland of Texas, 2,000 feet above the sea."[27]

Because a band of timber offered some shelter, Johnston decided to try to wait out the bad weather. The temperature fell to 4 below. It was impossible to stay warm. Presumably no one received better care than Johnston's wife. Yet she reports sitting with her daughter on her knee, her sons rolled up in blankets, and everyone shivering. There was nothing to eat—the antelope roast had frozen so solid it could not be cut with an axe—so she gave a few crackers to the children and went to bed hungry. On

December 23 troopers distributed a scarce corn ration to their benumbed horses. The terrible weather continued, but rather than have the horses die of starvation, Johnston ordered the march resumed the next day. In the understated words of Johnston, "This was a hard day for all."[28] Fortunately, the direction of march was southwest, so the wind was at the column's back. It blew so hard that Johnston doubted they could have managed a march into the teeth of the wind. On Christmas Eve the column met its supply train, and so the horses again ate a life-sustaining corn ration. A sparse band of timber offered the best available shelter, but it was none too good. Christmas dawned clear, bright, and the coldest yet. Snow covered the ground. The ice was so thick that it was hard to break through to let the animals drink. There was no question of resuming the march on a day like this.

Massachusetts-born Captain Charles Whiting was the duty officer on December 25. He was determined to show the southerners that they did not have an exclusive hold on hospitality. Along with Lieutenant William Lowe, another of the northern-born officers, he somehow managed to concoct a holiday eggnog, albeit with frozen eggs. Whiting served the libation to his fellow officers and provided a gut-warming apple brandy to wash it down. Because it would not do to imbibe without inviting his colonel, the somewhat impaired Whiting insisted that Johnston partake on the grounds that regulations said it was not possible for both the duty officer and the unit's commander to be under the influence. He hoped that if Johnston had a drink or two, the relative difference in their sobriety would diminish and regulations would be honored. When Captain Smith relieved Whiting that evening, their greatly exaggerated ceremony of guard mounting entered into regimental legend.

Johnston was quite willing to ignore, up to a point, certain irregularities. To spread the cheer he ordered a dram of whiskey

51

per man for the enlisted soldiers. Alcohol begot music. That evening the regimental band's buglers serenaded the Johnstons with holiday tunes. One inspired musician even attempted some Swiss yodeling. To reward them for their effort, Mrs. Johnston gave the band warm rolls and ham, while some officers sent them along with a tad more whiskey.

To celebrate Christmas the regiment had put the best face on a difficult situation. However, in spite of the cold, the lack of forage again compelled the column to continue the following day. Lack of water left men and horses thirsty. After one last bleak bivouac in the open, the regiment arrived at Fort Belknap on December 27, two months to the day since it had departed Jefferson Barracks. The post lacked sufficient accommodations for the entire unit, so the regiment camped in a sheltered place about a mile from the fort. The weather was an awful mix of snow and sleet, with the temperature hovering around zero. Although Johnston received an invitation to house himself and his family inside Fort Belknap, he declined and instead bivouacked in a tent in order to share his unit's discomfort.

In a testament to army couriers, a dispatch rider had braved the subzero weather to ride 35 miles to deliver War Department orders to Johnston the day before Christmas. They required him to split the command. The colonel correctly feared that the regiment might never assemble as a whole again. Dutifully, he sent Major Hardee and four companies to the Indian reserve on the Clear Fork of the Brazos River, forty miles southwest of Belknap. Hardee's mission was to protect the peaceful Indians living there against raids by the "uncivilized" Comanches to the north. Johnston led the balance of the regiment on a final, 150-mile trek southwest to Fort Mason.

The cold weather persisted. The last week of December and all of January would prove to be one of the coldest spells ever recorded in Texas. Eliza Johnston reported that the water froze in her cup before she could drink it. Johnston's column traveled through a beautiful country with live oak groves. Had they entered this territory during a different season, they would have seen why it drew so many new settlers. It was a vast area of gently rolling grassland that in any but drought years was covered with a luxuriant growth of grass. Every valley seemed heavily timbered. Herds of buffalo fed on the hillsides, and deer and turkey were unusually abundant.[29] Passing over a deeply frozen stream, the troopers saw schools of torpid fish moving sluggishly beneath the ice. They provided a welcome fish fry.

It was the last meal for one twenty-one-year-old soldier. He had been complaining of feeling unwell for several days but had been able to ride with the column. After his fish supper, he lit his pipe and sat down to talk with a comrade. Suddenly he fell over and exclaimed that his bowels pained him. He died within minutes; it was the second death from cholera since leaving Jefferson Barracks. The next day his comrades buried him in his uniform with his cloak wrapped around him. They heaved large logs into place to prevent wolves from digging up the body, and Eliza Johnston wrote this epitaph for the young man, whom she called an excellent soldier:

> No useless coffin confined his breast
> Nor in sheet nor in shroud they bound him
> But he lay like a warrior taking his rest
> With his martial cloak around him.[30]

As the column marched past his roadside grave, Eliza reflected upon how his family was probably anticipating his making a name for himself and returning after his tour of duty crowned with laurels.

On January 14 the column marched the final twenty miles to Fort Mason. After a 750-mile trek lasting two and a half months, the Second Cavalry had arrived at its assigned posts in Texas.

3

War without Scruple

*The history of our Indian affairs clearly proves that the friendship of
Indians cannot be bought; and I still entertain the opinion that I did a
year ago, that nothing but a sound chastisement will have the effect of
bringing the Indians of the plains to their senses.*

> —Indian agent John Whitfield, September 1855
> (in Whitfield to the Commissioner of Indian
> Affairs, September 4, 1855, in 34th Congress,
> 1st Session, Executive Document No. 1,436)

—— I. Texas in Terror ——

The word "Comanche" came from the Spanish, a corruption of
the Ute description *kóh-mahts*, which translated as "those who
want to fight all the time," or more simply, "enemy." Spaniards
had been the first Europeans to meet these nomadic people and
applied the name to distinguish them from other Plains Indians.
Spanish settlers in New Mexico began regularly encountering
Comanches during the first years of the eighteenth century. From
the beginning it was an uneasy relationship. Depending upon circumstances unfathomable to the New Mexicans, mounted Comanche warriors appeared intermittently, sometimes to trade,

sometimes to raid. The horse was their article of trade. Initially, Spanish authorities seldom questioned where the horses came from. Over time, they allowed the Comanches access to Spanish markets as long as their raids occurred out of sight. Then came a stern and forceful Spanish governor of New Mexico named Juan Bautista de Anza. He imposed a treaty that the Comanches found expedient to adhere to. For the next hundred years or so, Comanches made considerable efforts to preserve their good relations with the authorities in New Mexico. Texas was an entirely different arena. The Comanches quickly learned that the best way to turn a profit was to steal a horse in Texas and trade it for European goods in New Mexico.

After founding San Antonio in 1718, Spanish missionaries had moved out to spread the gospel to the Apaches. The Apaches had little use for their religion but recognized a useful ally in their death struggle against the Comanches. Of course, the Comanches viewed this alliance differently. Henceforth, outside of New Mexico the Spanish became both victims to be plundered and a military enemy to be killed when possible. A key event occurred in 1758, when a large band of mounted Comanches, many carrying French firearms, successfully raided the Apache mission on the San Saba River. A bungled Spanish retaliatory raid the following year taught the Comanches that the Spanish were not to be feared. Until the end of the Mexican regime in Texas, Comanche attacks on the Spanish settlements were frequent and intense.

The Louisiana Purchase of 1803 brought a new player onto the stage to vex harassed Spanish officials. Anglo-American traders swarmed the territory, replaced the French, and began aggressively establishing trading relationships with the Comanches, or Camanches as they labeled them. The Americans exchanged arms and munitions for horses and then created a market in the east for Texas horses. People in Louisiana were no more likely to ask about the provenance of a fine-looking horse than were the Spanish in New Mexico. The newly developed American market stimulated the Comanches to raid Texas with greater frequency since they could trade the Texas horses in both New Mexico and Louisiana. In turn, the need to compete with the Americans caused New Mexico traders, the so-called *Comancheros*, to begin traveling onto the plains to conduct business with the Comanches. The unanticipated consequence was that the Comanches lost the incentive to preserve peace with settlements in New Mexico since they no longer had to travel there to trade. Now New Mexico too became a target. From a Comanche perspective, all they had to do was conduct business with individual traders or trading consortiums. They did not have to satisfy distant Spanish or American governments with the appearance of peace.

By the early 1820s, large numbers of American settlers were entering Texas. There were periodic efforts at treaty making with the Comanches. Both parties weighed the advantages: for the Comanches, opportunities for trade; for the settlers, opportunities to acquire land. Both adhered to the treaties as long as they judged it to be within their self-interest. But the inexorable tide of white settlers flooded Comanche lands, bringing them into increasing conflict with the Comanches.

Westward expansion prompted the federal government to make a show of force on the southern Great Plains. A combined military and diplomatic expedition departed Fort Gibson in June 1834 under the command of Brigadier General Henry Leavenworth. The expedition had the primary objective of stopping the Kiowa-Osage war and the secondary objective of establishing contact with the major tribes operating in the relatively unknown country of present-day Oklahoma. When illness incapacitated Leavenworth, Colonel Henry Dodge pursued the mission. Few Americans outside of Texas knew very much about the Comanches. From his Indian guides, Dodge learned that the Plains tribes considered the Comanches to be the most skilled horse thieves going. Their sign language designation for the Comanches was a backward, wiggling motion of the index finger to signify a snake and to indicate the Comanches' silent stealth.

About ten miles north of present-day Fort Sill, Dodge's U.S. Dragoons and Comanche warriors encountered each other. The two lines of riders stared at each other for close to thirty minutes. Then the head Comanche chief "came galloping up to Colonel Dodge, and having shaken him by the hand, he passed on to the other officers in turn, and then rode alongside of the different columns, shaking hands with every dragoon in the regiment; he was followed in this by his principal chiefs and braves, which altogether took up nearly an hour longer."[1]

No one appreciated that Comanche-American relations had just reached a high-water mark.

The sight of the Comanches impressed a Dragoon officer who left this word picture: "Appearance of a Camanche fully equipped, on horseback, with his lance, bow, quiver, and shield by his side—beautifully classic. This has been an interesting day for us."[2] During an ensuing council, Dodge told the Indians that he had come on a friendly visit in the name of the president. He urged them to return east with him to make a firm and lasting peace. Various tribes complied, including the Wichitas, Kiowas, and Osages. A small party of Comanches also briefly accompanied the Dragoons on their return trip. But they dropped out, citing the illness of one of their squaws as a reason. Although later pledges of friendship were exchanged, only a fraction of all Comanche bands formally encountered Americans along the western frontier during the period leading up to midcentury. Meanwhile, in Texas, relationships formed from deeds, not words.

*　　*　　*

"One of their party galloped out in advance of the war-party, on a milk white horse, carrying a piece of white buffalo skin on the point of his long lance in reply to our flag." Catlin describing the 1834 meeting of American soldiers and Comanches, the high-water mark in cavalry-Comanche relations. (George Catlin, *Letters and Notes on the Manners, Customs, and Condition of the North American Indians,* 1844)

IN 1837, the year after the attack on Parker's Fort, an agent for the Texas government visited the northern Comanches in an effort to negotiate a treaty. Although the Texans did not fully appreciate it, the Comanche's lack of tribal organization made negotiation difficult. Whereas there was a group who knew themselves by dress, speech, thought, and action and who shared a common way of life, they were a loose-knit band inhabiting a large and changing geographic area. There was neither a single chief nor a ruling council that spoke for the entire tribe. Traders and frontiersmen came to identify different Comanche bands, but soldiers and politicians tended to conceive of them as a single entity or as two groups: the "lower" Comanches, who lived in Texas, and the "upper," or "wild," Comanches, who resided beyond the settled frontier.

The absence of a tribal organization was only one obstacle would-be negotiators confronted. Ever since the founding of the Texas Republic, Mexican agents had worked industriously to undermine Indian faith in the Anglo word. They found willing audiences because the Comanches already had had enough contact with whites to be deeply suspicious of their words and promises. It gave them a solid understanding of what white encroachment portended. As one Comanche chief explained, "so long as he continued to see the gradual approach of the whites and their habitations to the hunting grounds of the Comanches," he would believe to be true what the Mexicans had told him, "that the ultimate intention of the white man was to deprive them of their country." Thus he and his band "continue to be the enemy of the white race."[3]

The Comanche culture also militated against meaningful negotiation with the whites. They considered themselves the "lords of the plains." They were accustomed to getting their way and had little notion of the latent military might of the United States. Nine years before the Second Cavalry arrived in Texas, a sympathetic Department of the Interior Indian agent observed, "The spread of our population will, in a very few years, so crowd upon the Camanches' ancient hunting grounds as will compel them either to recede westward, or to resist by arms a progression which is perfectly irresistible to their feeble powers."[4] Violent resistance to outside pressure was entirely in keeping with Comanche culture. To carve out their foothold on the buffalo plain and then to retain it, they had had to fight very hard indeed. Thereafter, the Comanche emphasis on war stemmed from their vision of the potential reward: if successful, they could conquer the rich hunting grounds of the southern plains. To fulfill this destiny, every male was a warrior.

From childhood on, a boy's ambition centered on coping successfully with his enemy in war. "When a chief wishes to go to war he mounts on horseback, holding erect a long pole with a red flag tipped with eagle's feathers attached, and rides through the camp singing his war-song. Those who wish to go fall in, and after going round for a while they dismount, and the war-dance commences. This routine is gone through with several days until sufficient volunteers are collected."[5] A young man was not admitted into the ranks of the braves until he had successfully stolen horses and mules or taken scalps. Since it was considered a disgrace to return to camp empty handed, if an expedition proved otherwise unsuccessful, the warriors dispersed to rob and kill whenever opportunity permitted.

They were superb riders, in the saddle from boyhood to old age. A warrior's equestrian skills—"such as throwing himself entirely upon one side of his horse, and discharging his arrows with great rapidity towards the opposite side from beneath the animal's neck while he is at full speed"—astonished American soldiers.[6] The Comanche warrior carried a lance, a straight piece of tapered steel two and a half feet long and an inch wide fixed into a slender wooden handle about four and a half feet long. He often painted the handle red and adorned it with tufts of colored cotton yarn and strips of cloth worked with beads. To his left arm he tied a brightly painted round shield, two feet in diameter, made of wickerwork covered with deerskins and then a tough piece of buffalo hide. He decorated the shield with a circle of feathers and ornamented it with human scalps and other hunting trophies, such as a grizzly bear's claw. The shield was arrow-proof and provided some protection against firearms.

Thus armed, Comanche war bands set out on raids whose prime objective was to procure horses. Horse stealing assumed enormous cultural importance because the Comanches well knew that the horse had been their key to unlock access to the rich buffalo plains. Besides being a valuable trade commodity, horses allowed them to hunt the buffalo and to dominate the battles against other Indian tribes to control the hunting grounds. The acquisition of horses became a strategic objective above all others.

In 1840, over four hundred Comanches raided all the way to the Gulf coast, burning Linnville, sacking Victoria, killing twenty Texans, and stealing more than two thousand horses and mules. In 1843 they drove off most of the settlers in the Austin area. Two years later some six hundred passed San Antonio as they rode to raid Mexico. To protect the frontier, Texas legislators supported a policy of offensive action against the Indians living on the republic's northern frontier, while asserting an interest in making a lasting peace. During times of peace, the Texas Rangers, at this time a militia organization, patrolled an arbitrary line for the nominal purpose of keeping settlers and Indians apart. In fact, they prevented Comanches from hunting south of the line but did not stop whites from crossing it to settle to the north. Indian agent Robert Neighbors complained that white settlers who illegally crossed the line caused much more difficulty than did Indians. Among many he cited a certain transplanted New York lawyer named Spencer who disregarded the boundary line to settle near the Brazos River. When Neighbors tried to intercede and explain to Spencer that he was encroaching on Indian lands, Spencer replied that he would "shoot the first Indian that came on the land."[7]

A sympathetic white recorded the protests of an elderly Comanche named Old Owl who was trying to coexist with the Texans: "You told me that the troops were placed there for our protection . . . that I know is not so." Old Owl explained that he had been told he could apply to the Ranger stations for permission to hunt below the line, yet when he applied to Captain Ben

McCulloch (the future Confederate general) and explained that he had no warriors and merely wanted to hunt where there was still game, McCulloch replied in the negative. "This made me angry, and I quarreled with him. I told him that I was an old man, and had hunted in these prairies before he was born, and before there was any white for a long way below."[8]

For Texans, the coming of statehood seemed to promise an end to Indian terror. Companies such as the Texas Emigration and Land Company were not slow to use the army's forthcoming presence as a lure to attract settlers. Increasing numbers of settlers accepted the risk of living on the border in the belief that the presence of the U.S. Army would provide the necessary security. Instead of enhanced security, the admission of Texas into the Union in 1845 proved the first of several false dawns for the white settlers along the Texas frontier. They found that the Comanche moon brought raiders with a greater frequency than ever. In part, the intensified raids came because of federal policy outside of Texas. When the federal government evicted numerous tribes from east of the Mississippi and relocated them on the edge of the Great Plains, the Comanches experienced additional pressure and encroachment. Delawares, Creeks, Shawnees, Seminoles, Cherokees, Kickapoos, and others settled in what is now Oklahoma and the country to the north. It happened to be in the midst of some of the best hunting grounds. In response, the Comanches had to live by hunting more-barren country or by pillaging the Texas frontier more heavily. In addition to competing for game and land, some of these relocated eastern Indians began raiding white settlements. Often blame for their depredations fell on the Comanches. Of course, this was a game many could play, and the Comanches were not averse to trying to cover their own raids by blaming them on the lesser tribes. Events would show that outlaw Texans could also be tempted into this practice.

When Texans began to realize that statehood would not provide security, Acting Governor Horton informed President James Polk of the consequences: "The citizens of the frontier will protect themselves, and retaliate whenever occasion offers, and in a very short time a state of things will thus be brought about which will greatly retard, if not entirely defeat, the wish of the general government, to settle a boundary line between us and the Indians, or make any treaty with them."[9]

It could later be seen that the admission of Texas into the Union provided an opportunity for a new beginning. Although various bands of northern Comanches periodically expressed interest in negotiating, they insisted upon a definite boundary agreement. This was not something the Texans were prepared to yield. The Texans claimed they loved peace, but their lust for land transcended everything else. The Texas Indians took to calling the whites' surveying instruments "the things that stole the land."[10]

During the Mexican War, the regular army recruited in Texas and received an enthusiastic response. In addition, the most popular Indian fighters went to Mexico with their Ranger companies. The focus on Mexico left few men available for the less glorious duty of defending the state from the Indians. Indians raided with near impunity. Yet in surprisingly short order the Comanches' dominant position eroded due to the combined pressure of the resettled eastern Indians and the surging wave of American immigrants flooding the west. The California gold rush of 1849 brought thousands of whites trekking through some of the Comanches' finest hunting land, disturbing and slaughtering the game as they went. More devastating, the emigrants brought the Asiatic cholera. It killed off an estimated half of the Comanches and hastened their decline from lords of the plains to predatory raiders.

When Indian agents tried to establish reserves where the Texas Indians could reside and adopt the ways of civilization,

Texas legislators consistently maintained that neither the Indians nor the United States had any property rights within Texas's public lands. Since Indians could not legally own land, at best they were tenants subject to the whims of the white rulers. Consequently, the Indian agents had to locate their wards on land the whites did not want. Since there was virtually no such land, it was an impossible task. In 1852, several Comanche leaders explained their plight to a sympathetic visitor: "What encouragement have we to attempt the cultivation of the soil, or raising of cattle, so long as we have no permanent home, and in every attempt we have ever made to raise a crop, we have been driven from them before they could mature by the encroachment of the white man."[11]

Meanwhile, in spite of Indian troubles, the Texas frontier continued its rapid westward movement, encroaching upon land where the Comanches had once hunted. In the period from 1847 to 1857, the frontier moved about a hundred miles west from what had been the border village of Dallas. In July 1853, the treaty of Fort Atkinson established that the United States was to give the Indians goods valuing $18,000 annually, for ten years. The Indians, in return, agreed to let the government lay out roads through their territory and establish forts. They also promised to cease raiding into Mexico. In the event, the value of a treaty "negotiated"—if that word may be used when communication was via sign language, while third parties provided translations—with only a handful of the Comanche bands proved limited.

Concurrent with these events was the decline of the buffalo, the victim of hunting pressure from Indians and whites alike. Although the Comanches had made a transition from buffalo hunting to horse trading, they still relied upon hunting to provide some basic needs. However, as early as 1847 the Comanche hunters were having trouble finding bison and other game

COLORADO

KANSAS

Ft. Atkinson

⚔ Fight on Crooked Creek

NEW

OKLAHOMA

Antelope Hills

Canadian R.

MEXICO

Llano Estacado

Camp Radziminski

● Wichita Village

⚔ Ft. Arbuckle

Red R.

Camp Cooper

Double Mountain M

Ft. Belknap

● Jacksboro

Comanche
Reserve

Brazos
Reserve

Dallas

Trinity R.

Big Spring●

Ft. Chadbourne

Camp Colorado

● Site of
Parker's Fort

Horse Head
Crossing●

Approximate line
of frontier
settlements in 1860 →

TEXAS

Traditional
Comanche war
trail to Mexico →

Rio Grande

Devil's R.

Camp Hudson

Ft. Mason

Fredricksburg

● Austin

Brazos R.

Camp Verde

Colorado R.

Ft. Clarke

● San Antonio

Ft. Inge

MEXICO

Ft. Merrill

**Comanche Country
and Adjacent
Territory in 1860**

Laredo●

Ft. McIntosh

GULF
OF
MEXICO

© 2000 by D. L. McElhannon

Ringgold Barracks●

Rio Grande City

Edinburg
Reynosa●

Arroyo Colorado

● Brownsville
Matamoros

65

animals. Moreover, war with the Osages, who had firearms while the Comanches remained bow and lance armed, made hunting the northern ranges too dangerous. To the east was the barrier erected by the transplanted eastern Indians. To the south were the Texans. The decline of the buffalo, denial of access to traditional hunting grounds, and inability to establish farms or ranches plunged numerous Comanche groups into near starvation. Faced with starvation, they ate their horses and mules. To replenish stock, they raided into Mexico and Texas. From the viewpoint of the U.S. government, the Indians' only sensible recourse was to take up farming. Some years previously Indian agent John Rogers had tried to explain this to an assembly of Comanche, Lipan, and Mescalero Indians: "You must go to *work*, the Buffalo is gone the deer there is not any. The bear and Mustang are gone which you have heretofore Subsisted & lived upon—and without you go to work aided by the United States, you and your children must perish & die."[12]

Finally, in February 1854, the Texas legislature allowed the federal government to select some 53,000 acres for two Indian reserves. The limits of the reserves confined the Indians to a district from which the buffalo had almost entirely disappeared. A newspaper editor who accompanied the team that surveyed the reserves provided a dim forecast of the future. Having seen the Comanches confronting real hardship, he concluded that they faced three choices: become farmers on the reserve, steal, or starve. With their strong dislike of the white man and his customs, he had no doubt that they would continue to steal "until repeated chastisement accomplishes their destruction."[13]

In sum, during the time before the Second Cavalry arrived in Texas, the Comanches were being squeezed by pressure from three sides: to the east, by the resettled tribes; to the north, by the powerful Osage Indians; to the south, by white settlers. As had been the case east of the Mississippi River, the white thirst for land was unquenchable. Texans were unwilling to limit their territory for the benefit of the savages. This alone made all other arrangements futile. The Comanches, in turn, had long depended upon raids on Texas and the Mexican settlements to obtain horses. Stolen horses were the currency they used to obtain basic goods that ensured their survival. Some four to five hundred Comanches maintained an uneasy, poverty-stricken existence on the reserve. They received intermittent visits from family and friends who preferred living elsewhere, as well as from groups recruiting manpower for a proposed foray. To the north, along the Red River, various bands who had never entered into any treaty with the United States continued their nomadic life, a subsistence existence whose main prop was the horses and mules found in Texas and Mexico.

The Indian raiders presented settlers on the Texas frontier with an enemy whose methods were outside of prior American experience. The eastern Indian wars had featured an enemy who typically fought on foot and lived in fixed villages. A punitive expedition that destroyed their villages along with their stored foods, field crops, and orchards wreaked a devastating blow. A Comanche, on the other hand, had no permanent abode and moved his family and belongings upon a few minutes' notice. It was exceedingly difficult to overtake him. Never before had Americans confronted a situation whereby a dispersed warrior band, mounted on the hardy Indian pony, could harry a long stretch of frontier and escape with impunity. No one knew precisely how many Comanches were alive: an 1855 census giving the figure of ten thousand is undoubtedly too high.[14] From the perspective of the Texas settlers, whether two thousand or ten thousand made little difference. There were ample numbers to make life on the frontier terrible in the fundamental sense of the word.

*   *   *

TWO MILES from where the city of Austin now stands. A clear, starlit night. A waxing moon. The most dangerous of times: the Comanche moon. Worse in the autumn with a brightly lit harvest moon, but bad enough even now.

The young rider crossing the prairie knew he stood out in stark relief, but there was no alternative. Prudence dictated that he keep his horses and cattle behind his strong stockade fence, but the grass was bare, his animals grown thin. Turned out to graze—watched by his seven-year-old son, but not watched well enough—they had strayed, and he had spent the day searching for them. Now he headed home, where he expected, where he hoped, where he prayed he would find his wife and children. Because he was experienced, and experience taught caution, he approached a line of timber slowly until he entered distant gunshot range. Then a mad gallop parallel to the timber line. Rein and knee pressure, and the reluctant horse—sensing his rider's fear, ears back, white of the eye showing—entered the tree line. The rider's evasive course avoided a possible ambush.

Last year a neighbor—if the person living closest, six miles away, may still be called a neighbor—failed to follow this policy. No Indians had been seen for over a year. He had lost his caution and he had lost his life. The buzzards showed where he had fallen. They found his naked body, his hand, nose, and ears cut off. His breast had been cut open, his heart lifted and laid on his face.

The rider entered the tree line. Sudden movement. His horse startled. It was only an owl. He continued toward home.

Over in Eastland County, the Flanagan household was running low on flour. Mr. Flanagan hitched the wagon to his team and sent his son and another youth to the settlements on the lower Brazos. The wagon disappeared into the woods and the unseen watchers prepared their ambush. Young Flanagan thought he saw the horns of a deer showing above the brush. A deer hunter since he was old enough to hold a gun, his pulse quickened. "Do you see that buck?" he asked his companion.[15] He was mistaken. The horns belonged to a Comanche war helmet. The first volley killed Flanagan and struck his companion in the knee. Although hobbled, the companion escaped. Content with their scalp, the Comanches moved on.

The Reverend Jonas Dancer said good-bye to his wife and family, gathered his tools, and rode to meet his neighbors. They were to rendezvous to work on a new road from Llano to Austin. Ever punctual, Dancer arrived first. He hobbled his horses and set to work. Five or six Indians suddenly attacked. Being unarmed, Dancer fled through a deep ravine. From overhead poured a volley of arrows. Overcome, Dancer sat on a rock ledge, composed himself, and died. Searchers found his scalped, mutilated body the next day.

In Bosque County, a man named Renfrew was out looking for his horses with his son. Comanches ambushed them, killing and scalping the boy. Renfrew had a good horse and fled four miles before falling to Comanche arrows. The return of the riderless horse informed Mrs. Renfrew that she was a widow.

So it went, season after season. The people of Texas prayed that the cavalry would bring them deliverance.

—— II. First Blood ——

To the troopers of the Second Cavalry, it seemed that the winter of 1856 would never end. A five-inch snow fell on March 1, and it remained exceptionally cold a week later. Major Hardee, with the four companies on the Clear Fork of the Brazos, endured a succession of severe northers. An officer described the storm's arrival: "Suddenly there appears in the north a light, windy-looking cloud, which approaches with fearful rapidity. Within twenty minutes after the cloud is observed the storm is at hand. There is no rain, only wind, and it is so cold that one imagines it just down from an iceberg."[16] The storms generally continue for three or four days, during which time the air is full of dust and sand. Houses and tents cannot be built to keep the dust and sand out. There is dust in everything: eyes, ears, mouth, sugar, coffee. After a lull of a day or so, a gale from the south blows, driving the dust back in blinding sheets.

In between storms, the men built a semipermanent post. Mindful of which side to butter his bread on, Hardee named it in honor of the army's adjutant general, Samuel Cooper. Hardee sited Camp Cooper inside the Comanche reserve. Captain Kirby Smith tried to give his mother an idea of the post's locale: "Fifty miles west of Belknap, and about eighty beyond the line of settlements, is an elevated region of bare, rocky hills, open to the north winds which sweep over the central plateau of the continent three-fourths of the year. Sheltered by a bluff in the bottom of a little stream called the Clear Fork of the Brazos, and in one of the most dreary spots of this dreary section, Camp Cooper is located."[17] Only the wolves prowling Camp Cooper's perimeter seemed to thrive during the harsh winter.

Moreover, someone had blundered. The commanding general in Texas had made no preparations for the arrival of the Second Cavalry. The absence of provisions compelled troopers to grind corn in a mortar in order to make meal for baking. Lieutenant Charles Radziminski arrived in late March and wrote that the men had nothing to eat "but ground corn & starved beeves—without any small rations whatsoever; they were without clothes . . . and several in consequence have died, and the horses had no shelter, and no forage, so that when corn was procured, they died by hundreds of blind staggers, and on the first appearance of grass they continued dying of scours."[18] To Captain Van Dorn's chagrin, the effort to stay warm in the leaky tent led to a fire that destroyed his Company A's books and papers.

The six companies that Colonel Johnston led to Fort Mason were only slightly better off. Fort Mason offered lovely, expansive vistas and little else. Dragoons had established it back in 1851 and it had been occupied intermittently since. The few intact buildings were barely sufficient for the hospital and storerooms. The married officers' families took over the remaining dilapidated quarters and tried to make a home of it. Johnston reserved only one room for his own family. His wife complained about a lieutenant's howling children who inhabited the adjacent room, and too often her own, but Johnston was determined to set an example by sharing in the hardship. Except for one mild day, the remainder of January was a mix of heavy rain, cold northers, and frequent snow. Here, too, the troopers' Sibley tents offered poor shelter. Within the first two weeks three men died, their deaths undoubtedly hastened by exposure. Frozen sleet covered the shivering horses, who suffered piteously and grew ever thinner. One hundred and thirteen oxen hauling the trains to deliver supplies to the regiment died from the cold.

In spite of the weather, Johnston rotated the companies out on frequent patrols. Those that remained behind received daily drill because Johnston was determined to hone them to the sharpest point of discipline. He instilled in his subordinates the desire to make the Second a crack regiment. "All the officers were young and ambitious," recalled Richard Johnson, "and the enterprise and energy displayed by them soon established a fine name for the regiment." Sidney Johnston did not want mere pipe-clay soldiers, men who looked splendid at inspection and on the drill field but were inept while on campaign. He knew that a unit's reputation had to be based upon performance. Its first test came in mid-February, and the ensuing combat set the tone for the type of fighting the Second Cavalry would experience for the duration of its time in Texas.

A civilian rode to Fort Mason to report that a band of Waco Indians was raiding the nearby settlements. On February 14, Captain James Oakes set off with his Company C troopers to try to intercept them. Oakes had won two brevets for gallantry during the Mexican War. He remained eager to demonstrate to the regiment that he had not changed. On his third day out, trackers showed Oakes the hostile Indians' track. Oakes led a six-day pursuit that finally overtook the raiders, who numbered seven or so warriors. With the enemy in sight, his troopers chased furiously, their big bays straining hard against the flat bits, the men firing their revolvers whenever a shot presented itself. With each miss, the Indians turned in their saddles to shout and gesture defiantly with their bows and arrows. Their return archery fire killed one of the company's big horses and wounded another. The pursuit continued unchecked. As the cavalry drew closer, arrow fire severely wounded Sergeant Reis and Private Kuhn, while Privates Farrer and Fleegel had their uniforms pierced. Four more horses were hit. Small-arms fire from the saddle, particularly while on the move, is notoriously inaccurate. So far, mounted archery was besting carbine and Colt.

The troopers' return fire finally wounded one of the Indian's horses. The warrior sprang from his horse to continue the fight on foot. A trooper whose own horse was wounded dismounted to engage him. A hand-to-hand grapple ensued when the Indian attacked in an effort to capture and mount the trooper's horse. According to Eliza Johnston (who received two trophy arrows stained with the blood of this Indian), since the trooper had fired off all his ammunition, he used the nearest weapon at hand and killed the Indian with a stone. Almost certainly, the trooper wounded the Indian with his revolver and then dispatched the prostrate but still struggling warrior with a rock.[19] Whether pistoled or bludgeoned to death with a rock, the victim was the first foe to be killed by the regiment. The remainder of the Wacos escaped.

The conclusion of the skirmish marked the beginning of an ordeal for Oakes's detachment. The joy of the hunt had helped them ignore unpleasant conditions. Now they had to return to Fort Mason while enduring more cold, wet weather. Then trackers discovered another trail. The determined Oakes followed it for three days until the completely knackered horses were unable to carry their riders and the men ran out of food. They had to make two days' rations of bread and coffee last for seven. They killed several lame horses for food. The detachment staggered back to Fort Mason to claim victory, having routed the foe while killing or wounding several Indians. However, the certain casualties were one Indian killed and two cavalrymen seriously wounded. The claim to have put the enemy to rout was misleading, since the Wacos' objective was to flee as rapidly as possible. Still, the casualty inflicted represented the Second's first opponent killed, and army headquarters responded enthusiastically by commending Oakes and his men for "their gallant conduct . . . under circumstances of great hardship and privation."[20]

Over time, the Second's soldiers would learn how their foes operated. Upon leaving their assembly area, the Indians dispersed into small parties, with each one taking a separate route to the objective. They seldom followed the same trail twice. Mounted or dismounted, they traveled light and fast, taking no equipment or provisions except their weapons. Because they typically traveled on an empty stomach, when they halted and enjoyed a successful hunt they ate enormously and then slept. These old habits contributed to their neglect of camp security. They provided an opportunity for the Second to garner its first unqualified success.

Most of the regiment's patrols went out with little expectation of meeting hostile Indians. But the officers believed that patrolling was useful to instruct the men in field service. However, a routine scout like that of March 8 near the Guadalupe River could change into a deadly combat in very short order. A band of Lipan Apaches were resting after a successful raid, having killed two settlers, looted cabins, and driven off livestock in the San Antonio area. A Company I patrol led by Sergeant Henry Gordon came across them unexpectedly. The Apache camp was in a dense cedar brake. Since the terrain did not permit a mounted charge, Gordon led his troopers on foot. Their first carbine volley surprised the Apaches, who fled without offering much resistance. Gordon's men killed three men, recaptured a number of horses and mules, and suffered no losses themselves. The department commander hailed this "brilliant success" and cited Gordon and two other noncommissioned officers for their "gallant conduct."[21]

If enough such victories occurred, the cavalry would be well on its way to overcoming the scorn with which many Texans regarded the U.S. Army. Too often in the past, Indians had successfully raided the very forts housing the frontiersmen's nominal protectors. While the Second had been organizing in Missouri, the Mounted Rifles had suffered the humiliation of having horses stolen from the stables at Fort Inge in spite of the presence of four sentinels. Likewise, a sergeant bringing a load of hay was within one mile of Fort Duncan when the Indians struck. They cut three mules from the traces of his wagon before he could rally his escort. Many Texans thought that living near a fort was more dangerous than elsewhere simply because the soldiers' fine horses and weapons acted like a magnet attracting Indian raiders.

Texans believed that not only was the army unable to defend against raids, but it was hopelessly inept at pursuing and catching the raiders. The regulars typically arrived on the scene anytime from six hours to several days after the event, by which time the trail had grown cold. Thereafter, it seemed to the Texans that they lacked the skill and zeal to chase down the Indians. As one observer sardonically wrote, "The deliberate slowness of the national sword is as notorious along the frontier as the good-natured blindness to official larcenies. Justice always comes lumbering one day behind the rogue."[22] The Second Cavalry's initial skirmishes gave hope that justice could overtake the rogue.

LEADERSHIP WITHIN the Second Cavalry demanded both military judgment and the ability to supervise the unit's internal management. By March 1856, Colonel Johnston faced an ugly challenge to his supervisory skills when he realized that he could no longer contain the emerging scandal over the conduct of Captain Charles Travis, stemming from charges Lieutenant Wood had proffered against Travis back at Jefferson Barracks. The conflict had escalated during the unit's march to Texas, at the time of the difficult crossing of the Canadian River. Thereafter, the slow wheels of army justice ground inexorably to a court-martial that convened on March 15. Because of Travis's name, the trial created an enormous sensation throughout Texas. The state's most prominent newspapers enjoyed stirring up journalistic blood feuds between public figures. Travis's trial perhaps promised something better, so the papers followed it attentively.

The prosecution charged Travis with "conduct unbecoming an officer and gentleman." There were three specific accusations: Travis had cheated at cards on October 1, 1855; he had been absent without authorization on November 16, 1855; he had circulated false and slanderous imputations against Lieutenant

Wood. Travis pleaded not guilty to the charge and all three specifications.

Like his father, Travis was a lawyer. Consequently, although he employed another lawyer to assist him, he mostly acted as his own defense counsel. This gave him numerous and embarrassing (at least from the regiment's viewpoint) opportunities to speak publicly. The court-martial dragged on for almost a month, which is perhaps a testament to Travis's legal skills, since the evidence against him seemed overwhelming. Fully half of the regiment's company commanders acted as witnesses against him. Far worse was the testimony of Johnston himself. The colonel asserted that Travis had lied to him more than once. This effectively sealed the case. The court handed down a guilty verdict and sentenced Travis to dismissal from the service of the United States. It was a harsh sentence that West Pointers might not have inflicted upon a fellow graduate. In any event, President Franklin Pierce upheld the decision.

Having at a minimum exhibited his father's poor judgment, the son now showed his father's fighting spirit as well. He took his case to the Texas legislature. In the hopes that legislators in Austin were more likely to be sympathetic to the son of a great Texas hero, a onetime Texas Ranger and a former legislator himself, Travis demanded a copy of the testimony from his court-martial and gave it to the legislators. They reviewed the testimony and recommended that he be publicly exonerated. They asked President Pierce to reconsider, but he refused. Travis then tried to make several officers who had spoken against him change their testimony. It was such a sordid, ham-fisted effort that all he accomplished was to lose public esteem. Discredited, disgraced, and humiliated, Travis slunk into the shadows and out of public view. He died of consumption in 1860.

If cheating at cards was manifestly conduct unbecoming an officer and gentleman, getting another man's wife with child and then openly living with her was apparently not, at least if the perpetrator was a West Point graduate. During the march to Texas, Eliza Johnston had heard pretty convincing stories that Lieutenant Charles Field had seduced a married woman and then somehow brought her along with the baggage train. Still, her principal source for such intelligence was Captain James Oakes's gossipy wife, "who I verily believe would cause trouble in Heaven."[23] However, when Mrs. Johnston's cook confirmed that one of the garrison's laundresses had borne a child who had the same sandy-colored hair and blue eyes as the handsome Charley Field, Eliza accepted it as fact. Indeed, the voluble Mrs. Oakes reported that after the woman recovered from childbirth, Field lived with her openly. The regimental officers enjoyed Field's fine sense of humor, but this was a bit too much. And here is where Field's West Point lineage helped, for as an indignant Eliza wrote, "I can never talk to the man with pleasure or patience again & yet he is considered a gentleman and a fine officer."[24]

To rid the regiment of scandal and to relieve himself from his wife's carping, Johnston assigned Field to recruiting service back east, with his post of duty at West Point. By so doing he lost a valuable, experienced officer, a man who knew how to care for his men and how to inspire fortitude.[25] For the five years prior to the Civil War, Field was a professor of cavalry tactics at West Point. Although the lieutenant missed a chance to distinguish himself with the Second Cavalry, his military talents emerged during the Civil War. He earned an outstanding reputation in Lee's Army of Northern Virginia and rose to major general. His charm and affability persisted into middle age. Following a stint in the Egyptian army, he returned to the United States in 1878 and achieved a handsome sinecure in Washington, D.C., as doorkeeper for the House of Representatives. Ironically, his last public post was as superintendent of the Hot Springs, Arkansas, Indian reservation.

___ III. Colonel Lee's Campaign ___

After a cold winter, spring came late in 1856. Not until the end of March did the grass around Fort Mason begin to green up. But it did not green up much, because a droughty spring followed the wet winter. It was so dry that corn had not emerged by May 1. Because extended patrols were problematic until the horses could find graze, Johnston had devoted much time to company and battalion drill. After hours he frequently met with his officers to review military matters. Spring's arrival meant that the time for instruction was over. It was time for the Second to take to the field. Then, on March 31, Johnston unexpectedly received orders elevating him to temporary command of the entire Department of Texas. It was quite a leap for an officer who just one year earlier had been mired in the routine of carrying money from post to post. His close association with the regiment ended. But he had formed it in his own image. Officers' letters and memoirs emphasize how his desire to make the regiment the finest in the army inspired them. Had he been a mere martinet, or simply an ambitious soldier, he would not have had such influence. But because he was a fair-minded, considerate man, his young subordinates "not only respected but loved him."[26]

Johnston's promotion gave him an opportunity to put into practice his strategy for dealing with the enemy. While traversing Texas as an army paymaster, Johnston had witnessed the aftermath of Indian raids—horses and mules stolen, cattle butchered, the people forced either to fort up or to flee. As early as 1850 he had seen that merely chasing the raiding parties was not a viable tactic. "To give peace to the frontier . . . the troops ought to act offensively and carry the war to the homes of the enemy."[27] Accordingly, he ordered the Second to patrol aggressively. If an officer encountered the Comanches, he was to pursue them relentlessly. One of the first officers to try to implement Johnston's orders was the regiment's lieutenant colonel.

During the time the Second Cavalry had been marching to Texas, Robert Lee had been serving on the court at Fort Riley, Kansas. It was an ugly trial, featuring charges that Dr. James Simons had deserted the post in the midst of a smallpox epidemic. Lee and his fellow judges found Simons guilty and condemned him to be dismissed from the service. The court might as well have saved its breath. There were only twenty-two surgeons and seventy-two assistant surgeons in the entire army. The army was so short of medical officers that the cowardly Simons was reinstated the following year, eventually managing to become a lieutenant colonel of surgery.

Court-martial duty had kept Lee away from his regiment for the past half year. He finally arrived by steamer in Galveston in early March. A ride inland brought him to San Antonio for a pleasant two-week sojourn. Here he met one of his regiment's most unusual officers, First Lieutenant Charles Radziminski. Born in Poland in 1805, Radziminski had taken part in a revolution against Russia in 1830–31. The revolt's failure condemned him to three years in prison—at which time a man who knew firsthand about the value of freedom, the marquis de Lafayette, negotiated an agreement that allowed the defeated to exile themselves to the United States. Radziminksi arrived in New York, where, in surprisingly short order, he proved himself to be a man of talent. He served as a civil engineer until the outbreak of the Mexican War. He received a second lieutenant's commission in the U.S. Dragoons, and thereafter utilized his engineering skill while serving with the Mexican boundary commission. Radziminski was in Texas completing the final border survey when he received notification that the War Department wanted him for

For second in command Lieutenant Colonel Robert E. Lee, service in Texas provided a first opportunity at field command. (National Archives)

the Second Cavalry. He was another example of Jefferson Davis's thorough search to find the best possible officers for his pet unit.

The extent to which Lee appreciated Radziminski's talents is unknown. In San Antonio, Lee assigned him the not too challenging task of procuring supplies for the journey to regimental headquarters at Fort Mason. Lee explained that his own needs were simple, consisting of only boiled ham, hard bread, molasses, and coffee. If this was a duty slightly beneath a former Polish revolutionary, civil engineer, and combat veteran, the lieutenant also understood his place in the chain of command. He discharged his duty and accompanied Lieutenant Colonel Lee on his five-day journey to Fort Mason.

Here Lee reunited with Colonel Johnston and learned about some of the changes within the regiment. The unit's senior lieutenant, Nathan Evans, had replaced the disgraced Travis as commander of Company H. More surprising was the departure of Major Hardee. As an officer with the Second Dragoons, Hardee had conducted numerous small patrols against the Indians in Texas. Furthermore, over a three-year span from 1849 to 1851, Hardee had led large-scale mounted operations involving mounted infantry and Rangers. No other officer in the Second Cavalry had such experience. Yet before the unit's first campaign season began, the War Department decided that this valuable officer could be better utilized as commandant of cadets at West Point. It was a position Hardee would fill until September 1860. His brief service with the regiment had come during its formative time. Most believed that his training and discipline had helped positively mold the regiment. Captain Brackett disagreed: "His career in the regiment was unmarked by a single thing which could go to show that he was anything more than a vain and conceited martinet."[28]

With Hardee recalled, Johnston ordered Lee to take command of the two squadrons based at Camp Cooper. So Lee and Radziminski set off to ride over an uneven Texas frontier road that wended between hills and across creeks and ravines. Some of the flats supported post oak thickets. Connecting them were frequent carpets of green grass through which protruded the yellow splashes of the spring's first primroses. After traversing a mesquite tableland, the riders approached a steep bluff overlooking the Clear Fork of the Brazos River. On April 9, 1856, Lee arrived at the post he was to call his "Texas home." His view of Camp Cooper was far more benign than the winter scene first beheld by Hardee's command. He entered the wide, level valley of the Clear Fork, passing through a chaparral desert of mixed vegetation—dwarfed mesquite, stunted hackberry, ubiquitous prickly pear. Only the riverbank supported something resembling an eastern vista, hardwood stands of elm and pecan trees spreading their branches over the placid river. Emerging from the trees, he saw towering metallic cliffs streaked with gray, as if to remind him that this was surely not his beloved Virginia. Beyond those cliffs was a wild region, bordered to the west by a desolate land that stretched to the Staked Plain.

The Llano Estacado, or Staked Plain, was an elevated, desolate, and barren tableland up to two hundred miles wide, cut up by numerous rugged canyons. Here game was scarce, trees rare, and the infrequent water usually unpotable. The Spanish had staked a road across it for the use of traders, thus giving it its name. Mounted men could enter, but unless they had a superb guide, they emerged lost and on foot. If a diligent cavalry trooper had read the report of the first U.S. Army officer to cross the Staked Plain, he would not have been encouraged:

> The sun was pouring down heat as heavy clouds do rain. . . . We travelled some hours . . . but found no sign of water. Our tongues seemed to cleave to the roofs of our mouths, and our throats were parched with dryness. The rude jokes and boisterous laugh had long since died away, and the "hep" of the driver, as he urged his panting team, under the scorching sun, grew fainter and fainter, until we moved on in dead silence.[29]

The cavalry would learn that the rugged terrain of the Staked Plain provided raiding Indians with a safe invasion route into Texas.

Camp Cooper had no buildings and lacked lumber to construct any. So Lee, like all his troopers, lived in a tent. The snakes were so plentiful—men often encountered rattlesnakes up to eight feet long with as many as eleven rattles—that no free-range domestic chicken could survive. Lee had to build an elevated chicken coop and surround it with a protective barrier of woven twigs to shelter his seven hens. A nocturnal visit to the latrine required care to avoid stepping on the venomous serpents. Lee would have liked to keep a pet cat, but the abundant wolves eliminated that choice. Even Lee's pet rattlesnake did not thrive at Camp Cooper. It grew sick, refused its frogs, and died one night.

Many of Lee's neighbors, the reserve's Comanches, were pariahs within their own tribe. Numerous others, although Lee did not yet know this, contributed manpower to the very raiding bands that Lee was charged with killing. Whenever a chief from outside the reserve decided to assemble a raid, he sent runners to the reserve to recruit. Regardless of the inclination of the tribal leaders on the reserve, it was impossible to restrain the young warriors. If someone participated in a raid he usually lived with his relations beyond the frontier until the disturbance subsided and he could return to the reserve. The Department of the Interior's agents knew that the Comanche reserve sheltered a floating population, with the young men departing for a raid when the mood struck. Some of them concluded that this was an unfortunate situation that could be rectified only by a more generous and better-supported federal policy. To army officers, the idea of maintaining a hostile population near to white settlements was ridiculous. Bureaucratically and philosophically, the Indian agents and army officers were at odds. When Secretary of War Jefferson Davis had promoted the idea of Texas Indian reserves, he predicted that it would greatly simplify the army's problems. With the Indians confined to their reservations, the military would be free to assume that any Indians found elsewhere were hostile. As the army was to find in subsequent guerrilla wars, solutions that appeared neat and clean in Washington worked rather differently when put into practice.

Lee personally regarded the reserve's Comanches to be nearly as disagreeable as his physical surroundings. His first contact came when Chief Ketumse paid a ceremonial call. A long and, from Lee's viewpoint, tedious conversation ensued. Lee believed that he delivered a pithy warning to the Indian: "I hailed him as a friend, as long as his conduct and that of his tribe deserved it, but would meet him as an enemy the first moment he failed to keep his word." Ketumse, in turn, assessed Lee as another rude, overbearing white. The relationship did not improve when Lee visited the tepees and found conditions distasteful. The sight of thin, unkempt children living amid camp refuse—bones carelessly strewn, flies swarming—appalled this exceptionally orderly man. When Ketumse paraded his six wives before Lee, the colonel found them "hideous." The conditions on the reserve made Lee doubt the wisdom of the reservation experiment. Moreover, he concluded that the Comanches were a debased people; "extremely uninteresting," he wrote his wife.[30]

Lee found it far easier to cooperate with the supervisor of the Texas Indian reserves, Robert Neighbors, since after all, both were native Virginians. Neighbors keenly wanted the reserves to succeed. He tried to apprise Lee of the movements of hostile Indians and offered to provide skilled scouts to guide any expedition. Neighbors's offer proved welcome when Lee received an order from the departmental commander. Army headquarters in San Antonio had been besieged with complaints from the border settlements. Lee read that the Tenawish, Noconas, and Sanaco's band of southern Comanches, the Penatekas, were the suspected culprits: "Their continual rejection of the privilege of settling on the Reservations under the protection and control of the government, will be considered sufficient evidence of their unfriendliness; and it is the order of the Department Commander that they shall be pursued to the utmost limit that the means of your command will permit."[31]

Accordingly, orders provided for Lee to assemble two cavalry companies of not more than forty men per company, take thirty days' provisions and no more than two tents per company for the sick, hire guides and use pack mules, and set off for Fort Chadbourne. After marching the hundred miles to Fort Chadbourne, Lee would merge his command with two more cavalry companies. Indian trailers from the Brazos Agency would join him. He was to consult with Neighbors as to likely Indian locations.

The Comanche leader Sanaco was well known to Neighbors. A haughty, difficult Indian, at one time Sanaco had sent a message to the agency to announce that he would come to the reserve if the agent would provide plentiful good whiskey and that he would stay as long as the whiskey lasted. Since that time he had been implicated in numerous Indian depredations. Most recently, his band had killed some settlers, stolen livestock, and hurried off to the sanctuary of the country bordering the upper Red and Canadian Rivers. When officers and men learned that their objective was to hunt down Sanaco, they nodded their heads with pleasure. He was just the sort of enemy they expected. Probably none knew that Texans had killed Sanaco's father back in 1840 while he was attending a peace negotiation and that revenge motivated the son.

So, at age forty-nine, Lieutenant Colonel Robert E. Lee embarked upon his first independent combat command. His two company commanders were Van Dorn and O'Hara. Neighbors provided valuable assistance and forwarded the celebrated Jim Shaw and fifteen of his Delaware trailers to scout for Lee. Jim Shaw—Bear Head—was a Delaware Indian adopted into the Caddo tribe of Texas. He was "about fifty years old, full six feet six in height, as straight as an arrow, with a sinewy, muscular frame, large head, high cheek bones, wide mouth, and eye like an eagle—his countenance indicative of the true friend and dangerous enemy."[32] Shaw and men like him would prove indispensable to the Second Cavalry.

The four-day march to Fort Chadbourne took the cavalry across a monotonous succession of barren, rocky hills onto an elevated tableland where short grass, stunted mesquite, and little else grew. However, unlike many areas, this region had frequent watering holes, around which grew enough grass to provide grazing for the horses. Lee's column united with companies commanded by Captains Smith and Bradfute—the latter the officer who had nearly drowned back when the unit crossed the Canadian River the previous December—at Fort Chadbourne on June 17. Named in memory of Lieutenant Theodore L. Chadbourne, who had been killed at Resaca de la Palma during the Mexican War, it was one of the forts built to protect emigrants who chose the southern route to California. Although none of the troopers had seen Indians during the march to Fort Chadbourne, dense plumes of smoke rising from the prairie to the south and west suggested that Indians were present.

In fact, around this time of year the Comanches habitually moved north to hunt buffalo along the Arkansas River. Somehow Lee never learned this. Not realizing that his quarry was reduced to tiny bands of horse stealers, Lee formed up his two squadrons and their supporting wagon train and set out to find the enemy. Captain Kirby Smith knew something of this desolate country. Among the company commanders, Smith had unequaled practical experience on the Texas frontier. He had served with the Dragoons along the Mexican border, and then his company was chosen to escort the boundary commission that surveyed the permanent line between the United States and Mexico. This experience had taught him a good deal about the nature of Indian warfare. He anticipated a wearing, fruitless search. His prophecy proved all too true.

Over the ensuing days, the Delawares found old campsites and trails used by Yamparikas, one of the major Comanche bands, on their way south to raid Mexico. But no one found any enemies. The smoke plumes turned out to be caused by prairie fires. For many, the march was the first prolonged exposure to a Texas summer. Across the drought-stricken land the column rode. Huge horseflies, of which a dark blue variety was nearly the size of a small hummingbird, tormented the men. They endured omnipresent dust and heat. Game was scarce. Since they typically found the streambeds dry, they drank whatever water they could find. Experience taught them that upon reaching a water hole they had to place a guard around it so the humans drew the water before the animals rushed into it to make it even worse than it already was. Even coffee could not disguise the taste of water drawn from a badly fouled pool. That knowledge came later. On this campaign troopers fell sick with raging diarrhea. At night, officers and men alike slept in the open on their saddle blankets with their saddles serving as pillows. The column spent three miserable nights around Double Mountain while troopers searched adjacent draws and canyons out to a distance of thirty miles. There still was no contact.

Lee resolved to cut loose from his wagons. He loaded them with the sick and sent them back under escort. He ordered the troopers to carry seven days' rations—salt pork (a particularly delectable sustenance when water was scarce), flour, and coffee—and planned to rely upon game for most of the unit's food. Their horses would have to survive on parched prairie grass. To sweep a broader area, Lee divided his command and sent Captain Van Dorn, his senior captain, ahead with Captain O'Hara's company in support on his right flank. When his trackers found more recent Indian signs, Lee made the assumption that the enemy was heading for water. Accordingly, he led the remaining two companies on a search of the upper Brazos and Colorado Rivers. When the whiskey-loving Captain Evans returned from one reconnaissance to report that he had found a fine camping spot with plentiful wood, water, and grass, Lee replied, "Captain, your report is quite satisfactory; but did you drink of the water to ascertain if it was good?" Evans recognized the joke and instantly replied, "By Jove! I never thought to taste the water."[33]

After some more fruitless searching, Lee concluded that there was nothing in this terrritory to attract Indians. His conclusion speaks more to his frustration than to his wisdom, since Evans's discovery—plentiful wood, water, and grass—was of obvious interest to Indians on the invasion route to Mexico. Some of the same deep canyons that Lee's patrols found barren in the summer offered the Indians protection from the cold north winds in the winter. Ignorant of his enemy's habits, Lee decided to turn back. He reunited with Van Dorn, and that officer reported a modest success. Van Dorn's trackers had found a recent Indian trail. They led the command on a 200-mile pursuit. Days of hard riding climaxed in a stealthy approach toward yet another smoke plume. This time the troopers encountered, if not quite a fearsome predatory band, then at least four men and one woman. Nonexistent camp security allowed the troopers to attack with surprise, kill two Indians, and capture the woman. She related her experience to Van Dorn's Indian guides. Some four months earlier, she and twelve Yamparikas had left their homeland north of the Arkansas to raid Mexico. After capturing numerous horses they began a return journey, only to be attacked by white men north of the Rio Grande. The whites killed nine of the warriors and recaptured the horses. The five survivors fled north with only the horses they rode. To avoid the shame of returning after utter failure, the men raided a Texas settlement and stole eight horses. Around Big Springs, they stole cattle from a California train and moved to Double Mountain to rest and jerk beef for the return home. Thus, after Van Dorn's men attacked them, the Comanches lost ten of twelve warriors who had departed the north, and all of their supplies. Just as Lee's expedition was like the futile Vietnam-era search-and-destroy operations, so was the experience of many Comanches akin to the "lost generation" of North Vietnamese youth who were sent down the Ho Chi Minh Trail and never returned.

Based on the woman's tale, Lee suspected that the Big Springs area served as a staging area for Indians on their way to raid Mexico. His assumption was accurate—at a different time of year, Big Springs did provide a large-scale assembly area—but his timing was off since he failed to enter Indian logistics (the seasonal nature of the forays) into his calculation. A seven-day sweep along both banks of the Concho River proved fruitless. Even Jim Shaw could find no fresh Indian signs. The dispirited column spent a forlorn July 4 huddled beneath improvised tents to escape the heat. The Texas sun did not respect rank. Lee described his Fourth of July celebration as "spent, after a march of thirty miles on one of the branches of the Brazos, under my blanket, elevated on four sticks driven in the ground, as a sun-shade. The sun was fiery hot, the atmosphere like the blast from a hot-air furnace, the water salt."[34]

The forty-day mission ended in the same heat and dust that had shrouded it throughout. Patrols had traversed some sixteen hundred miles. For their efforts they had killed two Indians and taken one female prisoner, along with recapturing twelve horses and mules. Upon the return to Camp Cooper, Kirby Smith described the results: "We travelled through the country, broke down our men, killed our horses, and returned as ignorant of the whereabouts of Mr. Sanico [*sic*] as when we started."[35] Recalling Lee's service in the Mexican War, General Winfield Scott had described him as "the very best soldier that I ever saw in the field."[36] In contrast, Lee's first independent command had been completely undistinguished.

For Kirby Smith the conclusion was obvious: when confronting a dispersed and elusive foe, large expeditions were an inefficient, unimaginative use of resources. But even smaller-sized expeditions were not necessarily the answer. In late August, Smith conducted a small patrol for two weeks and never saw another human being. One hasty bath in a blood-warm alkaline stream while guards stood ready was the only relief from the cloying dust. Weather-beaten and discouraged, the troopers returned to camp. The summer of futility taught Smith a lesson: only by adapting to the Indians' way of life and learning their habits can "we operate successfully against them."[37] In large measure, this is what they did. They lightened their loads even more and abandoned most civilized comforts. They exchanged formal uniforms for more serviceable dress: "Corduroy pants; a hickory or blue flannel shirt, cut down in front, studded with pockets and worn outside; a slouched hat and long beard, cavalry boots worn over the pants, knife and revolver belted to the side and a double barrel gun across the pommel, complete the costume as truly serviceable as it is unmilitary."[38] But the more practical uniform did not seem to make a difference either. In September Smith led another lengthy patrol that failed to discover anyone at all. So it was for most of the regiment.

Extended patrols were very much a hit-and-miss affair. By the late summer of 1856, many raiding bands had yet to experience the impact of the Second Cavalry's presence. Thus, the unit's mobility and persistence still could surprise. Captain Oakes—the officer whose wife provided Mrs. Johnston with her choicest bits of gossip—led a thirty-man cavalry patrol out of Fort Clark in August. Accompanied by nineteen infantry and thirteen artillerymen, the patrol headed for the mouth of the Pecos River to search for Comanches. Even by Texas standards it was exceptionally rough ground. No army units had previously penetrated this region, a sanctuary where the Comanches did not expect to encounter the cavalry. Ten days into the mission, the patrol arrived near the junction of the Pecos and Rio Grande Rivers. The Indians' lack of vigilance allowed the cavalry to surprise three separate bands during one eventful day. However, even with the advantages of surprise and numbers, the troopers managed to kill only four Indians. This was a low return for a twenty-day effort involving sixty-two soldiers. Furthermore, never again would any of the regiment's patrols fight three separate encounters during one day. Still, Colonel Johnston praised Oakes and his second in command, Lieutenant James B. Witherell, for their "judgment and energy."[39]

Yet, just perhaps, the patrols were unable to locate the enemy because there was no enemy to find. This notion came to Johnston's mind in August, and he conceived that his strategy seemed to be working. Certainly the number of Indian raids had dramatically declined. Apparently the Second's aggressive patrolling had driven the Comanches deep into the hinterland. When Texas had learned that the popular Johnston was returning to the state at the head of the Second Cavalry, it gave hope that the era of insecurity was over. The event seemed to equal the expectation. The reduction of the Indian threat encouraged such an influx of settlers in the region around Lee's "Texas home," Camp Cooper, that the state legislature confidently created the new counties of Erath, Parker, Jack, Palo Pinto, Wise, and Young to absorb, organize, and tax them.

Meanwhile, a grateful public lavished praise upon Colonel Johnston. Many prominent Texas leaders had felt neglected by the federal government. They pridefully believed that Johnston's efforts stemmed from the government's desire to make amends. Their accolades did not turn Johnston's head. Indeed, the Texans misunderstood his motivation. "The truth is," he wrote his son, "they felt unsafe. A feeling of security was due to them. According it to them was a simple act of duty, nothing more."[40] However, his brief experience at departmental command gave Johnston a new appreciation of the extent of the problem: "The country . . . is as open as the oceans—They can come when they like, taking the risk of chastisement. If they choose therefore it need only be a question of legs."[41]

Indeed, although the whites did not realize it, in the second half of 1856 the Comanches had withdrawn by choice. They had done this before. In 1851 and 1852, the army had extended its line of forts about one hundred fifty miles into Indian country, constructing at that time two of the outposts that the Second Cavalry would garrison. The subsequent year witnessed a marked reduction in Indian attacks, which, in turn, led to optimism and a false sense of security within the War Department. Concluding that the frontier had been pacified, the War Department shifted forces elsewhere. In fact, in 1853 the Indians had prudently withdrawn to assess the strength of the defense. Having figured out how to evade contact with the soldiers garrisoning the new line of forts, the next year they returned with a vengeance.

So it was again in 1856. The Comanches wanted time to take the measure of their newest opponents in the Second Cavalry. No army officer yet fully appreciated that in their pursuit of horse stealing, they would always seek to avoid combat with the cavalry. Consequently, to the men of the Second Cavalry it seemed that outside of the reservations, few Indians remained in Texas—they had eliminated the enemy threat.[42] It was perhaps an appropriate conclusion insofar as it applied to soldiers. They were always armed and usually in large enough force to avoid fear of annihilation. Such was not the case for the people of Texas, and they had a far different outlook. After an all too brief interlude of safety, the Comanches completed their assessment of their new foes and returned to raiding. They learned to infiltrate past the cavalry posts or operate in the hinterland beyond the range of cavalry patrols. Because the Comanches knew the countryside and operated in small groups, the settlers seldom detected them. They came on foot, and at an unguarded moment stampeded the horses, and then rode day and night until they thought themselves safe from pursuit. Typically the Comanches had rounded up stock and fled before most whites even realized that they were in the area. Since his stock lived on the open range, a rancher searching for his animals had to assess whether they had merely wandered or had been stolen. For a stockman, it was almost a daily decision, yet one fraught with the gravest consequences. A lone rancher or his children who were out searching for horses or cattle that had strayed did so in peril of their lives. The first indication of danger and perhaps the last thought of a lifetime was the hissing sound of an arrow approaching at horrible velocity. In spite of the cavalry's best exertions, the settlers continued to dread the approach of the Comanche moon.

THE RESIGNATION OF the regiment's post captain, Theodore O'Hara, on December 1 opened a place for Lieutenant Richard Johnson. Johnson had served as regimental quartermaster during the long march to Texas. He thirsted for greater glory. So Johnson happily welcomed his promotion to captain: "I had reached that rank which would ever exempt me from duty with mules, broken harness, and the accumulated trash and rubbish which drift into the storehouses in charge of a post quartermaster."[43] After stagnating for a very long time as second lieutenant, Johnson had joined the Second Cavalry and in little more than one year ascended to company command. He now held a combat assignment. Its challenge became starkly obvious when Johnson led the regiment's last patrol that encountered Indians during 1856.

Richard W. Johnson greeted his appointment as a first lieutenant to the Second Cavalry with joy: "It opened up a new life for me." Part of that life would include the rank of major general in the Civil War. (National Archives)

Johnson and twenty-five troopers departed Camp Cooper to search for the elusive Sanaco and his band of Comanches around the headwaters of the Concho River. A green second lieutenant just out of West Point, A. Parker Porter, received permission from Captain Van Dorn to accompany the patrol. Seven uneventful but cold days ensued. Then, on December 22, the patrol contacted the enemy. The Comanches were on the fringe of a dense thicket. If Johnson ordered his bugler to sound the charge, it was the last time Ryan Campion ever lifted his instrument to his lips. The regiment's leaders had learned that when a patrol encountered an Indian camp, their first maneuver should be aimed at separating the Indians from their horses in order to prevent them from escaping. This Johnson accomplished. His men drove the Comanches into the chaparral. He ordered the troopers to dismount and divided them into two groups. He gave command of one group to Porter. In a pincers movement, the two detachments surrounded the thicket and then plunged into the underbrush to pursue the enemy. Probably neither Campion nor Private Timothy Lamb ever saw the warriors who shot the arrows that drove through their chest walls and pierced their hearts. Still, the charge overran the Comanche camp. The troopers' carbine and pistol fire killed three Indians. The soldiers claimed to have wounded three more. They captured thirty-four horses and all of the Comanches' meager camp equipage, along with a Mexican youth who had been captured and raised with the band since boyhood.

Prisoner in tow—the hapless Mexican did not want to be taken back to his own people, since he considered himself a Comanche—the patrol began its return journey. First Sergeant Thomas Gardner, one of two troopers who had been slightly wounded, was still smarting from his own injury and mourning the death of two comrades. Thoughts of revenge remained uppermost in his mind. It bothered him to have to escort a live enemy—he called the Mexican captive a "naturalized Comanche"—back to Fort Cooper. Gardner saw that the prisoner remained alert for an opportunity to escape, his eyes searching the horizon for his Comanche brethren. This was too much. The sergeant asked permission to kill him. Johnson forbade it. The patrol returned to Camp Cooper, where it received profuse praise from Van Dorn. The commanding general of the entire army even commended the action in a general order. It had been a typical Texas combat: a sudden, unexpected beginning; a brief but violent melee; and then the foe broke contact and disappeared. It differed from the regiment's other encounter only in the amount of cavalry blood spilt. Campion and Lamb were the first soldiers in the Second Cavalry to die in battle.[44]

When they came to Texas, the men of the Second Cavalry entered a cruel environment of savage warfare. While there is no evidence that the troopers, unlike the civilians and the Indians, tortured their captives, they also seldom took male prisoners alive. Almost all wounded Indians continued to fight as long as they possibly could. Bitter experience would show that even a fallen warrior remained a formidable foe. Still, if the cavalry did not kill the enemy wounded, they left the task to their own Indian allies, who after a skirmish would methodically kill and scalp wounded Comanches.[45]

Then and thereafter, whether they encountered them in their eastern homes or in their quarters in Texas, people widely perceived the Second Cavalry officers as gentlemen. They in turn adopted the prevailing national ethos regarding the Indians. They cast aside most of the rules of civilized warfare. They fought without scruple. They fought to kill.

4

"Tell Robert I Cannot Advise Him to Enter the Army"

Little does the casual observer at West Point know of the after existence of its graduates, and their lives of exile and privation on the frontier, passed in lonely seclusion from the world, a stranger to its luxuries, almost a stranger to the ordinary comforts of civilization.

—A soldier's wife, 1858 (in Teresa Griffin Viele,
"Following the Drum": A Glimpse of Frontier Life)

—— I. Ordeal in Irons ——

A review of the Second Cavalry one year after its birth shows a regiment that had not performed any notable exploit to elevate it to the standard Sidney Johnston craved. It was not thoroughly battle tested. It was not yet *the* regiment in the army. Still, by midsummer 1856 constant patrolling had taught the unit's thirty-seven officers and 608 enlisted men how to adjust to the rigors of field service in Texas. It had also taught a fair number of men that cavalry life was not for them, and they deserted at every opportunity. Since the departure from Jefferson Barracks, eighty-seven new recruits had joined the regiment, but this did not compensate for the heavy desertion. The regiment was shy 247 recruits. However, this was far better than the situation in its sister regiment, the First Cavalry. Assigned the unpleasant duty of preserving peace in "Bleeding Kansas" as well as protecting emigrant trains moving west, Colonel Edwin Sumner's First Cavalry had shrunk to 404 enlisted men.

Desertions aside, the Second Cavalry's men were tolerating Texas's harsh environment. The same could not be said for the unit's select horses. They had suffered cruelly, with over half having died or become too weak to be serviceable. The younger animals in particular had been broken down by hard service.[1] No one dared acknowledge that the unlimited budget provided to buy the finest horses had obtained animals ill-suited to Texas warfare. The horses had to endure an environment very different from the bluegrass pastures where many had been born. In Texas, after a hard day crossing desert or prairie, the horses grazed on whatever wild plants grew near the bivouac, supplemented by a handful of corn if available. Overnight they had to be closely guarded to foil Indian theft, so they remained tied to the picket line. If the troopers were not in hot pursuit, the horses could browse for the first hours after sunrise on desert vegetation made tender by overnight dew. Otherwise, they were driven hard, day after day. With the mission complete, the horses returned to their rude stables to regain their strength on the corn delivered by civilian contractors. It was a life better suited to the Texas mustang. Since attrition had claimed so many of the blooded eastern horses, a board of officers led by Captain George Stoneman began buying replacements from northeast Texas as early as November 1856. Experience had taught some specific lessons. Hardihood was more important than appearance. Smaller animals between 15 and 16 hands fared better than the larger, showier horses. So, instead of big, handsome, young, color-matched horses, the board sought fully mature six-year-olds with good conformation because they were best able to withstand the hardships imposed by cavalry service.

The summer of 1856 marked the dispersal of the regiment along the northern and western Texas frontier. The unit's senior leaders lamented it. Like most military men, they reveled in the latent power of a massed force. But they also understood that Texas had a very extensive frontier and that it could not be defended by keeping the regiment concentrated. So, while a few companies remained at Camp Cooper and Fort Mason, the balance marched off to garrison outlying camps and forts. Referring to the cavalry outposts as forts conveys a false impression. They were not built for defense. The only structure suggesting a fortification was a stockade fence of mesquite trunks surrounding the stables. Indeed, this stockade protected the fort's most valuable asset, its horses. If Indian raiders were so bold as to strike at a fort, their objective was to steal the horses rather than to kill the garrison. Occasionally they would show their hatred of the horse soldiers by filling nearby grazing cattle with arrows, but overall, from a Comanche viewpoint, the risk of attacking the garrison was without tangible reward.

The army occupied many of its Texas forts only intermittently. In response to Indian raids, the cavalry in particular shifted duty stations frequently. Once they arrived at a post, the troopers spent most of their time in the field. Consequently, officers and men had little incentive to make physical improvements. Rather, they did the opposite by burning whatever wood was easiest to come by—fence rails and doors usually went first—spreading their filth, and generally ruining the place before they departed. Such conduct gave many outposts the look of a squalid ghost town. Even at more permanent posts, the lack of building material and the lack of will combined to maintain a shabby air. The army occupied Fort Clark for five years, including a two-month visit by Captain Albert Brackett's Company I, before anyone decided to build a permanent structure. Yet Fort Clark was considered one of the state's most pleasant posts.

At most posts the best-built structure was the magazine for munitions. Typically, outbuildings centered around the parade ground. They served as officers' quarters, barracks, bakery, hospital, and guardroom. At Fort Mason they were built of stone and logs, while officers and men alike lived in tents at Camp Cooper. Fort Mason featured open-walled thatched sheds to shelter the horses, and stables built from wood pickets. Camp Cooper was so primitive that it even lacked any sort of stable. Something of this desolate post's crude physical facilities is reflected by Colonel Lee's observation that after an absence of seven months he found that nothing had changed. Even his tent still stood as before because troopers had put it back up after each of the many times it had blown down. By 1859 conditions at Camp Cooper improved slightly: the men now lived in mud-sided, shingle-roofed shacks. The commanding officer enjoyed the luxury of a kitchen built of pickets and rough boards. Key buildings such as the commissary storehouse, assistant surgeon's quarters, and regimental quartermaster's had rough stone walls and shingle roofs.

Fort Inge was one of the posts established to protect the San Antonio–El Paso road. Named after a Dragoon officer who was killed at the battle of Resaca de la Palma, it was the sometime base for Captain William Royall's Company G and Captain Charles Whiting's Company K. This fort had the uncommon good fortune to be near the Leona River, a source of clear water. A fine grove of old live oak trees provided welcome shade. But the fort's log-built quarters were in an advanced state of decay. Closer inspection showed that the buildings were very rough and temporary, with even the officers' lodgings "mere jacals of sticks and mud." They featured dirt floors, thatch roofs, and walls chinked with rocks, sticks, and thin mortar. One military inspector denounced them as "hovels" utterly unsuited for human habitation.

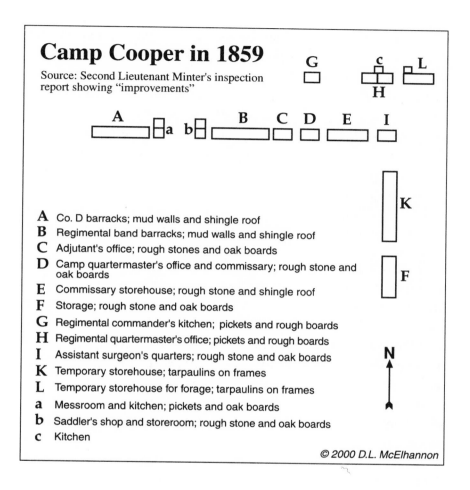

Camp Cooper in 1859

Source: Second Lieutenant Minter's inspection report showing "improvements"

A Co. D barracks; mud walls and shingle roof
B Regimental band barracks; mud walls and shingle roof
C Adjutant's office; rough stones and oak boards
D Camp quartermaster's office and commissary; rough stone and oak boards
E Commissary storehouse; rough stone and shingle roof
F Storage; rough stone and oak boards
G Regimental commander's kitchen; pickets and rough boards
H Regimental quartermaster's office; pickets and rough boards
I Assistant surgeon's quarters; rough stone and oak boards
K Temporary storehouse; tarpaulins on frames
L Temporary storehouse for forage; tarpaulins on frames
a Messroom and kitchen; pickets and oak boards
b Saddler's shop and storeroom; rough stone and oak boards
c Kitchen

© 2000 D.L. McElhannon

The few officers who had brought their families to Texas enjoyed housing little better than the common barracks. Captain Richard Johnson describes setting up quarters for his family: "The floors were prepared for carpets by throwing in clay so as to raise the ground on the inside about a foot above that on the outside. This was levelled off and rammed down to make it firm and smooth. On this old papers were laid, upon which grain-sacks sewed together were placed, and on the grain-sacks the carpet was stretched."[2] Back east, such structures would be the domain of the poorest class. In Texas, they represented luxury.

Rodents, reptiles, and insects routinely invaded the squalid living quarters. Although, outside, the tremendous number of rattlesnakes made walking about after dark dangerous, it was the fleas that made life particularly miserable. One army wife concluded that Texas was the birthplace of the flea; "Those found in other parts are merely occasional wanderers from this, their native land."[3] Johnson relates that in preparation for bed each night he put the foot of each bedpost in a pan of water, stood on a chair to undress and put on nightclothes, and then jumped from the chair into bed.

In his new capacity as departmental commander, Sidney Johnston labored to improve his regiment's accommodations. Mindful of his men's sacrifice during the previous winter, he asked the Adjutant General's Office for funds to build barracks for "the health, comfort, and efficiency of the troops."[4] Johnston's experience as an army paymaster had taught him that the regular army was a penny-pinching organization and that he had to be a strict economist to advance his proposal. So he pledged to keep construction costs low while begging that the job get done before another winter. Johnston's efforts made little difference. When an infantry officer, Samuel P. Heintzelman, inspected Fort Duncan in June 1859, the outdoor temperature hovered at 98 degrees. Inside, he found the company barracks still had dirt floors and primitive bunks. Given the enervating climate and squalid barracks, he concluded, "It is not surprising that soldiers at such frontier stations don't reenlist."[5]

Not only did they not reenlist, they deserted in droves. Some troopers had planned this all along. They joined the cavalry only in order to secure free transport to Texas. Numerous others found the deprivations and dangers of frontier service too much to endure. During 1857, the year when awareness of what frontier service really meant set in—long marches, short rations, brutal combat—a staggering 186 men deserted, nearly one man in four. The following year another 134 fled. Throughout its time in Texas, the regiment annually lost about 17 percent of its enlisted men to desertion alone.[6] To slow this hemorrhaging of strength, the army offered rewards to civilians who captured and returned deserters. One such episode created a national scandal.

It began when a trooper named Harrington deserted during the summer of 1858. Harrington was a new recruit who apparently changed his mind about the joys of cavalry service. He was either unlucky or stupid, because his bid for freedom did not last long. A civilian captured him and returned him to Fort Smith, Arkansas, within four days. Probably the civilian was an experienced bounty-hunting type, because he brought in two other deserters at the same time. Captain Nathan Evans went to collect them. Readers of the *Louisville Journal* learned how Evans made Harrington walk twelve miles while handcuffed and dragging a ball and chain. The recruit did not get fed until the end of the arduous march. The next day was worse. The march traversed a rough section of road called the Narrows. Evans ordered Harrington tied to a wagon's tailgate even though his fingers and wrists were so swollen he couldn't bend them. A sentry said that the recruit fell frequently with every jostle and that his breast frequently slammed into the back of the wagon. The sentry gave the weakened prisoner food and water and put him in the wagon until a sergeant intervened. The sergeant ordered Harrington out of the wagon and tied again to the tailgate. The prisoner endured three more stumbling miles and then even the sergeant took pity. He cut Harrington free, only to see the recruit collapse and die. "Harrington's breast was beat almost to a jelly and his back, from his chin down, was as black as could be," reported a New Orleans paper that picked up the account from the *Louisville Journal*.

Senior Lieutenant Nathan "Shanks" Evans ascended to company command and joined Lee in the regiment's first, fruitless campaign. Evans's rendezvous with destiny would come on the banks of Bull Run in 1861. (National Archives)

Papers throughout the east carried the story. Aroused readers complained to their congressmen about the shameful atrocity. Massachusetts citizens received the story through the pages of the *Boston Herald*. They did not much care for Jeff Davis's pet regiment anyway. This story confirmed their low opinion of a southern-dominated regiment. They wrote Secretary of War Floyd and General Scott to demand an investigation. Because Harrington was a Kentucky native, the story particularly angered people in the Bluegrass State. The *Louisville Journal*'s Texas reporter who uncovered this sordid tale forwarded his story to the War Department for investigation.

The War Department's request for information found Captain Evans at an isolated outpost named Camp Radziminski. Evans had just participated in the Second Cavalry's largest battle to date, a combat during which he personally killed two Indians in close combat. Evans was undoubtedly worn down by the experience and did not attend closely to the complaint. He did not exactly deny the incident concerning recruit Harrington but defended himself merely by observing that two other deserters handled the same way did not die! Evans added that when he examined Harrington's body he did not find any bruises or contusions.

Additional investigation by the army revealed that a good deal of the reporter's story was either wild exaggeration or outright fabrication. Evans's subordinates confirmed that "they were all in irons, as is usual with apprehended deserters," but that each prisoner had six feet of rope so he could choose his path and that the ball attached to his chain was carried in front of him in the wagon's feed trough so he could walk without injury. The subordinates asserted that the newspaper account was "without the slightest shadow of truth." Fitzhugh Lee, Robert Lee's nephew, had personally witnessed the episode and said that nothing untoward occurred. He reported that the three deserters began the march "laughing and talking" and that they were tied behind the wagons very loosely, with the balls resting in the feed trough. One by one, each officer who had any knowledge of the affair wrote out a statement. None said they found evidence to support the *Louisville Journal*'s account.[7]

The army never reprimanded Evans. Discipline in the frontier army of the 1850s was harsh, with sentences calling for whipping, branding, wearing of irons, or shaving of the head. A recaptured deserter typically received a sentence that confined him for two years with a ball and chain attached to the leg while he performed hard labor. During one investigation for misconduct, Colonel Lee assured a trooper, "You shall have justice." The soldier candidly replied, "That is what I am afraid of, sir."[8] In Harrington's case, what probably transpired was that a reporter heard the outlines of the incident and then added his own lurid details. Still, there was no doubt that recruit Harrington, in the learned phrase of the day, was "as dead as Julius Caesar."

If one man in five deserted, thereby sullying the regiment's name, the other four attended to their duty, or at least evaded it in a less notable manner. Theirs was a duty imposed by dedicated noncommissioned officers and ambitious lieutenants and captains who insisted that they preserve military form. Thus, from Fort Brown on the Rio Grande to Camp Cooper in the north, the day began before sunrise with reveille, the bugle's summons to duty. Just as fife-and-drum calls and the turning of the glass ordered shipboard routine, so the bugle's call divided the day at a Texas army post. The subsequent work might vary, but every day began with a ceremonial flag raising, followed by company roll call. Roll call was a serious matter. A discrepancy might be an officer's first awareness that one of his men had deserted. It triggered an immediate effort to apprehend the missing trooper. Everyone knew that this effort was unlikely to succeed. In spite of the rewards given to civilians who brought in deserters, a man running from the Second Cavalry had nine chances out of ten of making good his escape.[9]

Stable call followed roll call. Depending on conditions, the men exercised the animals, and then an officer and the stable sergeant supervised their grooming and feeding. In the U.S. Cavalry (until the War Department ended the cavalry era by replacing their mounts with trucks and tanks) a new recruit learned the paramount importance of horse care. At day's beginning and day's end, a trooper put his horse's needs before his own. Sergeants and officers lectured that unit efficiency depended upon the health of the horses. A recruit was also told in no uncertain terms that his own life might well depend upon the strength and endurance of his horse. Inattention, something as simple as a loosely seated saddle, produced a sore. The Texas heat and humidity and the plaguing, ubiquitous blowflies quickly turned a sore into a festering wound, rendering the animal unfit to carry a soldier. If lectures failed to make an impression, one day in the field spent walking beside a sore-backed or limping animal taught the trooper the importance of proper care for his horse. Laziness or carelessness around the post also produced horse troubles. If troopers allowed their animals to graze the same ground too long, the horses ate the grass to its roots and consumed adobe. The clay plugged their kidneys and killed them. It was up to the vigilant noncommissioned officers to ensure that the men attended properly to the regiment's horses. It was the responsibility of the junior officers, in turn, to insist that the corporals and sergeants find the right balance between disciplined efficiency and tyranny.

Within the regiment's hierarchy of care, sick call followed stable call. Many soldiers had real complaints. The unbalanced diet, poor sanitation, and inferior shelter took a continual toll. Typically the sick list bloomed during the worst of the summer heat. But sick call was also the opportunity for the unit's malingerers to step forward. It required an inventive mind to practice successfully on the regiment's veteran noncommissioned officers and on the post's surgeon. One chronic slacker reported that rheumatism had caused his knees to lock. Weary of dealing with this man, the post surgeon administered chloroform. An observer recalled, "Just as he regained consciousness out went that leg, stiff as a poker, but too late." The malingerer subsequently displayed "wonderful endurance and fortitude" while dragging a ball and chain around the parade ground with his "rheumatic" knees.[10]

107

Finally the men ate breakfast. They then repaired to the stables to water the horses. A routine of guard mounting, morning and evening drill, parade, another visit to the stable to feed and water the horses, and tattoo divided the remainder of the day. Each drill session lasted one to two hours. As a senior inspector observed, the officers attended to drill conscientiously because they, in this case Captains Stoneman and Charles Whiting, "were ambitious to advance their companies."[11] Occasionally the drill included target practice. Some notion of the troopers' marksmanship is suggested by their ability to hit targets a hundred yards away on the drill field. Troopers in two companies wielding the new rifled musketoons managed to hit anywhere from one in four to one in six times. Company K, armed with rifled carbines, managed one in three hits. Target practice with the Colt revolvers consisted of riding around a post and discharging the weapon at close range. In no way did such exercise replicate combat conditions.

The bored troopers assigned guard duty could only envy their comrades who participated in target practice. The officer of the day visited each sentinel at daybreak, sunset, and midnight, in addition to a noon inspection. The duty officer meticulously posted and relieved the sentinels as a matter of discipline and form rather than out of defensive need. The troopers, in turn, rigidly saluted and then manned their guard post with full knowledge that they would spend the next hours gazing upon an unchanging landscape.

While in garrison, troopers spent much time performing routine labor in order to maintain their bases. Daily tasks included gathering wood, tending the post garden, kitchen detail, construction work, cleaning, and hauling water. In Texas, this last chore was often particularly tedious because good water was so scarce. Most of the garrisons lay on the rim of the desert. Annual rainfall fluctuated greatly but averaged about 20 inches. Indiscriminate use of nearby water for bathing, cooking, cleaning, and watering animals quickly made slow-flowing water unfit for drinking. In 1859, for example, General Twiggs ordered Fort Belknap abandoned because of poor water. Camp Cooper's water supply came from the Clear Fork of the Brazos. It flowed through nearby gypsum beds, thus acquiring a strong, unpleasant smell and taste. In an era when patent medicines were typically unpalatable at best, Captain Kirby Smith suspected the water contained "all the drugs in the Medical Department."[12] Soldiers drove wagons considerable distances to find potable water, barrel it, and return. They learned to throw a prickly pear cactus onto a fire long enough to burn off the stickers. They sliced it open and tossed it into the water barrel to precipitate the dirt to the bottom. The result might appear satisfactory, but the water often contained bountiful microorganisms to ravage a soldier's bowels.

Food was often no better. Many officers knew how food ought to look and taste, but they did not know how to prepare it. They depended upon the culinary skills of cooks and mess orderlies. They may not have realized that they also depended upon these men's honesty. One day Captain Van Dorn told his orderly to save enough food for himself before serving the officers. The orderly candidly replied, "Oh, that's all right, Major. I always eats first. You gents only get what is left."[13] Kirby Smith had it better than most. He had asked his mother back in Florida to teach his boy slave how to cook and make himself useful as a bachelor servant. Once these skills were attained, Smith ordered the boy to join him in Texas.

According to Robert Lee, at its best, garrison food presented satisfying breakfasts of coffee, biscuits, steak, and occasionally peaches or stewed apples. Lunch featured boiled beef, potatoes, beans, and bread, and dinner the same. Game and fish supplemented the fare. If filling, it was far from a balanced diet. Lee's description represents the culinary heights of frontier Texas. It was different among soldiers at the isolated posts, particularly in drought years such as 1857, when the lack of rain parched the land, killed the company gardens, and made game scarce. Then beans, moldy flour, and rancid salt pork provided poor eating. Dining "became a dreadful ordeal . . . like swallowing a succession of pills," recalled a soldier's wife.[14] The commissary furnished only the barest necessities: coffee, flour, sugar, rice, pork. Staples of eastern fare—butter, milk, eggs, bread—were rare luxuries. Ubiquitous red ants, which some likened to the taste of caraway seed, flavored the food. Dust infiltrated all food containers. Although kept in stone jugs and in the warm season encased in wet flannel and suspended by a cord in the air to promote evaporative cooling, water was invariably served lukewarm. Butter, when available, was a soft liquid pool; cow and goat milk a too often strong-flavored drink. Hominy or beans provided the only vegetables. Even at Fort Clark on the Rio Grande, vegetables were rare and commanded fabulous prices. Here, hot peppers seemed to be the only one commonly available. In most garrisons southern-born officers had to endure the Christmas holiday season without eggnog for the first time in their lives.

The absence of eggnog highlighted a contrast: young men fighting a war while living in isolation and subject to military discipline versus their civilian counterparts living in the nearest towns. Captain Kirby Smith complained, "Our nomadic life and continual shifting of home cuts us off from all luxuries."[15] While the cavalry endured a bleak holiday season, a Texas newspaper was complaining about the pursuit of amusement by the idle young. It reported that Christmas week "was one continual scene of mischief and drunken uproariousness all about town."[16] Undoubtedly, the men in the Second Cavalry would have welcomed an opportunity to partake in the revelry.

When the Second Cavalry first came to Texas, the men could save most of their money simply because there were no nearby stores where one could spend money. Officers' pay varied; the aggregate factored in everything from rations and transportation to straw for servants. Captains drew a pay of between $400 and $500, while their colonels received twice that amount.[17] Lieutenant Colonel Lee had an annual salary of $1,205, or $3.30 per day. At this time on the Texas frontier, a white day laborer received $1 a day to cut hay or $12 a month to do general farmwork. Civilian contractors provided bacon to Fort Mason at 14 cents per pound and fresh beef at 6 cents per pound. Some sense of the cost of living is provided by Buck Barry, the noted Texas Ranger. He listed the prices for a variety of articles that he purchased in 1855: 20 cents for an elementary speller for his son; 25 cents for a pound of powder; 55 cents for a saddle blanket; 75 cents for three bushels of potatoes; $20 for two bedsteads; $25 for a horse; $30 for a five-shooter.

Some Texans welcomed the cavalry less for their promise of its protection than for the fact that in the army's wake came prosperity. Because the soldiers possessed the frontier's only ready cash, commercial establishments sprang up around the more permanent outposts. When Fort Belknap became the Second's headquarters, property values rose 200 percent and settlers poured in. A happy citizen commented, "We will soon have the regimental band here to discourse eloquent music to the good people of this city."[18] The army also provided settlers with a marketplace for their livestock, crops, and services. Economic relations with the army raised, but only just, the frontiersmen above a subsistence living. But money invested or saved did little good if one's livestock was stolen or if the Indians murdered a man's family. Still, drawn by a ready market, ranchers ran the "risk of being murdered by the Indians every trip they made" to travel fifteen or twenty miles to sell butter, eggs, and chickens to the soldiers.[19]

111

In Texas, as around all military posts, commercial establishments near the forts were heavily weighted toward drinking, gambling, and whoring. During its brief stay at Eagle Pass near the Rio Grande, Company H found that among the two-story adobe stores and thatch-roofed huts were businesses catering to the troopers' needs, including some nine groceries selling liquor and five gambling houses. A barkeep explained the marketing acumen required to appeal to soldiers:

> It don't cost much to set a man up in business here: three men will build a doby house in three days, roof and all; then all you need to be set up in business is a few boards to make a counter and some shelves, and some fancy bottles to put on the shelves, and red paint and gilt paper to set if off, a box of tobacco, and a single demijohn of good whisky, for them that's a judge of it, to start with, and a barrel of rot-gut to keep 'em going when they get tight and for common customers. A barrel of raw whisky goes a long way with these soldiers. A man can make a right good start for a fortune with it.[20]

The same clever men who received $50 a month rent from the army for the land on which sat Fort Mason also provided the fort's sutler service. This service sold liquor to the garrison, with predictable consequences. When troopers at Camp Cooper accused the Comanches on the reserve of killing a soldier, investigators learned that the trooper was beastly drunk and had probably killed himself. In an early example of what in the Civil War would be known as "spotting" and in Vietnam as "fragging," a trooper disguised as an Indian fired at an infantry lieutenant while he was in his bed at Camp Cooper. After what was probably another drunken brawl, troopers charged a prominent Indian with the murder. In this case the Indian's prominence saved him, since the Indian agent could confirm that he was on the reserve at the time of the killing. Purportedly, the cavalry in garrison near the Indian reserves actively aided or turned a blind eye to the sale and barter of liquor to the Indians. Among many, Robert Lee recognized the dangers of liquor. While advising his son to avoid it, he wrote, "I am sorry to say that there is great proclivity for spirit in the army in the field. It seems to be considered a substitute for every luxury."[21]

IF LIQUOR WAS abundant, women were not. Few women made it to the Texas frontier. Even aged spinsters of thirty-five and beyond were snapped up by the eager men of ports like Brownsville long before they set off inland. After three years of service in Texas, a lonely Kirby Smith complained, "We are all Bachelors beyond the reach of the luxuries of civilization and sadly feel the lack of the refining influences of female society." One soldier's wife observed that unlike in the East, "Wall-flowers are an unknown shrub in this part of the country; the men have too much gallantry to allow them to flourish."[22]

The lack of women made it difficult for officers wealthy enough to hire servants to secure a woman's services. Eliza Johnston brought her Irish servant, Ellen, with her from Jefferson Barracks. While en route, she learned that before departing Ellen had married the servant of another officer. The couple intended to avail themselves of free passage to Texas and then, just like similar-minded recruits, desert to begin a new life on the frontier. Unattached females were such a scarce and much-esteemed resource around the isolated frontier forts that they did not remain unattached for long. When Mrs. George Thomas brought two indentured female servants with her from New Orleans, one skipped out on her at first opportunity by engaging to marry a soldier at Fort Mason. Another officer reported that his two female servants married soldiers within a fortnight of their arrival in Texas. An army wife sniffed that "society" in Texas regarded lower-class women as "amiable" if they broke only one of the commandments. She hastened to explain, "We were obliged to overlook many vagaries and eccentricities of deportment, if we hoped to keep a maid on the frontier at that time."[23]

Whereas most cavalrymen longed for the company of women of any sort, the handful of officers who brought their wives to Texas confronted a different set of difficulties. Frontier hardships exacerbated the inevitable domestic squabbles. Couples strained to raise a family in a world unlike that back east. The habitual perils of frontier life promoted a recklessness uncommon in the East. One keen-eyed soldier's wife described Texans as combining heart-in-hand spirit with the raciness of the Kentuckian and the impetuosity of Louisiana Creoles. Violent bullies held the frontier in thrall. Witnesses were afraid for their lives to testify against them. Civic-minded people might deplore the violence, but they were powerless to check it. Richard Johnson said that the frontier people were "ignorant, destitute of any refinement, and have no respect for law or order."[24] He complained that horse stealing was a more serious offense than killing a man since the former was judged a more serious affront to the state's dignity.

It was difficult for army families on the frontier to assemble household goods. Basic furniture—beds and chairs—was scarce. Frequent changes of post compelled familes to begin anew with distressing frequency. Recalling his family's crude diggings in forlorn locations, Johnson mused about the strain a military career life placed upon his married life: "Looking back at my own experience I can but wonder why any young man endowed with ordinary business capacity, good habits, and reasonable ability should seek service in the United States army."[25] Regardless of their post, most wives eked out family income by raising cows, goats, and chickens. The elderly grandmother of a Tennessee immigrant family spoke for most when she summarized her experience for the folks back home: "Tell them that Texas is all right for men and dogs, but hell on women and horses!"[26] Of course, male tactlessness sometimes interfered with domestic bliss. "Those hot prairie winds were very trying to a woman's complexion," recalled an army wife, "and husband often compared the color of mine to a new saddle."[27] Yet outside of their own marriages, wives of officers in the Second Cavalry found that other officers treated them with invariable "courtesy and politeness."[28] In partial compensation for the difficulties of service on the frontier, they discovered that the treatment offered by the army's officers compared most favorably with what they were used to back east in the civilian world.

A handful of officers managed to marry while in Texas. Lieutenant James Harrison, one of four southern-born officers who would remain Union-loyal, consistently exhibited coolness and dash on the battlefields of Texas. He demonstrated sufficient romantic dash to outcompete his comrades. During the winter of 1859, he received permission to leave isolated Camp Radziminski to travel to Fort Belknap, where he married the daughter of Matthew Leeper, the agent for the Comanche reserve. As officers became familiar with their duties, a handful found that they missed their wives and invited them west to join them. Not Captain Earl Van Dorn. The dapper Van Dorn admired the fairer sex greatly. He kept his wife back in Mississippi because he had found early on that he preferred the company of other gentlemen's wives. With startling foresight, Van Dorn predicted to a comrade, "Lee, if I am ever killed, it will be over a woman."[29]

Social deprivation and the monotony of garrison life made an event like the one that occurred at Fort Mason in the summer of 1856 memorable. At that time officers assembled to attend yet another general court-martial. Among them were Colonel Johnston and Major Thomas. The restless spirits of the junior officers stirred, and Second Lieutenant Robert Wood, fresh from his legal triumph over Travis, proposed a race pitting Captain Evans's Bumble-Bee against Lieutenant Walter Jenifer's Grey Eagle. Jenifer well knew that at the proposed distance of a thousand yards, Bumble-Bee enjoyed a powerful advantage. Indeed, Bumble-Bee was already renowned as one of the fastest horses in all of Texas. Explaining that he preferred one-mile heats, where Grey Eagle's superior endurance would tell, Jenifer tried to decline. But Wood understood how to engage a comrade's pride, particularly if they were to perform in the presence of their seniors. Moreover, he knew that Jenifer welcomed an opportunity to exhibit his own invention. By this time all the regiment's officers who could afford to do so had replaced the government-issue saddle with a Texas version called the Hope saddle. It was patterned after a Spanish model and featured a saddle horn that in the modern world distinguishes a western saddle. In 1857, troopers in two lucky companies would receive the Hope saddle. Meanwhile, unsatisfied with all of the designs he had tried, Jenifer began experimenting with a design of his own. The race gave him a chance to demonstrate his light, comfortable saddle.

The race attracted remarkable attention, becoming the regiment's social event of the year. Bumble-Bee was a powerful but rather ugly horse. The ladies greatly preferred the smaller, strikingly handsome gray. They wagered gloves and handkerchiefs on Jenifer's horse. Officers divided their backing, betting baskets of champagne and even their entire back pay on the outcome. Evans selected Second Lieutenant Cornelius Van Camp to ride his Bumble-Bee because Van Camp was as fine a close-seat rider as the regiment possessed. Lieutenants Richard Johnson and Wood served as starting judges. At their word the rivals took off. The ladies waved their handkerchiefs, the officers cheered themselves hoarse. It was quickly apparent that the bigger animal had the advantage on the straightaways, while the gray gained at the turn. Entering the home stretch, Van Camp applied the whip, drawing blood from Bumble-Bee with each stroke. Still, Grey Eagle gained with every stride. At fifty yards from the finish, the gray's head was straining at Bumble-Bee's tail. The crowd's excited delirium spilled across the track. But Bumble-Bee exerted his last reserve and passed the coming-out judges—Lieutenant Field, who had not yet been exiled back east, and Captain Bradfute—to win by a short length. No one doubted that had the race gone a longer distance, Jenifer's horse would have won.

The combination of superb horses and riders, competitive men and alcohol, and the attendance of the fairer sex made the Fort Mason Derby an event to be told and retold within the regiment for the next seventy-five years and more, until unlovely, death-dealing machines replaced the cavalryman's beloved horse.

—— II. "Who Can Blame Them?" ——

When the officers of the Second Cavalry had learned that Texas was to be their duty station, they naturally inquired about the Texas Indians in general and the Comanches in particular. Stories, both told and written, helped form their attitudes. The prevailing army attitude is revealed by an incident a decade before the regiment began its trek to Texas. A lieutenant in charge of a topographical expedition scheduled to cross Comanche territory gleaned what advice he could. Traders told him that the "Camanches" were greatly to be feared. The officer consulted with Captain John Frémont, the renowned Pathfinder himself. Frémont sadly regretted that he could not lend the lieutenant a howitzer, which he thought would be of great service since no one in the lieutenant's party could understand the Comanche language.

In the event, the lieutenant had but the briefest of encounters with Comanches. They displayed a nice discernment between Americans and Texans, making it clear that the latter were their mortal enemies. When they learned that the white men represented the United States and not Texas, they were truly puzzled. Why, they asked, would anyone traverse this territory unless they wanted to make war or to trade? Nonetheless, they let the topographical detail proceed unmolested. Their conduct still made a bad impression. The officer reported, "The Kioways sustain a character for bravery, energy, and honesty, while the Camanches are directly opposite, being cowardly, indolent, and treacherous."[30]

William Parker's account, published nationally in 1856, provided an eyewitness description of domestic relations among the Tawakoni and Wacos he encountered near Fort Belknap:

> The chief—(an ugly old creature, a fac similie of a super-annuated monkey,) soon rode up, and dismounting near his half finished lodge, threw himself upon the grass, whilst his wife—about to become a mother—stopped her work, immediately, to unbridle, unsaddle and tether his horse, for of course, he disdained the smallest labour or assistance to her.
>
> The principal use the wild Indian makes of his wife or wives is to wait upon him, she . . . cooks his meals, puts up the temporary lodge or sheltering, and dresses what skins may be obtained in the chase, in fact, does all the manual labour necessary in their wandering life.
>
> Her lord lounges, sleeps, drinks, smokes, eats, fights, hunts, and not infrequently, *rewards* her with a sound drubbing, the only extra physical exertion he ever makes.[31]

A well-known humanitarian traveled through Texas around the same time as did William Parker, and he too published an account that reached a national audience. Frederick Law Olmsted would be best remembered as a landscape architect for his work on New York's Central Park, the grounds surrounding the nation's Capitol, and Chicago's World Columbian Exposition. In the 1850s he was best known for his opposition to slavery. The *New York Times* had sent him to tour the South to report weekly about how slavery affected the region's economy. In 1856 Olmsted's assignment took him to Texas.

His previous contact with Indians had been restricted to the New England region. With his curiosity "on the alert," Olmsted visited the Brazos Agency and was shocked at what he saw: "nothing but the most miserable squalor, foul obscenity, and disgusting brutishness." He quoted with approval a published description that depicted the Indians as "cruel, false, thievish, murderous; addicted more or less to grease, entrails, and beastly customs; a wild animal."

Olmsted told his readers that the Texas Indians routinely committed frontier murders, preferring victims who could not resist, filled the Texans' livestock with arrows, and drove off the cows and horses. They created "sleepless excitement and terror" throughout the frontier. Olmsted reflected upon the fact that the people he observed had been repeatedly forced to relocate until they had lost most of their traditional culture. The lamentable condition of the wandering tribes was due to a senseless policy practiced by all government, and thus "it is no wonder they are driven to violence and angry depredations." Yet in the end, this intelligent man who campaigned tirelessly against slavery candidly concluded: "If my wife were in a frontier settlement, I can conceive how I should hunt an Indian and shoot him down with all the eagerness and ten times the malice with which I should follow the panther."[32] Olmsted's self-awareness mirrored the sentiment of the far less thoughtful William Parker, who concluded that if his party were to kill Indians, "we would be doing a good service, for except for their greater capacity for mischief, there was no difference between them and the wolves."[33]

Teresa Viele accompanied her soldier husband to Texas in 1852. She apparently never saw a Comanche but published this description in 1858 based upon the attitudes of local inhabitants: "He is bloody, brutal, licentious, and an innate thief. Civilization will probably never reach him, as his feelings towards the white men are those of implacable hatred. . . . Actual extermination seems to suggest itself as the only remedy against this scourge. Nothing less will render many portions of the State of Texas a safe abode for white settlers."[34]

Given prevailing attitudes, it is easy to understand the cavalry's reluctance to exert itself to protect the Texas Indian reserves. Moreover, contemporary accounts reveal the tendency to dehumanize—the man looks like an aged monkey; the Indians are like wolves—those who were different. If everyone from experienced army veterans and journalists to humanitarians and soldiers' wives regarded the Indians as animals worthy of extermination, the men of the Second Cavalry could hardly be expected to be different.

BY THE TIME the Second Cavalry arrived in Texas there were perhaps fifteen hundred Indians living within the state, struggling to exist in the white-dominated world. Most were the remnants of once formidable tribes: Waco, Caddo, Wichita, Tonkawa, Keechi, Anadarko, Delaware, and Shawnee, people who had been forced repeatedly to relocate ahead of the advancing white tide. The first contact many troopers had with Indians came when these "friendly" Indians appeared at their camp to beg. Van Dorn wrote of them, "It is mortification to a soldier's pride to know that all his devotion to his country is wasted on such miserable devils."[35] Then there were the newspapers and dime-novel accounts of life on the western frontier, featuring lurid depictions of torture and rape, the pornography of the mid–nineteenth century. The Comanches became the scourge of the southern plains in popular consciousness. It is well to recall that in part, the image of "ruthless Comanche warriors killing and taking captive" settlers was used to justify occupation of the lands and the establishment of a force to deal with them militarily.[36]

Once the cavalry arrived in Texas, troopers were in frequent contact with white settlers, who freely expressed their views. The attitude of most Texans is well represented by a statement made after the massacre of Comanches during a peace council. The writer believed that the military had finally hit upon the appropriate policy and wanted "to treat the Indians at the next council with the six-shooters of the gallant dragoons."[37] Contributors to the newspapers openly recommended waging a war of extermination.

The Second Cavalry came to Texas at a time when Texans did not hold the army in high repute. Units belonging to the U.S. Army had previously established a reputation in Texas. Kirby Smith claimed that among Texans, Mexicans, and Indians, the regulars were "cordially hated" yet were "the only persons respected and feared."[38] More often they were laughed at for their ineptitude versus the Indians or criticized for their role in guarding the Texas Indian reserves. Such attitudes made the relationship between the Second Cavalry and the state's militia, the Texas Rangers, uneasy at best, a volatile mix of cooperation and respect, rivalry and scorn. Anytime a Texan wanted to abuse the cavalry, all he had to do was relate the tale of a race between a Comanche living on the reserve and a cavalry officer. Mounted on a half-wild ugly mustang, the Comanche challenged the officer on his purebred Kentucky racing mare. With a heavy bet riding on the outcome, the Indian easily bested the officer. Worse, during the race's last stage the Comanche rode backward so as to beckon the officer to come on.

When cavalry trooper met Ranger, the unease began with the difference in the horses they rode. Mounted on their big, blooded eastern horses, the cavalry literally looked down upon the Rangers, who rode the much smaller Texas horse. Among horsemen, an assessment of character and ability naturally follows an evaluation of someone's horse. Among many, Texas Ranger Buck Barry asserted that the cavalry did not understand how to fight the Comanches. He supported his opinion by claiming that cavalry horses were too big and not nimble enough for this type of warfare.

Barry elaborated that the troopers did not know the country and thus Indian raiders usually would lead them over "hill and dale" until the men and their mounts were exhausted.[39] Another Texas Ranger, William Henry, the grandson of Patrick Henry, made loud and frequent complaints about the failure of the regulars to protect the frontier. In Henry's opinion, the "dirty shirt Texas Rangers" outperformed the "tidy" regulars led by "dashing military officers on prancing steeds." About all the regulars accomplished was to clog the roads leading to military encampments with their "government ambulances, filled with champagne and all the luxuries of life."[40] Admittedly, Henry was no military paragon. The commander of the Department of Texas accused Rangers under his command of excessive pillaging and even robbing a post office. Nonetheless, Henry struck a popular chord.

The Second Cavalry was eager to burnish the army's tarnished image. In the past, the army in Texas had customarily not taken prisoners when fighting Indians. Back in 1849, the then Captain Hardee sent his Dragoons in pursuit of raiding Indians with the orders "to take no prisoners."[41] As a new regiment on the scene, the Second Cavalry had to prove themselves to the people they were supposed to protect and to the Rangers with whom they had to cooperate. It is unsurprising that when the regiment encountered hostile Indians, it too did not take male prisoners. To do so would be to fly in the face of the prevailing ethos, aptly depicted by a Texas historian who asked in

1889, "Who can blame a Texas ranger for placing his six shooter to the head of a wounded savage and pulling the trigger?"[42] Indeed, the cavalry quickly learned that a trapped and wounded Indian was not a potential prisoner but rather an exceptionally dangerous customer. Soldiers believed this stemmed from their religion. As they understood matters, an Indian's place in the hereafter—the cavalrymen invariably referred to this as the "happy hunting grounds"—depended upon the number of enemies he had slain. Thus, when cornered or even after receiving a mortal wound, the warrior would nerve himself to desperation and fight hard to increase his tally of enemy killed. Richard Johnson observed that when a trooper became wounded in battle, his comrades hastened to his assistance. Sometimes a wound took five men from the firing line: the injured man himself and four mates, each clinging to a limb as they carried him off to safety, while not incidentally removing themselves from harm's way. In contrast, a wounded Indian seldom received help and instead became a one-man fighting fury.

Both the cavalry and the Indians fought with the knowledge that being taken prisoner was not an option. The field of combat after a battle presented a particularly grisly scene. Not only did the allied Indians kill and scalp the enemy wounded, but the Texas Rangers did so as well. The Rangers claimed that the Comanches believed that a scalped warrior would inevitably be sent to hell. As a Ranger explained, "As we were not in the missionary business we sent everyone to hell we could by scalping them. We had seen so much of their brutality to our women and children that we had no qualms of conscience about serving them in such a way as would make them give our settlements a wide berth."[43] Although the memoirs never say so, undoubtedly some of the troopers acquired this habit.

* * *

DURING MOST of the time the regiment served in Texas, life was a monotony of drills and parades interspersed with arduous but otherwise uneventful patrols. The men lived an isolated existence unimaginable to the people back east. When the regiment first established itself at Fort Belknap, the nearest settler was nine miles away. An observer said of the officers at Fort Belknap that they bore isolation and privation with "the most Spartan spirit." He wished the politicians could visit the remote posts and see "a soldier's life in its true colours." They would be shamed to learn how they misrepresented a soldier's life while speaking in Congress. "Theirs is no carpet-knight service, but a stern reality" requiring great forbearance.[44] The officers understood that frontier service placed them in a world beyond the comprehension of their friends back east. "Not more than five men of a hundred who read in the newspapers that the regular troops had an engagement with hostile Indians," observed a regimental historian, "understand what it has cost in toil and suffering, life and money, to secure the result."[45]

Extreme isolation compelled a man to look inward. Lieutenant Kirby Smith, for one, was determined not to fall down. "I shall never become a bear, though I may love the bear hunt. I shall never drink whiskey though I be a dragoon. I may live in a tent but I shall never give up my books nor the refining influence of an intelligent mind."[46] Captain Earl Van Dorn turned to painting. Eliza Johnston gave him a new set of paints. Since West Point had stressed drawing, Van Dorn began sketching Camp Cooper and its environs. But he could not paint all day, and having read all of his books, Van Dorn, too, confronted boredom: "I am afraid I shall be 'hard up' for something to help me get through these long summer days," he told his wife.[47] The isolation of service in Texas also meant that officers serving there were unlikely to receive any plums offered by the War Department and Congress. When Lee's Mexican War comrade Joseph

E. Johnston received promotion to brigadier general, Lee wrote him a handsome congratulatory letter. Still, at age fifty-four, he must have wondered if he was all but forgotton. Lee's advice to an old friend reflected his discouragement: "Tell Robert I cannot advise him to enter the army. It is a hard life, and he can never rise to any military eminence by serving in the army."[48]

The glue that bonded the officers to their remorseless duty was a surpassing feeling of comradeship. The Travis affair was exceptional. Among officers, particularly among West Point graduates, there was a close feeling of fraternity. They were very much a band of brothers. Lee observed, "You have often heard me say the cordiality and friendship in the army was the great attraction of the service. It is that, I believe, that has kept me in it so long, and it is that which now makes me fear to leave it."[49] Mean-spirited young officers were rare, and the more senior leaders—Lee, Thomas, Van Dorn—were consummate gentlemen. They generously extended every possible hospitality to strangers. When a forlorn Texas Ranger rode into Camp Colorado after a hungry day and night, he related his misfortune to the temporary post commander, a stranger named Lieutenant Fitzhugh Lee. The Ranger explained that while carrying dispatches he had camped overnight in desolate country. He had practiced proper caution, eating his supper and resting in one spot until nightfall and then relocating a mile away to sleep in case Indians had been watching. He woke to find that all his provisions, which he had left hanging from a tree, had been eaten by wolves. Fitzhugh Lee "consoled me with a hearty meal and I rode on."[50]

Likewise, when a small group of army families arrived at Fort Duncan, Richard Johnson pitched a tent in the yard—the Johnson quarters were too cramped to admit overnight guests—and insisted that the travelers take their meals with them for their entire three-day stay. As an army wife observed, in the army outposts in Texas in the 1850s, "Nothing but stern necessity and duty took people to such a desolate place, so, when strangers did arrive, they were kindly welcomed and entertained."[51]

Visitors were uncommon. That made the arrival of the mail a special delight, with letters from home providing one of the few social diversions. It was a great event and the only connection with the outside world. When the regiment first arrived in Texas, mail service was erratic since it usually depended upon soldier couriers who rode mules on delivery routes of over 200 miles. An exception was Muley Stieler, a civilian hired to carry mail 125 miles between Fort Mason and Camp Colorado. Stieler rode his brown mule on two round trips per month, carrying the mail in one saddlebag and some food and an extra pistol in the other. He hid at night in a convenient thicket, striking a fireless camp regardless of the weather. Although chased occasionally by Indians, Muley Stieler escaped to deliver the mail.

In 1858 a visionary named John Butterfield began the semi-weekly Southern Overland Mail. Butterfield's sturdy "celerity" wagons and tall-wheel Concord coaches offered mail and passenger service from St. Louis and Memphis to San Francisco, with the journey completed in twenty-five days or less. Inside of Texas, the Overland Mail provided semiweekly service along the line of Fort Belknap, Clear Fork Station, Fort Phantom Hill, and Fort Chadbourne. The company established stations every 15 to 30 miles. The mail moved at the rate of 7 or 8 miles per hour, and in secure areas traveled day and night. When everything went smoothly, mail from the east arrived at Camp Cooper only eleven days after being posted. Much could go wrong. The mails were often the target of Indian and bandit attacks, which caused delivery times to average about thirty days. When Kirby Smith investigated why the regular correspondence from his mother had yet to arrive, he learned that the expressman had gotten drunk and "lost" the mail. In an effort to avoid the heart of Comanche country, the mail route out of Fort Belknap diverted more than a hundred miles to the south. The longer trail compelled stagehands and passengers to follow a route that was primitive even by Texas standards. Even by following this circuitous route and in spite of the cavalry's special efforts to guard the mails, the Overland Mail could not evade Comanche raiders. Attracted by the company's hardy mules and horses, raiders stole 233 horses and mules in 1858 and 1859.

Since the mail passed within four miles of Camp Cooper, when Robert Lee was present at his Texas home he could expect to learn about affairs back east about one month after they occurred. Because Lee was frequently on the move to attend court-martials, he was less dependent on the mail service than most. After twenty-seven consecutive days of travel—including one day during which everything from socks to epaulets became soaked in muddy water because he "had to swim my mules and get the wagon over by hand"[52]—Lee completed a 730-mile trip to Ringgold Barracks on the Rio Grande. Here he was closer to news. A steamer delivered papers, including the *Alexandria Gazette*. He eagerly read the paper and inferred that all was well at his home in Arlington. He also read President James Buchanan's message to Congress and found it reassuring that the Union was still in existence. But the great issue of the day remained unresolved: "The views of the President on the domestic institutions of the South are truthfully and faithfully expressed. In this enlightened age there are few, I believe, but will acknowledge that slavery as an institution is a moral and political evil. . . . I think it, however, a greater evil to the white than to the black race, and while my feelings are strongly interested in behalf of the latter, my sympathies are stronger for the former." Lee believed that the blacks "were immeasurably better off" in America than in Africa. "The painful discipline they are undergoing is necessary for their instruction as a race, and, I hope, will prepare and lead them to better things." He believed the length of their subjugation was in the hands of God. "Their emancipation will sooner result from a mild and melting influence than the storms and contests of fiery controversy. This influence, though slow, is sure."[53] The bitter presidential campaign of 1856 caused Sidney Johnston to react more gloomily: "Our compact of union seems to be drifting towards a lee shore."[54]

Thoughtful officers—the majority of the Second Cavalry—had to be concerned about the changes flowing from the new Buchanan administration. Conditions had been hard and primitive under Secretary of War Davis in spite of the fact that Davis had been both the unit's father and its most attentive patron. The new secretary, John B. Floyd, was a far less experienced man. Officers had to wonder if their lot would get worse, yet month after month they performed their duties with a surprising lack of complaint.

During its first year of service in Texas, the Second Cavalry made some thirty minor expeditions as well as numerous short patrols. The soldiers had now endured long pursuits, during which they sweltered during the day beneath a blazing sun and shivered at night beneath a saddle blanket arranged around straggling beds of cacti. They subsisted on bacon and hardtack and very little water. They learned the paramount need to remain alert since the monotony of patrol could be interrupted by violent fighting at almost any time. When they fought, they did so with the knowledge that defeat meant death by torture. This field service had begun transforming the enlisted recruits into hard-eyed, self-reliant combat troopers. A regimental historian who knew many of the officers and men who served in Texas wrote, "After a man has served a few years on the frontiers he becomes wary, suspicious of danger and watchful of its approach, until these become characteristics of his every-day life."[55]

In 1857, the literate public read about the composition of the new Buchanan administration and what it portended for he widening chasm between North and South. Adventurers mourned the overthrow of the Tennessee filibuster William Walker from the presidency of Nicaragua. *Harper's Weekly* thrilled the nation with its lurid drawings of massacre and revenge in British India, where the Great Revolt of the Indian army had begun. Buried in the swirl of events was the news that an obscure cavalry lieutenant named John Hood had fought a bloody encounter with the Comanches.

5

Hood's Epic

If soldiers suffer a defeat in civilized warfare the worst that can happen is a surrender. . . . If troops are defeated in Indian warfare there is no surrender. If they cannot successfully retreat, those of the number not fortunate enough to be killed outright in the combat will be subjected to cruel tortures. . . . It is, therefore, apparent that the officers who lead detachments of troopers against hostile Indians, where the chances are about equal, are the leaders of forlorn hopes, and that the men who follow them are heroes. Their only safety is in victory. The slightest indication of wavering is fatal.

—George Price, *Across the Continent with the Fifth Cavalry*

___ I. Revolver, Bow, and Lance ___

The severe winter of 1856–57 foreshadowed the worsening relationship between the Second Cavalry and the Indian agents associated with the two Texas Indian reserves. The supervising agent was one of the state's most controversial figures, Robert Neighbors. He was controversial because he took his job seriously and made a sincere investment in improving the plight of the reserve Indians, whereas most Texans saw nothing good in any live Indian and thought ill of any white man who tried to help them.

Neighbors went by the title Major, having served in the army of the Texas Republic, including a stint in Captain John Coffee Hays's Company of Mounted Gunmen. Born in Virginia, Neighbors had lived in Texas since the age of twenty. His blunt manner of speaking, particularly when confronting what he conceived to be the improprieties of others, made enemies easily. His assignment as agent to the Indians in 1845 started Neighbors down what proved a fatal path. The next year Neighbors helped negotiate the first treaty between the United States and the Texas Indians, and thereafter he tried to ensure that everyone adhered to its terms.

The fertile brain of Jefferson Davis had played a role in the creation of the Texas Indian reserves. Back in 1853, after pondering how best to defend the Texas frontier, Davis had advocated the concept in a letter to the state's governor. Neighbors was one of the few who believed it an eminently sensible suggestion. He had participated in the Texas Republic's four-year war of extermination against the Indians beginning in 1838. At that time Texas possessed both soldiers and leaders experienced in this special kind of warfare. Nonetheless, Neighbors declared that "the result was a perfect failure, and after exhausting all her resources, she [Texas] had to resort to the peace policy."[1] Even if only in economic terms, Neighbors was certain that it was cheaper to feed and shelter the Indians than to fight them. The federal government's Indian Department had a higher ambition. It wanted to teach the Indians to be self-sufficient through a combination of farming and stock raising.

When Texas joined the Union in 1845, it retained control of all vacant lands and declined to recognize any Indian ownership within its borders. After years of prodding, the Texas legislature finally relented in 1854 and permitted federal surveyors to mark 53,136 acres of unclaimed land for use as Indian reservations. High on the Brazos River were two reserves; one for the Comanche and another, about fifty miles away, for some tribes who were bitter enemies of the Comanches, including the Anadarkos, Caddos, Tawakonis, Wacos, and Tonkawas. William Parker accompanied the men who surveyed the Comanche reservation on the Clear Fork of the Brazos. He judged it to comprise "every essential of upland and meadow, with fine water and timber."[2] But Parker was a New York City businessman whose assessment of Texas scrubland must be suspect. With hindsight, it is apparent that the idea of confining five hundred or so nomadic people to the 18,000-acre Comanche reserve, only a small part of which was arable, was ludicrous. Seventy-five years later the same land supported only about fifty whites.

The men chosen to supervise the two reserves possessed unsurpassed experience in dealing with the Texas Indians. Shapley P. Ross and John R. Baylor were also two of the deadliest Indian fighters in the entire state. Still, the attitude of some of the Comanches toward the reserve was initially positive. Having been driven into the state's most barren, sterile land, where they were unable to hunt for subsistence, they faced extermination. The reserve offered a lifeline. Several chiefs urged Neighbors to make arrangements for their destitute families. Their women and children needed food and a safe place to camp. Only about one-quarter of the southern Comanches entered the reservation. Their number seldom exceeded four hundred, but even among them it was a floating population, with people coming in during lean times and departing when things improved. Although a nucleus from several bands tried to make a go of life on the Clear Fork reserve, it proved difficult. The drought of 1856 that killed off the company gardens belonging to the Second Cavalry also killed the Comanches' corn crop well before harvest. It persuaded many that farming was not their calling. Such disasters made it all the easier for the "wild" Indians to recruit participants for raids against the Texas settlements and into Mexico. Consequently, agent Baylor found the Comanches to be "wild, restless, and discontented."[3] Only with difficulty would they be persuaded to remain on the reservation. In time, Neighbors would replace Baylor, in part because of Baylor's poor attitude. However, it appears that in this case Baylor spoke the truth.

Still, an Indian reserve offered Texas the best long-term solution to accommodating the state's resident Indians. But it would have to overcome profound cultural opposition among the Comanches. One old Comanche leader confided to one of the officers who surveyed the reserve that his sons were a great comfort to him in his dotage because they could steal more horses than any other young men in the tribe. The reserves would also have to confront white demagogues who made political capital out of the Indian depredations. Supervising agent Neighbors believed that his reserve policy successfully demonstrated the practicality of settling down and civilizing even the wildest Indian tribes. In many ways Neighbors would prove an enlightened humanitarian, but one who fatally underestimated the hatred of his opponents.

Complicating everything was a federal policy at cross-purposes with itself. As long as they did not interrupt travel along the emigrant trails heading west, the Kiowas and Comanches received annuities including food, weapons, and ammunition from Indian agents living at army posts on the Upper Platte and Upper Arkansas Rivers. This arrangement satisfied the local army commanders since it kept the Indians quiet within their jurisdiction. It delighted the Indians because it gave them a secure base from which to continue their raids against Texas and Mexico. In essence, they were at peace with the white man on the Arkansas and warred against him in Texas. Simultaneously, they began to trade with their brethren living at the Comanche reserve in Texas. The gun running grew so brazen that Comanches on the reserve openly boasted of using government presents against the federal troops in Texas.

Into this tense situation stepped a stubborn cavalry officer named George Stoneman. Stoneman was from New York and had been Tom Jackson's West Point roommate. He was popular at West Point, particularly in comparison to the taciturn Jackson. Comrades called him a "generous-hearted, whole-souled companion."[4] However, he neither was particularly wise nor cared much for any Indians, regardless of whether they lived within or outside the reserve. After replacing Robert Lee as commander at Camp Cooper, Stoneman picked a quarrel with the Comanche Indian agent. Both men fired paper volleys containing charges, denials, and countercharges to their respective headquarters in Washington. Then Stoneman decided upon an impetuous action to win a point in the battle against the Indian agents.

Stoneman believed that the Indian agents were fraudulently drawing supplies for nonexistent Indians. Oblivious to the fact that the Indians were shy around soldiers at the best of times, without the knowledge of the agents he took a cavalry detachment and barged onto the reservation to make a physical count of the Comanches. Naturally his action produced a panic that threatened the fragile trust between the Comanches and the whites. It also did not produce the count Stoneman desired. Yet another exchange of written accusations between Stoneman and the agents ensued, each charging the other with failure to cooperate.

Officers like Stoneman might be uncooperative with the Indian agents, but they were more than willing to cooperate with other governmental authorities. When a Department of Interior road-building expedition reached Camp Cooper, Stoneman offered its members army quarters. This was routine frontier civility. But he also allowed the expedition to exchange a broken-down wagon for an army wagon, which was an act of generosity outside of army regulations.[5] In Stoneman's view, helping the Department of the Interior build a road to be used by white settlers was desirable, helping the Department of the Interior settle Indians in Texas was not. His insufferable attitude finally provoked supervising agent Neighbors beyond endurance. Neighbors requested that the department commander, General David Twiggs, transfer Stoneman and replace him with someone who would "not interfere with the proper duties of the agent or circulate *false reports*."[6] Twiggs obliged by sending Stoneman and his Company E to Camp Colorado. Before he departed, Stoneman fired his Parthian shot, asserting that Neighbors's Indian policy would fail everyone connected with it except for men charged with distributing the government money.

Robert Neighbors had won an important bureaucratic skirmish by forcing Stoneman's transfer. By so doing, Neighbors demonstrated anew his singular genius at making enemies. He also caused the breach between the cavalry and the Indian agents to widen. When the Second Cavalry had established Camp Cooper, those Comanches who were truly dedicated to becoming farmers and stockmen had welcomed the troopers in the belief that they would protect them from both their wild brethren and hostile whites. The cavalry, of course, always preferred chasing wild Indians to protecting those Indians living on the reserve. The growing rift between the officers and the agents made the cavalry ever more neglectful of its duty toward the reserve.

Neighbors's annual report for the year 1857 contained a mixed bag of information. At the Brazos Agency over a thousand Indians were making great progress adjusting to the farming and stock-raising life. Neighbors proudly cited the number of acres cultivated by each tribe alongside their corn and wheat yields. The agent referred to these Indians as "settlers" and predicted that they were well on their way to self-sufficiency. Neither had the army been required to intervene on the Brazos reserve, nor had any depredations been traced to this reserve. For Neighbors the conclusion was clear: from the viewpoint of both whites and Indians alike, working to ensure that the Indian reserves succeeded was the wisest policy. Neighbors believed that the success spoke for itself. He challenged anyone to propose something better.

The news from the Comanche reserve was less good. The number of "settlers" had declined by 133. The 424 Comanches who resided along the Clear Fork had made some progress at farming, but drought stunted their crops. Many were eager to have the children learn English and wanted a school to be started. The malignant presence of the wild Indians threatened to undo all progress. Neither the Indian agents nor the cavalry who guarded the reserve had been able to prevent the reserve's young men from joining the continued forays against the Texas settlements and over the border into Mexico. Reinforced by the reserve Comanches, the wild bands plundered ranches, interdicted roads, and destroyed the mails. Thus, Neighbors continued, "Our frontier still presents the anomaly of peace with a small portion of a tribe of Indians [the Comanches on the reserve] and continual hostility with the balance of the same people."[7]

THE OPTIMISM Colonel Johnston had expressed in August 1856 regarding his regiment's success at driving the Comanches to the interior did not survive past the autumn of that year. After assessing the capabilities of the Second Cavalry, the Comanches returned. Once again, their raids exploded along the border from the Brazos to the Rio Grande. In the winter a band of Comanches descended on the settlements on the North Bosque and killed members of two different families. They surprised two women, a Mrs. Woods and a Mrs. Lemley, within two miles of their homes and then raped, scalped, and killed them. The next day they encountered two farmers clearing a field and killed them. That night, fifteen miles farther on, they killed a young man named Knight. The next day they mortally wounded a Baptist minister before fleeing the region in the direction of the Indian reserves. The size and tempo of raids caught the Second Cavalry by surprise.

In March and April, Lieutenant Walter Jenifer led thirteen men on a two-week search that covered nearly 300 miles. On April 4, 1857, the patrol came across a fresh trail near the headwaters of the North Fork of the Nueces River. They followed the trail through the hills for most of the day until the ground became so rocky that Jenifer resolved to continue on foot. Leaving five troopers to guard the horses, he led seven men on a difficult four-mile march. Suddenly they spied a large Indian camp. A quick glance revealed about a hundred Indians. Exhibiting exceedingly poor judgment, Jenifer stealthily led the patrol to within 250 yards of the camp. What he hoped to accomplish is unclear, but he might as well have announced his presence with a bugle call. When the Indians detected the cavalry, scores of warriors poured out of the camp to charge toward the patrol. Only the fact that the Indians' ponies were off being watered and that night was rapidly approaching saved Jenifer's detachment from suffering Custer's fate in miniature. The troopers opened fire and successfully conducted a fighting retreat until darkness shrouded the terrain. Showing supreme arrogance, Jenifer led his full detachment back the next day. Fortunately for him the Indians had decamped. Jenifer had so mismanaged things that during the return march his men ran out of food. Admirers praised Jenifer's conduct. He had exhibited pluck and courage. General headquarters cited the patrol's gallantry, writing that the men were "entitled to high approbation."[8]

"Foolhardy" and "lucky" apply more appropriately to Jenifer's leadership.

Such incidents imbued the cavalry with enormous confidence. As Captain Richard Johnson observed, "In Texas we rarely ever heard of Indians attacking any organized force where there was the slightest chance of defeat. When pursued by superior numbers, they invariably attempted to escape by flight, and this gave rise to the belief that they were all cowards."[9] In fact, the cavalry possessed overwhelming superior firepower, and this gave it a tactical advantage over the Indians. It also gave the troopers great confidence. Regardless of the situation, the troopers trusted that Samuel Colt's six-shooter would allow them to win out.

It had not always been so. When they had first begun fighting against the Texans, not only did the Comanches enjoy superior mobility but they also possessed greater firepower and a weaponry advantage in close combat. Their short bows shot bone and flint arrows. Each warrior carried a quiver with about fifty arrows. A rifle- or pistol-armed opponent could answer the fifty arrows with but one or two shots. Furthermore, the Comanches carried shields that often deflected a rifle or pistol ball unless the ball struck at something close to right angles. Once his foe discharged his weapon, the Comanche closed to employ his seven-foot lance. It was a tactic that worked time and again. Whether confronting a desperate family forted up within their log cabin or a party of emigrants defending behind their circled wagons, the warriors would maneuver just outside effective range. They skillfully leaned to the outside of their horse to interpose its body between them and the enemy until the whites fired. Then they charged.[10] Once the lancers closed, a man armed with sword or knife could not defend himself. So the lords of the plains held sway over a vast range of land by dominating all enemies, whether Indian, Mexican, or Texan. Then, in the 1830s, Samuel

Colt introduced a five-shot revolver that quickly made its way west to the struggling Republic of Texas.

So much of the initial production ended up in Texas that Colt later called this model the Texas Arm. After an initial encounter with revolver-armed Texas Rangers in 1844, a Comanche warrior reputedly stated that he never wanted to fight them again since every one "had as many shots as I have fingers on my two hands."[11] In June of that year came a decisive test. Fifteen Rangers led by Jack Hays met a Comanche force that outnumbered them at least five to one. It was a close-range contest pitting arrows, spears, and shields against five-shot revolvers. Two Rangers were run through with lances; most of the rest received flesh wounds. But within fifteen minutes the combat was over and at least twenty-one Comanches lay dead on the ground. Hays's victory ended the era of Comanche tactical dominance. The subsequent model of Colt's hand cannon featured a depiction of Hays's fight engraved on the pistol's rotating cylinders. The extent to which the Colt revolver tilted the tactical equation to the advantage of a pistol-armed white man over a bow-and-arrow-armed Comanche became even more apparent two years later. In an astonishing three-day pitched battle, Hays and his Rangers again confronted a seemingly overwhelming number of Comanches. They killed more than a hundred Indians while suffering no fatalities themselves.

Lacking a production facility, Colt initially contracted with Eli Whitney to manufacture his weapons. Colt's business breakthrough came during the Mexican War when Colt-armed Texas Rangers impressed army officers. Demand so outstripped supply that officers offered up to $140, six times Colt's sale price, to outfit themselves with this wonder weapon. Thereafter, Colt assiduously collected testimonials from Zach Taylor, Sam Houston, and the newly celebrated Texas Rangers. Jack Hays affirmed the revolver's reliability and accuracy. He recommended that

The navy-issue 1851 model .36-caliber Colt revolver gave the Second Cavalry a decisive tactical advantage. (Museum of Connecticut History)

"soldiers should be practised in the use of them. They soon become easy to the hand; the aim you wish to draw can be easily caught; and when placed in the hands of those who understand the proper use of them, they are unquestionably the most formidable weapon ever used in battle."[12] The single-shot dragoon pistols of the past had been notoriously inaccurate. Not so the revolver with its rifled barrel. A Royal Army trial at the Woolwich Armoury in 1851 demonstrated that at fifty yards' distance, forty-six of fifty-four shots struck within a two-foot square, while six hit the bull's-eye.

The Colts soon also earned a reputation for quality and durability. In a skirmish with Comanches, Ben McCulloch fired three rounds before accidentally dropping his weapon. The action then carried him some distance away. Three months later he returned to find his revolver still on the ground, having been exposed to a season's worth of storms. After he put new caps on the nipples of the loaded chambers, "they were discharged as though they had been loaded but the day before."[13] Competitive trials by the Ordnance Department confirmed this reputation. Colt, in turn, perfected his production line so that all arms of the same model used interchangeable parts. Thus a trooper in Texas could take a part from a broken revolver and use it to replace a worn part in another revolver without having to wait for a replacement to arrive from the East. By 1850, Mexican War veteran General Harney concluded that Colt's revolver was the "perfect" arm for mounted service. Referring to the western Indians, he wrote, "It is the only weapon with which we can hope ever to subdue these wild and daring tribes."[14]

A Texas Ranger veteran described combat against the Indians and how best to utilize the Colt:

> These prairie tribes ride with boldness and wonderful skill, and are, perhaps, unsurpassed as irregular cavalry. They are so dextrous in the use of the bow, that a single Indian, at full speed, is capable of keeping an arrow constantly in the air, between himself and the enemy; therefore, to encounter such an expert antagonist, with certainty of doing execution, requires an impetuous charge, skillful horsemanship, and a rapid discharge of shots.

Although encounters with Indians seldom lasted long, they required "a steady nerve, the greatest possible precision and celerity of movement." There was no time to reload, "even were it possible to do so, and manage your horse, in the midst of a quick and wily enemy, ever on the watch and ready to lance the first man who may have lost the least control of his animal."[15]

Faced with the outbreak of Indian raids, Colonel Johnston reversed his opinion that the army was winning the battle for Texas. Much like the American high command in Vietnam, who believed their efforts had squashed the enemy, only to see them rise again, by February 1857 Johnston doubted that even four or five more regiments would suffice to protect the settlements. To make better use of what he had, Johnston wanted his troopers to have a clear idea of who was friend and who was foe. Identifying active enemies from passive inhabitants is one of the major challenges in any guerrilla war. At the time the Second Cavalry arrived in Texas, there were perhaps fifteen hundred Indians living on the two reserves, trying to exist within the white world. Johnston wanted authority to declare as hostile all Indians found outside the reserve. They should be considered enemies to be shot on sight.

The colonel received support for this bloody-minded notion from a surprising source, Robert Neighbors. Neighbors's subordinates were having great difficulty keeping their charges confined to the limits of the reserves. They wandered off to collect their animals that had strayed, to hunt and fish, and to visit relatives. And the young men on the Comanche reserve departed to participate in raids. No American had more experience in working with the Texas Indians than Neighbors. He had reached certain immutable convictions:

> Free intercourse with the Camanches for years has fully convinced me that it is absolutely necessary either to whip them or continually overawe them with a strong military force, in order to hold them in subjection and to make them peaceable. Their chiefs have but little control, and I have never known them to make a treaty that a portion of the tribe do not violate its stipulations before one year rolls around.[16]

To provide a sanction strong enough to confine the Indians to their reserves, Neighbors also recommended that all Indians found off the reserve without a permit from an Indian agent be declared hostile. This draconian measure simplified the cavalry's duty. Yet even so, confusion could occur, as Second Lieutenant Hood's engagement in the summer of 1857 demonstrated.

—— II. The Fight at Devil's River ——

It began when Hood made a resolution: "Having grown weary of the routine duties of camp life, I determined to change the scene and start on a scouting expedition in search of the red men."[17] His impetuous decision was entirely characteristic of the man. As a rambunctious lad growing up in Kentucky he had acquired a reputation as a bad boy. It was a reputation he thoroughly enjoyed, reputedly boasting to a relative, "Other boys don't lead me into trouble. I lead them."[18] He had entered West Point at age eighteen, at the time when Robert Lee was superintendent. Knowing that the youth might rebel under military discipline, Dr. Hood purportedly delivered a stern, parting injunction to his son: "If you can't behave, don't come home. Go to the nearest gatepost and butt your brains out."[19] The cadet was the type of person who was more than willing to like and be liked. At West Point he proved popular, prone to mischief, and no kind of student, graduating forty-fourth out of fifty-two.

So far, cavalry duty for the twenty-six-year-old officer had been uneventful. No sooner had he arrived with the regiment in Texas than he received leave to return home to care for his dying father. Nine months later Hood was back in Texas, reporting to Lieutenant Colonel Lee at Camp Cooper in January 1857. Routine duty ensued, a duty enlivened by Lee's habit of inviting his junior officers to accompany him as he explored the area around camp. Hood recalls that not only did Lee discuss military topics during these excursions, but he also dispensed advice about life's choices. Fearful that the handsome young lieutenant might become entrapped by some of the local girls, Lee told

Crippling war wounds reduced onetime Second Lieutenant
John B. Hood to a gaunt shadow of the aggressive cavalry
officer who conducted the fight at Devil's River. (National
Archives)

Hood, "Never marry unless you can do so into a family which will
enable your children to feel proud of both sides of the house."[20]

The following summer Hood transferred to Fort Mason for
duty with Captain Bradfute's Company G. Several weeks passed
with no opportunity for action. It was a problem the restless lieutenant sought to rectify by requesting permission to lead a scout
into Indian country. His superior, Major George Thomas, would
earn a Civil War reputation as an exceedingly cautious officer.
But in this case Thomas had no qualms. He ordered Hood to

proceed. The strapping, handsome, 6-foot, 2-inch man looked like a warrior. But no man knows how he will behave in combat until the first shots are fired.

After a celebration of Independence Day, the bugle sounded "Boots and Saddles" early on July 5. Sergeant Joseph Henley inspected the patrol's equipment—saber, carbine, revolver—and checked their saddlebags. Each trooper had hardtack, bacon, and coffee in one bag and his mess kit and personal gear in the other. The sergeant handed out twenty-five rounds of ammunition per man. Pack mules carried a reserve supply as well as extra food and forage. Hood led his twenty-four-man detachment out the Fredericksburg Road and turned south toward the Llano River. His objective was to explore a recently discovered Indian trail that lay fifteen miles beyond Fort Terrett, about a three-day march to the west. To locate the trail and pursue any Indians who might have passed along it, Hood relied upon the famous Delaware scout John McLoughlin.

Upon receiving word of an impending scout, McLoughlin invariably got so drunk that he could not depart with the cavalry. He always managed to overtake the patrol by the end of the second day. When queried about why he behaved this way, he replied that he well knew it would be thirty days or so before he could obtain more whiskey! Once on patrol, McLoughlin was all business. He taught the troopers the rudiments of his trade. On rocky hills, a dark-colored stone indicated that a mule or horse had overturned it while passing. Otherwise, the surface would have been washed clean by rain and bleached by the sun. A light-colored streak extending through grassland also revealed a trail because an equine had turned the grass and the underside appeared lighter. Some of this craft the cavalry could master. They learned that a collection of turkey buzzards meant carrion, perhaps the remains of butchered buffalo. Closer inspection revealed whether the animal had come to its death by the bullet of a white man or the arrow of an Indian. "Thus the flight of birds, movements of wild animals, a stick, a stone, or even a bruised reed, speak volumes to the practised eye."[21] Lacking such an eye, most officers relied upon Indian guides or a handful of exceptionally experienced whites.

Guides knew that the only animal that ate mesquite seeds was the wild mustang. After a mesquite seed soaked in a horse's bowels and was dropped, it germinated quickly. Mustangs seldom grazed more than three miles from water. So a mesquite bush indicated the near proximity of water. To find out precisely where, the guide looked at the animals. An experienced guide could tell by watching animals whether they were going to or coming from water. If there were no grazing animals, he looked for birds. If the low-flying swallow had its mouth empty, it was heading toward water; if its mouth was muddy, he was coming straight from water. "You can blindfold me, take me anywhere in the Western country, then uncover my eyes so that I can look at the vegetation, and I can tell about where I am," boasted an experienced guide.[22]

Hood's detachment was particularly reliant upon its guide's fieldcraft because the summer of 1857 brought drought. Kirby Smith called the Texas plains "the abomination of desolation" because there was no grass and the streams were down.[23] At Camp Cooper, Lee wrote that 100-degree and hotter days seemed to have set in permanently. Three days out, once the patrol turned away from the Llano, water holes became scarce. That night they occupied the abandoned ruins of Fort Terrett. Dick Hopkins, the patrol's best hunter, went out in search of something more tasty than hardtack and bacon. He cornered a bear in a cave and returned to camp for assistance. One of his helpers, a Sergeant Deaton, managed to wound the beast. The enraged animal chased Deaton. The sergeant contrived to dislocate his knee while fleeing. Fortunately for him, his comrades killed the bear. Deaton's injury prevented him from continuing on the mission. Hood detailed a corporal to escort him back to base. So, in exchange for a bear meat supper and breakfast, Hood lost two valuable men. The loss almost proved fatal.

The unit failed to find the reported Indian trail. Hood resolved to carry on toward the headwaters of the Middle Concho. After twelve days of riding across a cactus and sagebrush desert, scout John McLoughlin found signs indicating that a party of fifteen to twenty mounted Indians had passed by within the last three days. It appeared to be a raiding party moving south toward Mexico. Hood ordered a pursuit. The cavalry now entered an even more barren wasteland. The unit covered 40 miles that day. In this arid region the water holes extended like beads on a necklace with distances of 35 to 50 miles separating one from another. It was a brutal march conducted beneath a hot July sun. Approaching each water hole, the men perked up in anticipation of possible contact. Instead, for four days all they found were scum-covered, salty mud holes so foul smelling that they had to hold their breath to drink. Troopers filled the sleeves of their gutta-percha capes and tied off the ends so they could carry extra water. Even when combined with the three-pint capacity of the troopers' standard-issue canteens, this was not enough water. A trooper recalled: "We pushed on out to the dry plains, and soon the cry for water was heard among the men. It was the hottest weather I ever experienced and our horses suffered beyond measure."[24] For four days Hood maintained a killing pace that averaged 50 miles per day. Only the fact the the Indian trail grew progressively more distinct—they were now on one of the great war trails leading to Mexico—encouraged the patrol.

On July 20 McLoughlin led them to a water hole several miles above the head of Devil's River. The command buzzed with excitement because the embers from the fires were still warm, while strewn about the campsite were the bare bones of a

Arid conditions tormented Hood's men and their animals during their march to Devil's River. (National Archives)

freshly eaten mule or horse. However, McLoughlin told Hood that two bands had merged; their quarry now numbered up to forty warriors. If he continued, he would face odds on the order of two to one against. Moreover, his unit's horses were jaded, the troopers themselves fatigued. The enemy had been moving at a slower pace and would certainly be fresher. Hood ordered his sergeant to inspect carefully the troopers' weapons and prepare the command for combat. He could not help but notice that several of the horses were so leg weary that they could scarcely maintain their places in the column of march. The terrain had grown hilly, further tasking the horses' endurance. Around 3 P.M., Hood reluctantly decided to abandon the chase. The troopers followed their Delaware scout to find badly needed water. After they had traveled a mile, they suddenly saw motion on a ridge about two and a half miles away: horses, dismounted men, a large white flag flapping in the breeze.

Before departing Fort Mason, Hood had read a circular from the War Department notifying the cavalry that a party of Tonkawas was expected to come to the Brazos Agency. The Tonkawas were some of the cavalry's best allies. They hated the Comanches. Their expert trackers provided superb guides. The circular stated that if the Tonkawas spotted United States soldiers, they were to raise a white flag and be allowed to proceed unmolested. Hood asked himself, could the Indians waving the white flag be the Tonkawas? The liklihood was remote, given that the Brazos Agency was a fifteen-day hard march away. However, two of the effects of dehydration are reduced alertness and impaired decision making. "Notwithstanding the condition of the men and the horses," Hood wrote, "I determined to pass over upon the ridge . . . move toward them, and ascertain the meaning of this demonstration."[25]

Only seventeen troopers advanced. Hood told the six men with worn horses and the Delaware scout to remain behind to guard the pack mules. He formed his remaining seventeen men in line and cautiously advanced toward the mound atop of which waved the white flag. He could see several Indians, but they seemed to be resting easily. The ground separating the cavalry from the mound was partially covered by growths of Spanish bayonets. The lieutenant could see that the vegetation provided possible concealment. Normally, this was ground unsuited for mounted men. But if he dismounted, Hood would suffer a further diminution in strength since at least a quarter of his men would have to remain behind and act as horse holders. Of course this realization should have occurred earlier, before he divided his command. He could have left the horses in the hands of the men guarding the pack mules. Hood's sequence of decisions again reveals a man whose judgment is clouded by fatigue and dehydration. It was also affected by the regiment's prevailing notion that any twenty or so troopers should be able to outfight four times their numbers.

The line continued its advance toward the mound; fifty paces, forty, thirty. The men now saw some ten Indians gathered around the mound. Five began walking slowly toward the cavalry, one of them holding aloft the white flag. With churning stomach the dry-mouthed troopers involuntarily stiffened. Their jaded horses sensed the tension. For the first time in many dreadful days they showed their purebred spirit: mane and tail erect, nostrils flared, jinking left and right. The men looked to their right, where Hood had taken the traditional post of honor. Ever since man had fought in formed ranks with spear and shield, the position of greatest danger was the line's right because here a man who held his shield with his left hand could not protect himself. Tradition demanded that the bravest occupy the right of the line, and here was Hood, his double-barreled shotgun loaded with heavy buckshot lying across the pommel of his saddle.

At thirty paces the Comanches and Lipans, for it was they, not the friendly Tokawas, threw the flag to the ground and opened fire with heretofore concealed weapons. Simultaneously, other unseen warriors ignited a blaze of dry grass and mesquite branches. Suddenly a wall of fire rose thirty feet into the air just in front of the Second Cavalry. Thirty warriors instantly rose up from hiding spots just ten paces away. With "a furious yell" they charged down the slope. At the same moment, a lance-armed mounted party attacked the left of the line. About forty-five Indians engaged eighteen men of the Second Cavalry in a near-perfect deadfall.

The warriors appeared as if in a nightmare. They were stripped to the waist, their faces and torsos painted in lurid colors.

Atop their heads were ghostly wreaths of feathers or crowns of buffalo horn. Such apparitions had unnerved more than one foe.

Now the discipline instilled by Albert Sidney Johnston and William Hardee came to the fore. The troopers fired their one-shot carbines and then drew their Colt revolvers. Already the Indians were at point-blank range. Some warriors ran up to the troopers' horses, grasped the bridles, and beat the horses over their head with shields. One quick-fingered Comanche grabbed a carbine that a trooper had discharged and then hung from the cantle of his saddle so he could operate his revolver. The warrior ran upslope with his prize clutched triumphantly overhead. To manage a horse and fire accurately a revolver amid the smoke and noise required a rare skill. Each trooper's world narrowed to the scene immediately before him, an immediate present filled by horrid-looking men grappling, screaming, and straining to kill. Inexorably, the enemy pushed the cavalry line backward. A trooper recalled:

> An Indian seized my horse by the bridle reins, another seized me by the right leg, and yet another had me by the left leg, trying to pull me off. I still held my gun [carbine], although it was empty, when an Indian from behind rushed forward and seized it and wrenched it from my hands. . . . When I drew my pistol, I shot the Indian that was pulling my left leg and he fell over. . . . I turned to attend the Indian on the right, but just at that moment one of the boys shot him.[26]

Sergeant Henley engaged a mounted chief. Henley parried a lance thrust and then split open his skull with his saber. Hood himself was beset by multiple warriors. His double-barreled shotgun dispatched the first foe. He drew a six-shooter—he was one of a handful who possessed two revolvers—and forced his horse into the middle of the fray. Hood's voice rose above the din as he shouted out rallying words, "Steady men, on me Second Cavalry!" while firing his revolver left and right. Twelve or so Indians maintained a steady rifle fire. As soon as a warrior squeezed a trigger, he passed his weapon to a waiting squaw, who retired, calmly reloaded it, and returned through the beaten zone to hand it back to the fighter. It was not a rifle ball but rather an arrow that pierced Hood. It passed through his reins and pinned his left hand to the bridle. Enraged, Hood broke the spearhead and tossed it aside. The shaft still transfixed his hand. In his frenzy, the lieutenant tried to pull the arrow through the wound's channel, only to realize that the feathers resisted his pressure. He seized the feathered end and yanked it free.

Most of the Indian fire missed the mark. Shooting downslope is notoriously inaccurate. The Indians on foot failed to adjust adequately for the height difference when they shot against the mounted cavalry. However, when the fire dropped one trooper's horse and wounded the soldier, some found the range. Three more arrows pierced the trooper's back as he staggered back toward the pack train. Through it all the cavalry maintained its disciplined resistance. Two troopers died in the first charge. Besides Hood, four others received severe wounds. Their revolver fire checked the initial Comanche surge at a distance of five paces. The cavalry's heavy fire drove back the Indians until the troopers squeezed their triggers and they merely snapped against empty chambers. The Indians rallied in turn and poured in their own heavy fire. Hood realized that he and his men could not reload under such a withering barrage. He ordered a retreat. The surviving troopers calmed their horses and withdrew some fifty yards. To Hood's surprise, the Indians did not persist. "Soon afterward arose from beyond the burning heap one continuous mourning howl, such as can alone come forth from the heart of the red man in deep distress. These sounds of sorrow revealed to me that we were in little danger of a renewal of the assault, and I was, I may in truth say, most thankful for the truce thus proclaimed."[27]

Hood later acknowledged that the unit's survival was fortuitous. If the horses had not been so jaded, they would have become unmanageable when the Indians beat their faces with their shields. Some troopers would have been thrown by rearing horses. The patrol's formation would have been broken. Alternatively, if the Indians had shown the self-possession to cut their reins, thereby rendering the cavalry's horses unmanageable, the detachment would also have met "a similar fate to that of the gallant Custer."[28] It had been a remarkable fight with an inferior force confronting a shocking suprise. Since most of their foes were on foot, the cavalry could have retreated safely. Instead the troopers closed with the Indians and then remained under an intense fire even as they took heavy losses. Hood's example undoubtedly inspired them during the initial shock. Thereafter, the fight degenerated into numerous individual encounters. The men possessed great confidence to fight so tenaciously under these circumstances. In large measure, that confidence must have been founded on their faith that they had a tremendous weaponry advantage with their Colt revolvers.[29]

Hood's command was in no shape to resume the fight. After they reunited with the pack mule guards, there were only seventeen unwounded troopers left. The excitement of battle intensified an already acute thirst. Blood loss is a form of dehydration. The wounded particularly suffered from lack of water. The command staggered off to Devil's River, where it bivouacked at about 10 P.M. Hood sent a courier to the nearest army camp requesting help and hunkered down for a siege. Fortunately, the Indians retreated instead. They too had suffered severely. Hood estimated that his patrol had killed ten. Later, the reserve Indians reported that their brethren said that they lost nineteen killed. Regardless, the Indians correctly calculated that the effort to annihilate the crippled cavalry would cost them additional casualties. From their perspective this would be pointless.

The next day an infantry relief column arrived. They loaded the wounded privates, John David, William W. Williams (surely the assumed name of someone who wanted to escape his past!), Thomas Tirrell, and John Kane, into a wagon and took them to nearby Camp Hudson. In spite of his own serious injury, Hood remained with his men because he believed his duty was not yet done. He led the survivors back to the field to bury the fallen and continue the battle if possible. They found Private Thomas Ryan's body "horribly mutilated"; in addition to inflicting multiple wounds, the Indians had thrust a ramrod lengthwise through Ryan's body. In spite of a careful search, they did not find Private William Barry. Hood listed him as missing and presumed killed. It is likely that the Indians retreated with Barry as a captive and tortured him to death soon after the fight. Scout McLoughlin reported that the Indians had dispersed into numerous small groups. Given his horses' broken-down condition, Hood concluded that he would not pursue.

Almost exactly eight years after entering West Point, Lieutenant Hood had experienced his first combat. The fight at Devil's River could hardly be called a victory. Not only had his command suffered 25 percent casualties, but it had failed to check its foe. When Hood's crippled detachment limped back to Fort Mason, the Comanches attacked the California mail near the place where Hood had engaged. At Devil's River, Hood revealed himself to be impetuous to a fault, willing to take a chance against overwhelming odds. Once the fight began he exhibited an utter disregard for his own safety. It could be seen in his eyes; normally sad and almost fawnlike, in battle they blazed with a fearful intensity. Whether youthful rashness coupled with exemplary combat courage would mature into something more remained to be seen.

The unique obstacles Hood overcame—an enraged bear, drought—and the scale of combat may seem trifling when compared to challenges Civil War generals confronted. But consider: To reach the enemy, Hood had to make a fine assessment of his men's capabilities. He had to evaluate the endurance of man and horse under trying conditions. The fight began with a shocking surprise. Thereafter, Hood had to make rapid decisions with the knowledge that his choices could spell the doom of his entire command. In sum, the lieutenant made calculations based upon his evaluation of his unit's logistics and performed in a combat environment that demanded physical and moral courage. Hood's exploit earned him promotion to first lieutenant. The fight at Devil's River also prepared a leader for the larger stages of Gaines' Mill, Gettysburg, and Chickamauga.

Military men generally reckoned that it required two years of service to convert a cavalry recruit into an effective trooper. Hood's combat showed how far the Second had progressed. Had the men not performed reliably, the entire outfit would have been exterminated. Hood paid them handsome praise in his official report: "It is due my non-commissioned officers and men, one and all . . . during the action they did all men could do, accomplishing more than could be expected from their number and the odds against which they had to contend." General Twiggs, the commander of the Department of Texas, and General in Chief Winfield Scott both called Hood's epic a "gallant" fight. Among the Second Cavalry's fourteen engagements during 1857, the fight at Devil's River was by far the most costly.[30]

A FRESH PATROL led by Captain Charles J. Whiting and Second Lieutenant James P. Major returned to Devil's River shortly after Hood's fight. They followed the Indian trail of retreat from the battlefield and they too faced harsh conditions. Twice during their five-day chase their horses went without water for more than twenty-four hours. At last they encountered a band believed to include warriors who had attacked Hood's men. Whiting's troopers skillfully separated the Indians from their horses and drove the Comanches into a wooded ravine. Unlike Jenifer and Hood, at this point Whiting halted the pursuit. Suffering no losses themselves, the cavalry killed two Indians and captured thirty-three horses.

Whereas Hood's fight was the regiment's most dramatic engagement during 1857, there were many other encounters. In addition to numerous small patrols, the regiment occasionally still conducted "big sweeps." Major George Thomas led one such mission involving soldiers from four different companies. A summary of the manpower involved says something about the scale of the Second Cavalry's operations: in addition to Thomas, three commissioned officers, nine sergeants and corporals, eighty-three privates. The expedition left Camp Cooper on July 23, 1857, to search the headwaters of the Concho. Thomas fared even less well than had Lee's similar operation of the previous year. His troopers failed entirely to encounter the enemy.

By now the veterans in the Second Cavalry had acquired a pretty clear notion of how their adversaries fought. Since the cavalry was reacting to Indian raids, the troopers were compelled to conduct long pursuits of a fleet, mounted enemy. However, the Indians typically entered the settlements on foot, their silent presence unknown until they had already stolen horses and made their escape.[31] Like the Viet Cong, whom the descendants of the Second Cavalry would fight in Vietnam, a handful of fighters could terrorize a large civilian population:

> The savages would come in by the mountain trails . . . until they would get far down in the settlements, when they would scatter out in small parties of from two to ten, and, by traveling in the

dead hours of the night, they would reach points which they considered secure; then by a preconcerted signal, they would raise havoc in perhaps a dozen different places, at the same time. This kept the country in a constant fever of excitement, and, as is usual on such occasions, no one knew who to trust.[32]

After a raid, the Comanches usually left a warrior to serve as a rearguard vedette. He watched for any pursuit, and if he reported none, then the main band grew careless of security. Thus a patrol that followed an Indian trail several days could sometimes catch up with the raiders and surprise them in their camp. Although burdened with stolen horses and mules, during their retreat the Indians' initial dash covered an enormous distance, sometimes up to ninety miles without a halt.

In addition to being horsemen, the Comanches were superb archers, as Hood and his men could attest. To show off their skills, they would draw circles in the dirt and then unleash a barrage of arrows that rose a great height before descending to fill the target circle. When chased closely, a warrior could dismount in a flash and accurately fire his bow at his pursuers.

Hood's combat was exceptional in that the Indians invited battle with the lieutenant's detachment. Although the Comanches fought numerous pitched encounters with their special enemies, the Texas Rangers, and would even attack Ranger camps at night, like most guerrilla forces they avoided battle with regular army units. This restricted the cavalry to a handful of tactical responses, none of which were particularly satisfying. They could occupy static defenses. This made nearby settlers happy but was impractical given the expanse of territory that needed guarding. Leaders preferred to use the regiment's mobility to search actively for the enemy. At considerable cost in wear and tear to men and horses alike, the regiment patrolled through desolate regions in the hopes of crossing a track along which Indians had recently moved. The cavalry's Indian guides were particularly adept at "cutting track" and then leading the cavalry in pursuit. Most of the cavalry's encounters with Indians occurred in this manner. Additionally, there was the direct pursuit, in which the cavalry responded to a raid by riding to the scene and then trying to follow the Indians' escape route. This approach continued to be an exercise in "justice arriving too late to catch the rogue."[33] An entirely different tactical approach, carrying the war to the enemy, would not come until 1858.

After Texas became safe from raids, new settlers who gazed upon the region's numerous towns, roads, and settled ranches asked why it had been so difficult to provide security. The experienced Indian fighter Buck Barry struggled to describe how it had once been. Barry observed that the entire country from the Canadian River in the Panhandle southward to below the Staked Plain had once been familiar hunting land for the Comanches. Numerous ravines and small canyons bisected the land east of the Staked Plain, and they provided entrance and exit routes for Indians intent on raiding the settlements along the upper Colorado and Brazos. Small bands moved through these routes undetected. The land around the headwaters of the Little Wichita, Wichita, and Pease Rivers was even more rugged and desolate, covered with hills, small ravines, and dense thickets. These features provided convenient assembly points for raiding parties and a sanctuary in the event of white pursuit. Consequently, neither the Texas Rangers nor the Second Cavalry nor its Confederate successors in the Texas Mounted Rifles could effectively intercept raiding bands. Their recourse was to respond to raids by pursuing the raiders. Because the Indians typically enjoyed a considerable head start and were superb horsemen who moved very rapidly, it usually was impossible to overtake them. The cavalry's best chance came when officers organized a chase while the trail was still hot. Even then the challenge remained formidable. Buck Barry explained, "The country was so irregular that a war party might scatter and the warriors hide themselves until the pursuit had passed, overlooked them, or been abandoned."[34]

BRIEFLY IT SEEMED that Lieutenant Colonel Robert Lee would have an opportunity to exhibit the regiment's growing tactical prowess. Because the War Department ordered Sidney Johnston to report to Washington, on July 29 Lee ascended to regimental command. After conducting his first field operation the previous year, Lee had spent much of his time traversing Texas, riding from one post to another to participate in court-martials. Lee's great biographer, Douglas Southall Freeman, called this time "Education by Court Martial," a valuable opportunity to study the army's inner workings. Lee himself found it exceptionally tedious. He wrote his wife how "Major Porter had for his counsel two Texan lawyers . . . very shrewd men, accustomed to the tricks and stratagems of special pleadings, which, of no other avail, absorb time and stave off the question."[35] Only the fact that he periodically passed through San Antonio relieved the boredom.

Most of Lee's travels took him through thinly populated countryside. Even villages and towns were small and primitive by eastern standards. Only 430 people lived in Dallas in 1858. Affluent west Texas businessmen still lived in crude, dogtrot-style cabins. Decent hotels had to post requests asking guests to refrain from spitting on the walls and asking them please to keep booted feet off chairs and bedspreads. The Johnston and Thomas homes in San Antonio offered a welcome refuge. "The supper last night was so good," Lee wrote, "and so much to my taste, venison steak, biscuit and butter, that I had little appetite for my breakfast, though waffles, eggs and wild turkey were three dishes it presented; and when the dinner of wild turkey, tomatos, French peas, snap beans, and potatoes was followed by plum pudding, jellies and preserved peaches, I despaired."[36] At this time, Lee also forged an enduring bond with another Virginian who was to play an important role in his future. Major Robert Hall Chilton served as an army paymaster. Like his predecessor Sidney Johnston, Chilton delivered money to army posts. He brought the pay for the Second Cavalry at Camp Cooper. In turn, when Lee was in San Antonio he enjoyed the hospitality of the Chilton family. Lee would name Chilton as his chief of staff when he became commander of the Army of Northern Virginia. The two served together through to Appomattox.

Outside of San Antonio, Lee shared his troopers' continuing hardships. He arrived at Fort Mason in April 1857 and pitched his tent in the most sheltered place he could find. A cold norther blew in and the water bucket inside his tent froze solid. No man cared more for horses than Lee. He carefully stretched their picket line under the lee of a dense thicket, but when he visited them during the night he found the animals suffering intensely from the cold. Yet no hint of complaint issued from Lee's pen when he related this incident to his wife:

> The changes of weather here are very rapid. Yesterday, for instance, I was in my white line coat and shirt all the afternoon, and the thermometer in my tent, with the walls raised and a fine breeze blowing through it, stood at eighty-nine degrees. I could not bear the blanket at night, but about twelve o'clock a "norther" came roaring down the valley of the Clear Fork and made all my blankets necessary. This morning fires and overcoats are in fashion again.[37]

He was becoming inured to physical hardship, a hardihood that was to serve him well.

When Lee returned to Camp Cooper from court-martial duty, he learned that during his absence the cavalry had had four fights with the Indians, in which two troopers and perhaps a dozen Indians had been killed. In contrast to Lee's attitude toward his physical environment was his developing attitude toward Indian warfare. It depressed him. He viewed it as a distressing state of affairs while acknowledging that killing Indians on sight seemed "the only corrective they understand, the only way in which they can be brought to keep within their own limits."[38]

His own men's suffering also discouraged him. At Camp Cooper, a sergeant's one-year-old boy died. The sergeant approached Lee, tears streaming down his face, to beg him to read the funeral service over his body. Although Lee believed the baby was bound for a better place, the ceremony still upset him. Then heat-induced lethargy set in. In the summer of 1857, the coolest tent's thermometer read 112 degrees. Beneath the great heat, the sick list bloomed. There was not a great deal to occupy a lieutenant colonel's time, to distract him from the overpowering heat, since actual field service fell to the junior officers. Thus, Lee's assignment to regimental command proved a welcome diversion. Although his new duties were supervisory, Lee took pride in the fact that he was in charge of a strong fighting regiment. The July 1, 1857, returns showed 38 commissioned officers and 793 enlisted men. Desertions remained troubling, but the flow of fresh manpower successfully replaced most of the missing. The unit needed only 61 recruits.[39]

How Lee would have utilized this powerful force is unknown. After less than three months in command, he learned that his father-in-law had died. He received a leave of absence and departed for Virginia. His nineteen months in Texas had provided underwhelming experiences. He never personally led troops in combat, although through close association with common soldiers he did learn more about their attitudes and motivations. Court-martials consumed much of his time. However dull and tedious, this experience was instructive. In Freeman's words: "As he listened to case after case, he understood better than ever before how weak, jealous, indolent, and sensitive men reacted to army life. He saw why they lapsed in their duty, and what were the temptations before which they most often fell."[40] This complemented his previous experience as superintendent of West Point, during which time he had associated with the army's young gentlemen. Much of Lee's success in the Civil War was due to his ability to evalute character and leadership and select officers for appropriate commands. His first tour of duty in Texas provided the underpinnings for this talent. The regiment would next hear about their lieutenant colonel in connection with an ugly affair at the federal arsenal at Harpers Ferry and a man named John Brown.

With Johnston recalled to Washington for special assignment, Lee absent on leave, and Hardee serving at West Point, regimental command devolved upon the broad shoulders of burly Major George Thomas. Thomas hailed from Southampton County, Virginia, about five miles from the North Carolina border. Southampton County was a hardscrabble region, economically distinct from the plantation life of Virginia's tidewater region. His family was hardworking and solidly middle class. They jointly owned nine slaves, but this did not keep George's father from participating in farm labor. When George was thirteen, his father died in a farm accident. Two years later came another dramatic, deadly event when Nat Turner's slave insurrection swept through Southampton County. Young George and his family fled before the mob arrived and were among the fortunate. Some fifty-five of Thomas's neighbors died in the violence. Given this experience as well as his Virginia birthright, Thomas's future conduct—his resolution to remain with the federal army when Civil War ignited—marks him as an unusual man.

His character and ability did not shine during his cadet days at West Point, although he did graduate in the top quarter of his class of 1840. Following service in the Seminole War, Thomas won two brevets in the war against Mexico, yet still nothing marked him as an exceptional leader. However, something about him had impressed Braxton Bragg sufficiently so that Bragg recommended him for duty in the Second Cavalry. It also impressed Lieutenant Hood, who served for a time as Thomas's acting adjutant. Exhibiting his own generosity of spirit, Hood described how in Texas the man who would destroy his army in 1864 "won my high regard by his manliness and dignity."[41]

Under Thomas's leadership, the remainder of 1857 witnessed the continuation of a tactical trend that changed the nature of cavalry-versus-Indian combat. Much in the way the navy awarded prize money to sailors who captured an enemy vessel, the army allowed the troopers to divide the proceeds from the resale of horses and mules they recaptured from the Indians. Captain Whiting's detachment, the men who had pursued the Indians from the scene of the fight at Devil's River, divided $400 among themselves. This was a powerful incentive stimulating a trooper's zeal. It inspired Captain Brackett's men in Company I to ride hard through an arroyo feeding into the Rio Grande as they chased a band of raiders. The Indians sought shelter in a dense thicket, to no avail. The troopers pressed five miles through badly broken terrain. Prickly pear, Spanish bayonets, and mesquite bushes injured several of their mounts but the cavalry carried on. The Indians fled across the river to sanctuary in Mexico. However, to the troopers' satisfaction they abandoned most of their property. That evening Brackett deployed his men in ambush positions in the hopes that the Indians might return to collect their possessions. It may have been a pro forma exercise. At any rate, the enemy did not return. Prospects of earning extra money helped motivate Sergeant Charles Patrick to drive his twelve-man detachment through heavy September rains during a seven-day chase. In one sixty-hour span, the cavalry rode 160 sodden miles. This extraordinary feat ended with an encounter in which the cavalry killed one Indian and captured eleven horses.

When officers led the patrols, monetary gain was less likely to play a role in tactical decisions. Since officers earned considerably more money, possible financial reward was proportionally less significant. The respect of their peers, promotion, glory, and dedication to duty motivated the officers. Thus, in one of the regiment's last engagements during 1857, Lieutenant Witherell set out on a four-day pursuit of a band of Lipans and Comanches who had stolen eight mules from the mail company. Riding hard, Witherell's detachment overtook the Indians. In a short, sharp fight the cavalry killed one Indian and recaptured the eight mules. The value of the mules was clearly disproportionate to the risk the cavalry endured. Witherell and three privates were wounded in the fight.

As head of the regiment, George Thomas continued Johnston's policy of aggressive patrolling. Noncommissioned officers led an increasing number of the patrols, and the results suggested that many were more interested in recapturing horses than in fighting Indians.[42] It may even be that the Indians and the cavalry arrived at some tacit understanding. If the cavalry's pursuit seemed likely to overtake the raiders, then the Indians could abandon their stolen animals, in effect trading lives for horses. Experienced fighters, whether red or white, may have concluded that this was a reasonable way to conduct business since it preserved lives on both sides. At any event, 1857 and 1858 featured the lowest number of troopers killed during the regiment's tour of duty. In both years, only twelve men died in combat.

6

The Reputation
of the Regiment

My young friend, think twice, and think seriously, before taking this step; because, in all likelihood, it is the turning-point in your life.
—Albert Sidney Johnston, 1857 (in William Preston Johnston, *The Life of Albert Sidney Johnston*)

———— I. "The Matured Vigor of Manhood" ————

One of the responsibilities of leadership for a regimental colonel was to act as a father figure. So a Robert Lee dispensed sage advice to handsome John Hood to select a wife carefully. So an Albert Sidney Johnston addressed a potentially lethal quarrel. Johnston's special challenge stemmed from the fact that the culture of the duel was firmly embedded in Texas. With routine violence commonplace and prickly pride the norm, only with difficulty could differences be composed amicably. Johnston had personal knowledge of this. Back in the days of the Texas Republic, Sam Houston had ordered him to replace an incompetent firebrand named Felix Huston as commander of the field army. Huston resisted and challenged Johnston to a duel. In principle Johnston opposed dueling as an arbiter of honor. In this case he judged that he could not avoid the challenge without losing face before the entire army. The antagonists met for their showdown

165

at Camp Independence. They exchanged five or six shots before Johnston fell with a ball through his right hip. Little had changed since that time. A Texas newspaper reported how a dispute between rival editors ended without mortal combat and concluded: "We are decidedly opposed to the shooting mode of settling such disputes. It is very apt to derange the nervous system and destroy the appetite."[1]

While serving as acting departmental commander in San Antonio at a time when "Nicaragua fever"—plans to relieve Walker's beleaguered filibusters—was sweeping the city, Johnston heard about a personal altercation between one of his officers and a civilian. The controversy had purportedly escalated to such proportions that each felt compelled to kill his antagonist on sight. Johnston tried to intercede by speaking with the civilian's second, a personal friend and a lawyer. He asked the lawyer, Were the rumors true? The lawyer asked if the colonel intended to use his position to stop the fight. No, replied Johnston, his intercession was personal, not official. The lawyer stated that each man was pledged to kill the other on sight. Johnston asked if they could not compose their differences. No, they could not. It must reduce to "a bloody street brawl."[2] Exhibiting a fine understanding of the code duello, Johnston, "by the mathematical argument of *honor* and the inexorable logic of 'the code,'" induced the lawyer to adopt a plan to defuse the duel.[3] His masterful exhibition of tact allowed two hotblooded young men to live.

Johnston's service in San Antonio ended in the spring of 1857 when Brigadier General David E. Twiggs became the permanent commander of the Department of Texas. Johnston reluctantly returned to Fort Mason to command his regiment. "This is rather a falling off," he privately complained.[4] Two months later he received a surprise summons to report to the secretary of war in Washington. He turned command of the regiment over to Robert Lee and departed. Officers in the Second Cavalry admired Johnston and regretted his transfer. Both Lee and Major George Thomas wrote Johnston affectionate good-byes. Richard Johnson spoke for them all when he wrote how the regiment suspected that the colonel was bound for higher responsibilities and would never return to the Second Cavalry. He noted that while the men rejoiced at Johnston's chance for promotion, they "deeply regret your loss, for the Cavalry arm can not replace you. . . . Your Regt. Looks to you as its father and your reputation is the reputation of the 2 Cavalry."[5]

Arriving at the War Department, Johnston learned that there was trouble in the Utah Territory, home to some forty thousand Mormons. The Mormons belonged to the only evangelical movement of wholly American origin that ever blossomed into a great religion. Persecuted for their unconventional views, their founder lynched in Illinois in 1847, they followed Brigham Young to the desolate West, where they hoped to create a new Zion. The problem came when they refused to obey any federal official not of their own religion. President Buchanan ordered Johnston to command a military expedition with the objective of reasserting federal authority in Utah. In Johnston's words, his mission was "to urge" upon the people of Utah "the necessity of obedience to the Constitution and the laws," including presidential proclamations.[6] That Johnston could enter upon this mission in 1858 but resign rather than perform a similar mission in 1860 perhaps suggests that he and many other southerners had an elastic notion of states' rights.

In its haste to suppress an embarrassing revolt, the Buchanan administration had already sent an ill-prepared expedition across the Great Plains. Johnston caught up with the column west of Fort Laramie in the barren high plateau of southern Wyoming. Much as he had done while leading the Second Cavalry from Jefferson Barracks to Texas, he exerted himself tirelessly to untangle the wagon trains, encourage the weakhearted, and push the column forward westward. "Colonel Johnston is now in the matured vigor of manhood," reported *Harper's Weekly.* "He is about six feet in height, strongly and powerfully formed, with a grave, dignified, and commanding presence. His features . . . denote great resolution and composure of character. His complexion, naturally fair, is, from exposure a deep brown. . . . His manner is courteous, but grave and silent."[7] The march became a race against winter. By mid-September, Johnston realized that winter would win. Snow blanketed the camp on the Sweetwater River; the temperature dropped to 16 degrees. Rather than try to force the fortified Mormon position guarding the pass into Utah, Johnston resolved to establish winter quarters at Fort Bridger, 125 miles northeast of Salt Lake City.

The day the column began its march to this fort, a mountain blizzard struck. Now began an epic struggle for survival. Conditions were worse than those experienced by the icebound Second Cavalry back in north Texas. Blinding snowstorms reduced progress to a crawl. Daytime high temperatures hovered around 2 degrees, falling at night to 16 below. Axle grease froze solid and the horses, mules, and oxen perished by the hundreds. As the column forced its way through the snowdrifts the scene resembled Napoleon's catastrophic retreat from Moscow in 1812. Yet Johnston's driving energy got the column to Fort Bridger with the loss of only one soldier. He walked with the men through innumerable blizzards, sharing their hardship, inspiring them by example just as he had inspired the Second Cavalry. An infantry captain spoke for the entire Utah expedition when he said, "Col. Johnston . . . is a man."[8]

During a difficult winter at Fort Bridger, Johnston prepared for a spring campaign to crush the Mormons. In January 1858, Johnston's command numbered 2,588 officers and men, including dragoons, infantry, and artillery. The War Department dispatched reinforcements. The Second Cavalry assembled at regimental headquarters in preparation for a march to Utah. In the meantime, events intruded and it remained in Texas. Over time, Johnston's strength rose to 5,606. This was the largest concentration of force since the Mexican War, and a heavy responsibility.[9] General in Chief Scott thoroughly approved of Johnston's operations and praised him lavishly. Johnston was hardly aware of Scott's satisfaction because he was at the end of a very precarious line of communication, if that term may be used to dignify a succession of mounted couriers riding over the Rocky Mountains in winter. As of March 10, 1858, Johnston had not received orders dispatched from Washington since his departure from that city the previous September.

His request for instructions yielded a model reply from Winfield Scott: "At this distance from the scene of operations, and on imperfect information . . . he [Scott] doubts whether you will have sufficient numbers to force the passes to Salt Lake" before receiving reinforcements. Scott did not intend "to apply the curb" to aggressive action but rather to relieve Johnston of a possible notion that his orders compelled him to advance as soon as possible. Johnston had to decide for himself how and when to proceed. Scott wanted to avoid issuing specific orders that would be out of date and probably impractical by the time they arrived, and thus to leave his subordinate as "untrammeled as possible" by the heavy hand of distant authority.[10] Consequently, Johnston confronted the very essence of independent command. He had to make important decisions in the absence of complete information. Independent command required a certain type of moral courage, and few men possessed it. The War Department had chosen Sidney Johnston because it had faith in his abilities. Now Johnston faced a complex military-political environment and he had to confront it alone.

Until the snows melted, his main challenge was to maintain the morale of bored, cold, hungry soldiers. Just as he had done with the Second Cavalry, he conducted unit drills and tactical exercises at the regimental and brigade level. During spare moments he held tactics classes for the officers. After a final heavy snow on June 10, spring came to the mountains. However, the Buchanan administration had changed its mind. It wanted to conclude the expensive, embarrassing conflict without further hostilities. Before Johnston could begin his offensive, skillful federal negotiation averted a bloody battle. In late June a somewhat deflated army marched into Salt Lake Valley without opposition. Because the Mormons had abandoned their capital, a queer triumphal march through a deserted city ensued. When the column passed Brigham Young's home, the band struck up a ribald camp tune named "One-Eyed Riley." After that, there was little to do but undertake an unusual military occupation of the Utah Territory.

Exhausted by the strain, on July 8, 1858, Johnston requested that he be allowed to return to his regiment. If that could not be done, he asked for an extended furlough, citing the fact that he had enjoyed no relaxation from duty for more than nine years. His appeal fell on deaf ears. He remained in Utah until the spring of 1860. Most of this time featured military-civilian discord exacerbated by the fact that Johnston detested the Mormon theocracy. He complained privately about a life "worse than any imagined horrors of a Siberian exile" but continued to perform his duty.[11] Bored and lonely, he was enormously relieved finally to depart Utah. By the time he reunited with his family back in Kentucky, three years had passed since he had last seen them.

IF ALBERT SIDNEY JOHNSTON had a legitimate complaint about his "falling off" from acting district commander to mere colonel of a regiment, then Captain Innis Palmer and his troopers of Company D had an even greater basis for complaint. It was their misfortune to be assigned to duty at Camp Verde for two years between the summers of 1856 and 1858. Whereas Johnston's complaint rested upon his diminished responsibility, Company D's complaint was based upon something entirely different, namely, the extraordinary and noisome presence of camels.

Back in 1853, Secretary of War Davis had promoted the idea of importing camels to serve as transport animals on the western frontier. His proposal stimulated laughter and some open mockery. Notoriously thin skinned, Davis would remember those who mocked him, but he was also notoriously stubborn. By 1854, he knew that the British army in the Crimea was using camels to carry up to 600-pound loads 25 to 30 miles per day. Davis asked, If camels were suitable for Russia, then why not the American West? So, he promoted the project with characteristic determination until Congress authorized funds in March 1855. A Lieutenant Edward F. Beale, then superintendent of Indian Affairs in California and Nevada, enthusiastically supported the idea. Beale encouraged his relative David Dixon Porter—the future Union admiral whose support for the army decisively assisted Grant's capture of Vicksburg—to apply for command of the camel-purchasing expedition. Then and thereafter, Porter possessed an active imagination. Accordingly, he took command of an expedition that set sail to the Levant for an improbable rendezvous with dromedaries.

Something that had seemed easy in concept back at the War Department proved a little more difficult in practice. Porter procured thirty-three camels in Egypt and Turkey. His sailors loaded the beasts onto transports and the expedition embarked for Texas. The hapless creatures sailed across a storm-tossed sea in great discomfort. For weeks on end they were tied in a kneeling position. To make room for the largest animal, a hole was cut in the deck to accommodate his hump. During the stormy voyage one camel died and two were born. On May 14, 1856, Porter

171

To cope with arid conditions in the West, another of Secretary Davis's innovations was the importation of camels to Texas. Troopers operating out of Camp Verde, "Little Egypt," disliked working with the camels. (National Archives)

landed them at Indianola, Texas, a small port about 120 miles south of Galveston. Returned to dry land, the camels "became excited to an almost uncontrollable degree, rearing, kicking, crying out, breaking halters, tearing up pickets, and by other fantastic tricks demonstrating their enjoyment of the 'liberty of the soil.'"[12] A second shipment of some forty animals later joined the herd.

At first the bewildered beasts were kept outside of San Antonio, where the army hoped they would breed and multiply. Two Turks and their three Arab assistants provided experienced care. When Colonel Joseph Mansfield inspected the camels the first summer, he found them in tolerable condition and predicted that isolated outposts and ranches would find them a very useful means of freight transport. The next two years did not treat the animals kindly. An inspector found the camels at Camp Verde, where they were in the hands of inexperienced men because "the only men in America who understand them," the two Turks, refused to venture farther inland than San Antonio.[13]

Moreover, the camel sellers had obviously managed to fob off on the unwitting Americans some less than stellar animals. It became apparent that they were in poor shape for heavy work. In response to complaints, a member of the American consulate in Egypt, Edward DeLeon, sent the secretary of war a lengthy treatise on camel management. Written by one Herekyan Bey, it was an informed, affectionate distillation of centuries of experience with dromedaries. DeLeon sent a copy to Jefferson Davis, "whose untiring energy and zeal under difficulties and discouragement" DeLeon commended.[14] But Davis was no longer secretary of war. However great his energy and zeal, he was not the person responsible for camel care in Texas and was thus unable to apply Herekyan Bey's very detailed instructions. The permanent camp for the camel experiment was Camp Verde, sixty miles northwest of San Antonio. Here they landed in the hands of Captain Palmer and his men.

The army established the post on July 8, 1856, on the north bank of Verde Creek, north of Bandera Pass. It lay in the heart of Texas hill country, with abundant water, shade, and mild summers. It was one of the most desirable posts in Texas, except for the presence of the camels. The troopers called it Little Egypt and did their best to avoid camel duty. Yet strange as they were, Jefferson Davis's theory was correct: the camels actually were better suited to draft-animal duty in Texas than the ubiquitous mule. Accustomed to arid conditions, they required a less regular water supply, were less likely to go lame, and could subsist on desert vegetation that would nourish neither a horse nor a mule. Often a great amount of the camel's 700-pound burden was rations for the corn-fed mules. Praise for the camels even reached the pages of *Harper's Weekly,* where one satisfied teamster reported that "one camel can do the work of four mules" and another asserted that he would rather manage a train of twenty camels over one of five mules.[15]

When Captain Charles Whiting led a patrol to Devil's River in an effort to pick up the track of the Indians who had fought Hood, he used a camel instead of the customary pack mules. Whereas the horses suffered terribly during two separate waterless days, the camel seemed unaffected. Many had openly mocked Secretary Davis's camels, but their service with the Second Cavalry proved them to be an excellent potential solution to the vexing problem of how to carry heavy loads across the arid Texas wastelands. The chaos of the Civil War would cause the collapse of the camel experiment and the dispersal of the herd. For a long time afterward, Indians would report sightings of bizarre, almost mythical animals roaming remote regions of the American West.

THE OFFICERS assigned to the Second Cavalry enjoyed breaks from the privation of service in Texas when they returned east on leave. What they encountered surprised them. Richard Johnson remembered how fashion had dramatically changed so that "my wife did not consider herself presentable in public. . . . The stylish bonnet she wore when we first went to Texas looked like a Conestoga wagon compared with the style of 1855."[16] An army wife who accompanied her husband during his leave back east had been so long deprived of everything but the bare necessities that she gazed with amazement at how luxuriously her friends lived. Not surprisingly, given the comforts of leave, some officers lingered. They could also spin out leave by requesting special duties. Over time, officers on detached duty had begun to take such liberties that the War Department decided to crack down. Henceforth officers had to report monthly to their post commander, their unit commander, and to the adjutant general with a statement of what they were doing and on whose authority.[17] This stern requirement quickly recalled the officers to their duty.

Unlike the officers, the enlisted men rarely received leave. They remained with the regiment until completing their three-year tour of duty. Because they lived in relative isolation and shared innumerable patrols month after month, year after year, officers and men developed a matchless camaraderie. Captain Johnson considered his men as without equal. He stimulated their pride by urging them to be the best-drilled and best-disciplined company in the regiment. On a practical level he knew that his own life depended upon them. The men he chose to accompany him on patrol were light, lithe, and athletic. They all weighed between 140 and 150 pounds, were excellent horsemen and fearless fighters. They had great stamina and cheerfully endured privation and hardship. Johnson imposed strict discipline. If the troopers offended, they knew punishment would surely follow. But if they were well behaved, Johnson gave them "the largest liberty, consistent with proper discipline."[18] In the case of his first sergeant, that liberty included turning a blind eye to his drinking binges when on post. Johnson considered the grizzled veteran, Sergeant Thomas Gardner, a splendid soldier, the type of noncommissioned officer whose force of character bonded a company together. If he indulged his appetite for whiskey while off duty, it was a tolerable weakness.

When the cavalry fought in the Vietnam War, the tour of duty was too short for the soldiers to become familiar with their environment. The extended tour of duty in Texas gave the unit the opportunity to adjust both to the physical environment and to the tactics of their enemies. To conquer Texas's vast distances,

Captain Kirby Smith had discovered the remarkable ability of the riding mule. It was in many ways a creature more suitable than the horse. It was not without vices. The mule knew he was smarter than a horse and thought he was smarter than the rider. Indeed, the mule's intelligence and hardihood made him a valuable asset. Smith wrote how he went out on scout mounted on his mule, "the dearest, gentlest, and most intelligent brute, small but round, fat as a dumpling, with sleek coat, bright eyes and two well developed and expressive ears, actively moving in every direction and speaking as plainly as an alphabet."[19] Not only did the mule detect danger more readily than the horse; it was capable of great feats of endurance. Smith reported that he rode seventy-five miles in twenty-six hours with a rest of only five or six hours. But a general prejudice among most troopers against mules prevented their widespread adoption.

Something the troopers had to adapt to was the presence of an extraordinary number of rattlesnakes. Their warning rattle sounded to an eastern ear like a loud August locust. Although snakebites were not uncommon, very few caused lasting troopers serious injury or death. Army physicians adopted the treatment regimen practiced by San Antonio doctors: for the professional class, ammonia; for the people, whiskey. Troopers who were afraid of snakes, probably 99 percent of the Second Cavalry, comforted themselves with the story of the Texas farmwife who walked barefoot to milk her cow and was bitten on the ankle. She ran back home and tossed off a pint of whiskey and recovered completely, albeit a little muddleheaded, the next day.

On a more practical level, troopers learned that when bedding down for the night they should spread their blankets on heavy grass whenever possible, since rattlesnakes seemed to prefer dry ground to dewy grass. Experience also taught small patrols to cook and eat at one site and then, in case the Comanches were watching, to wait until sunset before stealthily moving elsewhere to sleep. Veterans discovered that while they were out in the chaparral wilderness, corn ground fine between two stones, mixed with bacon fat, wrapped in green leaves, placed in a bed of ashes and hot coals, and baked was quite delicious. Better still was rabbit Texas Ranger–style: skewer a dressed rabbit on a green mesquite stick, generously rub with salt, lay on a bed of hot embers for a minute or so, remove, peel off any flaky bits and eat them, cook the other side for about one more minute, and tear into as many parts as required. After dining this way once, many concluded that this was the only way a rabbit should ever be cooked. With the saddle as a pillow, the revolver under the fork of the saddle to keep it dry and within quick reach, on a starlit night, life seemed tolerable. As the German immigrants said, the sky seems nearer in Texas than in Europe.[20] Although troopers on patrol learned how to make themselves as comfortable as possible, this did not interfere with their fighting capability. An army surveying team encountered a cavalry patrol out from Fort Clark. The patrol had been on scout for ten days without contact. One of the survey team described them as "a very hard looking party."[21]

—— II. Twiggs's Calculated Risk ——

The years 1858 and 1859 were the bloodiest since Texas had won its independence. In a ten-week span during the winter of 1857–58, Indian raiders killed seven settlers, kidnapped one boy, and captured an estimated six hundred horses. Between January 1 and February 8, twenty separate raids struck along a line from Jack County in the north to Cherokee Creek in the south.

The *Austin Intelligencer* reported in the spring of 1858 that five citizens of Brown County had been killed and thirty-two horses driven off. The governor of Texas appealed to General

Twiggs for help. Twiggs was one of the army's two permanent brigadier generals. The sixty-eight-year-old warrior was a veteran of the War of 1812 and of every subsequent war his nation had fought. He possessed unquestioned bravery; one of his nicknames was the "Bengal Tiger." Although he no longer possessed the physical vigor to take the field, he retained a keen strategic sense. He recognized that given the paucity of his resources, he held few options. He did order the cavalry to make a show of force around the places where the depredations had occurred. He probably knew that this was a hollow gesture. He applied himself with greater energy to complaining to army headquarters that "it is extremely mortifying to be placed in this situation with an inadequate force."[22] His strongest complaint arose after he received a government-issue firearm that had been taken from a dead Indian. It was confirmation of a long-suspected traffic in arms and ammunition between Indians receiving annual presents at Fort Atkinson, in the Indian Territory, and their brethren living on the Texas Indian reserves.

To the settlers, intensified Indian raids were all the more frightening for being unexpected, since the past two years had provided relative peace and security. Not knowing where to turn, angry Texans conceived plans to prove that the root of the problem was the presence of an enemy sanctuary in their midst. A Texas Ranger wrote the governor to suggest that the best way of implicating the reserve Indians was for the citizens to kill a few Indians and then watch who came to bury them. If the burial party was from the reserve, then it proved that the dead Indians were also from the reserve. But instead of satisfying public rage, the cavalry responded to the onslaught with an incomprehensible move. At a time when red men were killing white men, a cavalry detachment relocated to better protect the reserve's Indians. No one liked this idea less than Captain Nathan Evans, the commander at Camp Cooper.

"Shanks" Evans had enthusiastically continued his unit's quarrel with special Indian agent Leeper. In the spring of 1858 the cavalry had moved away from Camp Cooper. The reasons for the move are obscure, but Leeper believed it was in retaliation for his complaints about the troopers' conduct. In any event, when the reserve Indians began reporting frequent sightings of Comanches and Kiowas, Leeper asked the army for help to protect his charges. Evans reluctantly complied with orders and sent Lieutenant Hood, a noncommissioned officer, and nineteen privates to old Camp Cooper. Duty done—except, as Leeper pointed out, this was still eight trail miles away from where the reserve Indians lived. Then, in April, the reserve Indians informed Leeper that a big raid was pending. Leeper reported this to Evans, who disdained to reply. Shortly thereafter the reserve Indians reported a large band of raiders only three miles outside the reserve. Leeper immediately informed Evans, who replied that he would not send out his troops on the basis of such unreliable information. To Leeper's chagrin, the report did prove false. To the agent's credit, he also reported this fact to Evans, who now triumphantly retorted that henceforth he would not dispatch the cavalry unless there were verified reports of wild Indians actually fighting on the reserve.

The poisonous atmosphere between Evans and Leeper thickened in May. An elderly Comanche, along with his family, left his reserve to visit the lower reservation. They did not have a pass. Four Texans murdered him and took his horses. When Leeper applied to Evans for a military guard to escort the relatives of the deceased so they could find and bury the body, Evans refused on the grounds that he had no authority to protect Indians who were off the reservation.

Around this time, Ranger captain John Ford summoned a secret meeting of Ranger officers. Ford liked Neighbors and admired the success of the Brazos reserve, the lower reserve, from which both the cavalry and the Rangers recruited allied Indians to guide them against raiding the Comanches. He shared Evans's attitude toward the Comanche reserve. To the assembled officers Ford stated his desire to break up the Comanche reserve. He wanted to apprehend Comanches who committed depredations off the reserve. Someone remarked that if a trail from a raid led back to the Comanche reserve, that should be sufficient evidence. A Lieutenant Allison Nelson, a future Confederate general, observed, "That thing can be managed—the trail can be made."[23] Ford was too honorable a man to countenance such tactics, but the statement speaks to the prevailing attitude. Unless the Second Cavalry could do something dramatic to slow the pace of Indian raids, the relationship between Texas and the reserve Indians was likely to explode into violence.

August was an important month for the Comanche reserve. The reserve's school had finally opened, in a ceremony attended by all of the chiefs and heads of family. Thirty-seven students, aged seven to twenty-five, were present in class. The school was an encouraging symbol of the resolve of many prominent Comanches to make a new life for their people. It also brought the contempt of the wild Indians. One of their visits triggered an amazing blunder by a cavalry officer. The Second Cavalry routinely rotated the detachment assigned to protect the reserve. The regiment had never enjoyed this duty. General Twiggs spoke for them when he averred that if it were not for federal policy supporting the reserves, he would dispatch the troopers to take them all prisoners or shoot them if they resisted. The same month that witnessed the opening of the Comanche school found Lieutenant Cornelius Van Camp in command of the troopers guarding the reserve. It was the last day of his tour and he apparently relaxed discipline. Meanwhile, on the reserve an Indian chief named Katemesse had ordered a visiting pair of notorious Comanches to leave. Katemesse well knew that the visitors were intent on raiding, and he did not want his people to become involved. When the visitors refused, he asked for help. What transpired next probably would not have occurred but for the poor relationship between the agents and the cavalry officers.

Agent Leeper requested help from Van Camp. The young officer, in turn, assembled twenty-five troopers—two were off fishing, three were sick and left behind—and went to expel the visiting Indians. Besides being a superb horseman, Van Camp had shown real promise as a leader. Perhaps in this case he should have been less tactically clever and attended more to administrative detail. He divided his command, sending a non-commissioned officer and five men to take position in the hills, where they would intercept the Indians if they fled. He led the remaining nineteen to the cabin where the visiting Comanches were. Although the reservation Comanches wanted the visitors gone, by this time they disliked the cavalry even more.[24] Some fifty warriors grabbed their weapons to oppose the troopers. Thirty women and boys, armed with sticks and clubs, supported them. Van Camp tried to shoulder them aside. Failing that, he prepared to open fire. As the rival forces glowered at each other, a sergeant spoke softly to Van Camp: the troopers had only one round of ammunition for their carbines! He added the unbelievable intelligence that there was no more ammunition back in camp. Apparently, because they were about to be relieved, the sergeant had allowed his men to fire off their ammunition in a bout of target shooting. Rash inattention to duty on Van Camp's part had combined with the sergeant's dereliction of duty to produce an unwinnable situation. Van Camp ordered a retreat. His total loss of face emboldened the Comanches thereafter to use the reserve as a staging area and sanctuary with impunity.

The incident infuriated General Twiggs. It had been a "ridiculous affair."[25] To the Indian agents it was another example of military neglect. The army's blunder had made it impossible for them to discipline refractory Indians. To Van Camp it was much worse. He narrowly avoided a court-martial, but he carried the shame of the incident with him into the field. Van Camp resolved to erase the blemish on his name at the next opportunity.

The increased Indian raiding that predated this episode had little or nothing to do with the Indians residing inside of Texas. Rather, although no one realized it, the Indians living to the north had been quick to exploit the cavalry's assembly around Fort Belknap in preparation for marching to Utah. Their intensified raids into vacated areas prompted a stream of protests from alarmed citizens to their political leaders. Congressman John H. Reagan, the future postmaster general for the Confederate States of America, spoke for many when he contrasted the exploits of the Texas Rangers with "the whole of 3000 regulars, who live in comfortable quarters and are only serviceable in keeping up 'the pomp and circumstance of War.'"[26] Smarting in the face of such public insults, Twiggs resolved to do something.

BACK IN 1850, Twiggs's predecessor had reported to General in Chief Winfield Scott that Indian problems were out of control. Force was the only solution: "It is impossible to bring these deluded people to a sense of their weakness compared with the power of the United States—unless by severe chastisement."[27] Even the Indian agents agreed with this sentiment. For over a year Twiggs himself had been urging a change of policy. His recommendation made military sense but it also had a political component. Settlers were eager to occupy the heretofore unpopulated lands north of the Wichita River. In the summer of 1858, David Twiggs concluded that effective "chastisement" involved taking the war to the enemy in his home. The fortuitous concentration of the Second Cavalry for the march to Utah provided opportunity. When the War Department canceled the transfer of the regiment to Utah, Twiggs suggested that rather than have the cavalry return to its scattered garrisons, it should abandon its defensive posture and invade Indian country. He elaborated that the campaign should be sustained, summer and winter, to compel the Indians to defend their own homes and families. Occupied by the need to defend, the Indians would be unable to attack Texas.

Eighteen days after Twiggs made this suggestion, Assistant Adjutant General Irvin McDowell—the future Union army commander at First Bull Run—responded on behalf of Winfield Scott. McDowell primly observed that Twiggs already possessed the authority—he cited General Orders, No. 18—to dispose of the Second Cavalry as he saw fit. It was not the unequivocal permission that Twiggs sought. Scott was playing the time-honored army game of dealing with a possibly disastrous change of strategy by hiding behind formal policy. If Twiggs's idea worked, Scott might allow some of the credit to fall upon his own shoulders. If it failed, the responsibility was clearly with Twiggs. Twiggs accepted the responsibility. He set the cavalry to work accumulating the supplies necessary to support an extended expedition north of the Red River.

The regiment's lifeline was the road connecting Fort Belknap with San Antonio. The term "road" yields a false impression of this deep-rutted, hardscrabble track. Like most Texas roads, it had begun as a footpath, deepened somewhat by the poles dragged by the Indians' canine beasts of burden. When the Indians acquired horses, the old footpaths became wider, deeper tracks routed through less dense timber and, in west Texas, running from water hole to water hole. The first American explorers and settlers followed these same tracks. Beginning in 1849, the heavy wagon traffic caused by fortune seekers traveling to California further widened the track and deepened the ruts. Usually dusty and hard packed, occasionally flooded and muddy, the roads of west Texas connected the main cavalry posts in a way tolerated by the citizens and soldiers of the 1850s simply because there was no alternative. The surgeon general complained that Texas's rough roads destroyed medicines and surgical instruments before the wagons delivered supplies to the garrisons. One passenger aboard an Overland Mail wagon reported that his coach overturned three times in the vicinity of Fort Belknap alone. Undaunted, the army began running regular wagon trains from the settlements to Fort Belknap so the Second Cavalry could stockpile supplies.

Defending its own supply line is always a challenge for regular forces engaged in a guerrilla war. The route from the Second's base in San Antonio to Fort Belknap illustrates the problem. The fort's garrison depended upon the regular arrival of wagon trains to bring everything from beef cattle and hay to currycombs and ammunition. A typical wagon train assembled on the Alamo grounds in San Antonio. Pack mules carried brass-cased ammunition for carbines and percussion caps, lead, and powder for Colt revolvers. Soldiers loaded four wagons each with twenty kegs of gunpowder. Teamsters covered the ammunition wagons with tarps to protect against a chance spark or an occasional rain. Troopers loaded half of another wagon with fifteen cases of the newly introduced Sharps rifles. In addition to these ninety rifles, this wagon carried camp equipment. The men filled two wagons with large burlap sacks of salt pork and four more wagons with clothes. A last wagon carried medical supplies.

After the wagon train departed San Antonio, the first third of the journey passed through settled country that was relatively safe. Another forty-five miles brought the wagon train to Fort Mason. Beyond Fort Mason, each step brought the wagons into more rugged and dangerous territory. The freight rates for mili-

San Antonio's central plaza served as the staging area for the logistical buildup to support Van Dorn's march north. (National Archives)

tary supplies reflected this. It was four times more expensive to haul supplies from San Antonio north to Fort Belknap than west to Fort Clark. The northward trip required four river crossings where banks were so steep that men had to double the teams. One of these crossings was on the Colorado River. Because high water here often delayed entire wagon trains, thus making them vulnerable to Indian attack, two cavalry companies had built Camp Colorado to provide protection. After departure from Camp Colorado, an eleven-day trip brought the train to Fort Belknap. Troopers and teamsters unloaded the wagons beneath a sweltering August heat and sent the train on the return journey back to San Antonio. In this laborious fashion, the cavalry created a supply depot.

General Twiggs faced a conundrum. To secure the San Antonio–to–Fort Belknap road, one cavalry company occupied Fort Mason, two occupied Camp Colorado, while a fourth company provided the garrison for Fort Belknap. Thus, 40 percent of the regiment's strength manned static positions in order to guard the flow of supplies needed to accumulate a stockpile that was a prerequisite to sustain an offensive campaign. In order to mass strength for the offensive, the cavalry would have to strip manpower from key positions such as Camp Colorado. Twiggs resolved to gamble. Once sufficient supplies arrived at Fort Belknap, he would denude the garrisons defending his line of supply, abandon less important outposts, and send the cavalry north into Indian country. Hopefully the Indians would be so busy defending their own territory that they would not attack exposed positions in Texas. Twiggs's bold decision was a calculated risk thoroughly in character with the Bengal Tiger's reputation.

7

Chastising the Indians

In the State of Texas and upon its borders, there has been, and still is, at this time, raging an Indian war between our troops and that most formidable of all the tribes, the Camanches. [Their] depredations brought on at last a fight between our troops and their warriors, which for fierceness and determination was very remarkable in Indian warfare. The Indians were routed with considerable loss.

—Secretary of War John Floyd, 1858 (in Report of the Secretary of War, December 6, 1858, in Executive Documents, 35th Congress, 2nd Session, 5)

—— I. The Battle at the Wichita Village ——

Earl Van Dorn was a little man with a big ambition. At age sixteen he boldly wrote to General Andrew Jackson to request an appointment to West Point. How much of the curriculum he absorbed is problematical, since he graduated fifty-second out of fifty-six. But he did learn to admire another undersized officer who had once performed prodigies, and so, as an adult, Van Dorn kept a large vase adorned with the bust of Napoleon in his domestic quarters. Van Dorn was brave and impetuous. At the siege of Fort Taylor during the Mexican War, an enemy ball toppled the garrison's

187

Earl Van Dorn conducted the campaign that led to the regiment's greatest success over the Comanches, the fight at the Wichita village. (National Archives)

flag. Van Dorn volunteered to run across a hundred yards of bullet-and-shell-swept ground to raise the flag again. Later he begged off staff duty to join his regiment during the assault at Chapultepec. Reputedly he was the first man to scale the fortress. Sword in hand, he cut his way into the citadel. His conduct in the Mexican War earned him praise from his superiors and brevet promotion to major. A young second lieutenant who joined his cavalry company in Texas described him: "While a little below the medium height, his figure was strong and compact. He had a small waist and broad shoulders, and looked the gallant soldier that he was. Courteous, amiable, with a magnetic pres-

ence; agreeable manners, splendid head and handsome face."
Fitzhugh Lee concluded that among the regiment's captains, he
was "the most conspicuous officer."[1] The Mobile Grays concurred. For these veterans Van Dorn was a dashing, brave, and
beloved leader.

By all rights, the command of the expedition into Indian
country should have gone to the regiment's senior officer, Major
George Thomas. Instead, army politics interceded. During the
Mexican War, the then Lieutenant Thomas had made the mistake of moving his battery within sight of General Twiggs.
Twiggs remarked upon the battery's sleek mule team. He wanted
them for his headquarters. None of this was too extraordinary: an
overbearing, comfort-loving superior pulling rank on a hardworking junior officer. But Thomas exhibited a stubborn streak and a
detailed knowledge of regulations. After much discussion, "and
thus use of quantities of red tape," Thomas thwarted Twiggs.
Twiggs suffered this humiliation with poor grace. He was a vindictive man with a long memory. George Thomas had made a
lifelong enemy.[2] Twiggs extracted his pound of flesh more than
a decade later when he passed over Thomas in preference for
the regiment's senior captain. Scorned, humiliated, and deeply
angered, Thomas fired off a protest against such a flagrant out-
rage to General in Chief Scott. In time, Scott would decide
in Thomas's favor. In September 1858, however, Thomas remained at Fort Belknap with his tiny staff, the band, and the
regiment's sick.

Meanwhile, Van Dorn prepared for his first important inde-
pendent command. His orders required him to march north from
Fort Belknap into the Indian Territory. Here, on the edge of the
Wichita Mountains, he would establish a secure camp that would
become the base for punitive expeditions. Twiggs relayed to Van
Dorn the most recent intelligence concerning the enemy. On
August 9 the commander of Fort Arbuckle, Indian Territory, had

reported that large bands of Apaches, Comanches, and Cheyennes were on the Canadian River near the Antelope Hills. They had been raiding the settlements of the Choctaw Nation, reportedly to procure horses to carry them on a planned series of raids into Texas.[3] If the cavalry hit these Indians first, it might spoil the Indian plan. Van Dorn had the authority to pursue them wherever found, regardless of state or territorial boundaries or departmental limits. To accomplish this, Van Dorn received the largest force assembled since 1856: four cavalry companies, a fifty-four-man infantry detachment, and a contingent of Indian scouts.[4]

Not only was Van Dorn's three-hundred-man force the strongest expedition assembled since 1856; it was better armed and enjoyed improved logistical support compared to previous expeditions. Back in February 1858, an officers' board had convened at the Washington Arsenal to evaluate the utility of attaching a shoulder stock to the Colt revolver as a substitute for a carbine. Among those attending was Major Hardee, still formally assigned to West Point but retaining his posting in the Second Cavalry. At ranges of 100 to 500 yards, the officers blazed away at white pine-board targets to assess both accuracy and penetrating power. They recommended the immediate adoption of the Colt with shoulder stock for the cavalry service and then specified "that each trooper be furnished with two pistols . . . one pistol be worn on the right side of the soldier, in a pouch attached to the saber belt, and the other in the holster, on the right side of the saddle." The shoulder stock would be kept in a pouch attached to the left rear of the saddle.[5] Hardee and his peers urged that the Colt armaments be hurried to the troops in the field in time for the forthcoming campaign season.

Van Dorn's superior logistical support arose by good fortune. In preparation for the march to Utah, quartermasters had assembled fifty-nine wagons, each with a six-mule team, as well as an ambulance and a mobile forge. Van Dorn could draw upon this splendid train to haul supplies for his own expedition. The addition of a wagon train would slow the march. Ranger companies made do without them, preferring to use pack mules. Since Van Dorn's orders required him to establish an advanced base, he decided he needed the slow-moving wagons to carry both the tools to construct the base and the supplies to sustain it.

WHILE THEIR SUPERIORS devised a campaign strategy, the men of the Second Cavalry continued with their generally futile patrolling. It was particularly unpleasant duty during an exceptionally hot and dry August. During an eight-day heat wave beginning on August 24, troopers at Fort Belknap experienced daily temperatures of between 108 and 111 degrees. In September, Indian raiders believed to be Kiowas killed four men near the Comanche reserve and drove off more than a hundred horses. Ranger Buck Barry happened to be present when raiders struck again a few days later. He volunteered to direct the cavalry pursuit, and Second Lieutenant Charles W. Phifer, well aware of Barry's reputation as a skilled and ruthless Indian fighter, happily assented. Phifer took thirty troopers to chase the raiders. But even the presence of Barry, another experienced white, and some twenty allied Indians could not run down the raiders. To the disappointment of the pursuing column, the raiders simply maintained a fast pace and refused to offer battle.

Over the weeks preceding the march north, the troopers endured a harried and too-hot existence escorting wagon trains into Fort Belknap, rescuing stranded emigrants on the Marcy Trail, and protecting surveyors laying out new plats for settlers. They welcomed the news that they were going to leave the Fort Belknap furnace and return to real soldiering. At sunrise on September 15, 1858, the expedition departed Fort Belknap.

To avoid overgrazing the sparse grassland, Van Dorn divided his command into an advance guard of one company and a main column comprising another cavalry company, the infantry detachment, and the wagon train. The Fort Belknap contingent would unite with two more cavalry companies north of the Red River.

Scouting in the van of the column were some 135 allied Indians commanded by Lawrence S. "Sul" Ross, the son of the Brazos reserve's Indian agent, Shapley Ross. Although young for such a position of responsibility—Ross celebrated his twentieth birthday during this campaign—both family history and personal experience had prepared him for this duty. His great-grandfather had been taken from a Virginia frontier school at the age of six by raiding Indians; thereafter he had lived with the Cherokees until age twenty-three. Sul himself had narrowly avoided capture when Comanches attacked the family ranch in Texas. Clinging to his father's back, he survived a run through a shower of arrows until reaching the sanctuary of the family cabin. From that day on the Ross children received training on how to act when confronted by a surprise raid. In the summer of 1858, the young man interrupted his university studies in Alabama to return to the Brazos Agency.

Sul Ross learned how just this past May his father had led a hundred reserve Indians in an expedition commanded by Texas Ranger John S. "Rip" Ford. The reserve Indians led Ford's men north across the Canadian River. Together with about a hundred Rangers, they attacked a large Comanche village. The Comanches placed their faith in the heretofore invincible leader Pohebits Quasho, or Iron Jacket. Dressed in his resplendent coat of Spanish armor, which he supposed was proof against firearms, Iron Jacket challenged the Rangers to personal combat. They shot him from the saddle in the blink of an eye. Then Ford ordered his Colt-armed Rangers to charge. Demoralized by the loss of their leader, the Comanches put up a weak resistance. Seventy-six fell to the Rangers' revolvers. After this fight, Rip Ford—who had gained this name because of his habit of writing to the widows of Rangers who died under his command with the words "Rest in Peace," which he shortened to RIP as continuing casualties made the writing onerous—had to write only two letters to grieving Ranger families.

Texans suspected that Ford's lopsided victory had shamed the army into trying a similar expedition. In any event, the Brazos reserve's Indians had thoroughly enjoyed exterminating the hated Comanches and were eager to have another go when Van Dorn asked for their help. This time the respected Shapley Ross was unable to lead them. The Indians accepted Sul Ross as a substitute with the expectation that he too would prove worthy. So the young Ross discarded his university veneer and took his place among the Caddo, Delaware, and Tonkawa Indians. He had never been in the territory north of Fort Belknap. So he relied upon the Tonkawa Indian chief Placedo, an exceptional ally who was nearing sixty years of age, to choose the route. Placedo had fought the Comanches from the Guadalupe in Texas to the Arkansas in Kansas. Included in his wealth of experience was knowledge of where lay the all-important water holes and grazing areas, a matter of great importance in semiarid northwest Texas. Rather than directing the column due north toward the Red River, Placedo led it northeast.

Nighthawks flew above the plodding column, darting and swerving to feast on the insect life disturbed by the troopers' passage across the grasslands. On the Little Wichita River the troopers gazed over a splendid vista: "Towering in the background were the long battlemented bluffs lining the opposite shore of the river below, the green belt of timber making its course, and in front the wide prairie with its yellow coating of buffalo grass, studded with the pale green mesquite."[6] Along the

Wichita's banks the cavalry enjoyed a well-watered camping site in a grove of large oaks. It would prove to be their last comfortable camp.

After crossing the Wichita River, Van Dorn's command entered Indian country. The nearest white settlement was forty miles to the east. Yet already, white surveyors had partially divided this land in anticipation of eventual settlement. Indeed, a surveying team accompanied the cavalry and busily marked plats between the Wichita and Red Rivers even while the troopers were out searching for the Comanches. The cavalry crossed a wide span of prairie, extending from the Wichita to Otter Creek, where Indians had burned off all of the grass during a seasonal hunt. The lack of forage caused a logistical nightmare. Although the advance guard fared reasonably well, their animals ate up the available grass. By the time the main column crossed the burnt prairie there was nothing left. Their animals began to weaken from lack of graze. Troopers fanned out to either side to search for grass. Whenever they located a decent stand, soldiers unhitched the draft animals from the wagon train and led them to graze. Consequently, the train's rate of progress slowed to only twelve to fifteen miles per day. During this time the troopers' only fuel to stoke their cook fires was buffalo chips, the bisons' dried dung. At least it warmed the salt pork, albeit while adding a unique flavor. When Ross's Indian scouts located one still-green section along the Red River, Placedo led the column on a swing to the northwest to take advantage. The column proceeded across the Red River downstream of its forks. The Second Cavalry was now in present-day Oklahoma.

Scouting ahead, Ross located a site on the southeast side of Otter Creek suitable for a base. Good, clear water rose from nearby springs. A walnut grove provided hardwood timber for building permanent structures. When Van Dorn arrived he approved of Ross's choice and set the troopers to building a temporary base. The men laid out a tent camp and constructed a picket enclosure to confine the horses and mules. Van Dorn named it Camp Radziminski to honor the popular Polish lieutenant, who had recently died of tuberculosis. The infantry detachment provided Camp Radziminski's permanent garrison. Last into camp was a civilian named Duff who was fulfilling a contract to provide the command with corn. The march across the burnt prairie had depleted the expedition's horses. The corn carried by Duff's fifteen supply wagons and fifty pack mules partially restored them.

While the troopers established Camp Radziminski, Ross's Indians spread out wide to search for Comanches. With his horses strengthened by several good corn rations, Van Dorn anticipated that he would continue his march north to the Antelope Hills. The region along the Canadian River was a traditional assembly point for raiders bound for Texas and Mexico. He changed his mind when he received a surprising report from a pair of Wichita Indians serving in Ross's command. In times past, Wichitas had been among the warrior bands terrorizing the Texas frontier. In their present role as allies, a Wichita leader named Nasthoe and his son rode east to visit a Wichita village on Wild Horse Creek, where they hoped to obtain information about the Comanches. Nasthoe approached the Wichita village and saw its familiar dome grass huts surrounded by well-maintained cornfields. To his utter surprise, alongside the Wichita homes was a large Comanche camp. A quick count of Comanche tepees suggested the presence of four to five hundred visitors.

Nasthoe and his son hid until darkness. Then they entered the village to learn the reason for the Comanche presence. The Comanches suspected that the Wichitas had betrayed them by leading Rip Ford's Rangers to their camp back in the Antelope Hills. In the Comanche view, support for this notion came from the fact that they had previously stolen horses from the Wichitas.

Clearly the Wichitas had extracted their revenge. By the time Nasthoe arrived, his people had managed to convince the Comanches that they were blameless. Nasthoe found the Comanches comfortably living alongside the Wichitas, trading, gambling, and generally living a life of ease. He warned his brethren of Van Dorn's presence and then galloped back to Camp Radziminski.

Nasthoe reported to Sul Ross that a large Comanche band led by a chief named Pohchanahkwoheep—Buffalo Hump to American ears—was camped only forty miles to the east. All American officers knew about Buffalo Hump. On the Texas frontier at this time he was a feared and legendary character. Like all Comanche leaders, Buffalo Hump led an uninhibited life serving under no master. Like most, he was a haughty leader. Unlike many, he disdained white dress. A decade earlier an eyewitness described him as "the pure unadulterated picture of a North American Indian. . . . His body naked, a buffalo robe around his loins, brass rings on his arms, a string of beads around his neck, and with his long, coarse black hair hanging down."[7] Long ago, when representatives of the Texas Republic had tried to arrange a council with him, Buffalo Hump replied with the demand that the emissaries immediately order President Houston to be present and have everything ready. There must be no delay because he, Buffalo Hump, did not intend to wait. Of course, neither party reported to the meeting. Since that time, Buffalo Hump had conducted some of the deadliest raids into Texas.

Ross relayed Nasthoe's intelligence to Van Dorn. Van Dorn wondered if he could trust the report. It could well be false or, even worse, lead his men into a trap. Ross persuaded him that Nasthoe was a loyal ally. Accepting this assertion, Van Dorn issued a rapid series of orders. Troopers quickly herded the extra horses and draft animals into the paddock along with the expedition's wagon train. The infantry would remain behind to guard the base. Within two hours he had all four cavalry companies in the saddle. Each of the 225 troopers carried ammunition and rations for two days. The excitement of impending action was such that even the sutler J. Ward took a place in the ranks.

Van Dorn had confidence both in his men and in their leaders. Most of the troopers were veterans of numerous patrols and more than a few combats. Van Dorn well knew the capacities of the sixty-four Mobile Grays of his Company A. Although only a pitiful few of the splendid gray horses remained, the weathered, experienced troopers could be relied on implicitly. The hard-drinking, hard-fighting Nathan Evans led Company F. He, too, was an officer Van Dorn knew well. Van Dorn was less well acquainted with Captain Richard Johnson, the leader of Company H. But he did know that this officer had seen a fair number of fights against the Indians. Both Evans and Johnson had begun their service in the regiment as lieutenants. This meant that the senior captain, and Van Dorn's second in command, was Captain Charles Whiting, of Company K. A Maine native, Whiting was outspoken in his abolitionist sympathies. Van Dorn disliked him for this. In contrast, he welcomed the presence of Lieutenant Van Camp. Although Van Camp was also northern-born, his gallant conduct impressed everyone he met. General Twiggs had assigned Van Camp to the expedition before the lieutenant's blunder at the Brazos Agency. Van Camp's special duty was to map the country through which the cavalry moved. Whether Van Dorn sensed the lieutenant's burning desire to erase the shame of his humiliation at the Brazos Agency is unknown.

With a 40-mile march ahead of him, Van Dorn anticipated reaching the Comanche camp at dawn. He hoped to catch the enemy still asleep. He did not know that two Comanche scouts had already detected the cavalry's presence and conveyed this intelligence to their people. But what foiled Van Dorn's scheme was Nasthoe's inability to explain distances in white man's terms.

The Comanche camp actually lay about 90 miles east of Camp Radziminski.

The cavalry began the march in good spirits. Most of the men joked and talked as they rode. Not so the Mobile Grays. Van Dorn was something of a martinet. He insisted on adherence to his notion of martial bearing, which meant his company marched in silence. The column rode steadily through a first night. Dawn found them still far from the enemy. Van Dorn maintained a grueling pace until the afternoon of September 30. At that time he granted his jaded command a rest to boil coffee and allow the horses to graze. Only Captain Evans directed his men to unsaddle their animals so the horses could roll and wallow to ease their galled hides. At sunset, after a three-hour halt, they were back in the saddle again. Van Dorn and his fellow West Point graduates had studied the Napoleonic wars. The duke of Wellington once described his campaign strategy as a long rope stretching from his base to his objective. When something unexpected occurred—the inevitable friction of war—and his rope snapped, he gathered the ends, tied a knot, and pressed on. Having been inadvertently deceived about his enemy's location, Van Dorn adhered to his strategy. Instead of attacking at dawn on September 30, he would attack at daybreak twenty-four hours later.

Even this resolution proved impossible. The cavalry forced the march through the second night across rough, broken terrain. It seemed that no sooner had they climbed out of one deep ravine than they had to descend into another one. Since departing Camp Radziminski, the men had ridden for thirty-six hours, the last sixteen and a half without a break. A cold dawn found them entering a rolling prairie. A chilly mist clung to the low spots. Ahead lay a succession of ridges. Sul Ross's scouts reported that the Comanche camp was just ahead. The enemy still seemed to be unaware of the cavalry's presence. Their entire

Comanche camp security was notoriously lax. However, the Comanches at the Wichita village correctly believed themselves to be operating under a flag of truce. (Center for American History, University of Texas at Austin)

herd of about five hundred horses were grazing away from camp. To Van Dorn's mind, the tactical situation could not be improved upon.

The Comanches' complete indifference to camp security arose from a series of interactions with the U.S. Army that had begun more than a month earlier. Back in August, after resolving their differences with the Wichitas, the Comanches had sent emissaries to the nearest army garrison, at Fort Arbuckle. That garrison's commander, Captain Prince, was the officer who had sent a warning to Twiggs on August 9 about a dangerous gathering of Indians bound for Texas. Prince confronted his own set of Indian problems. They boiled down to something very similar to those facing the Second Cavalry in Texas: too few men to protect his jurisdiction against Comanche raids. Fort Arbuckle's main purpose was to protect emigrant trains moving west through hostile territory. Officers had learned that it was easier to make a financial arrangement with the warriors—gifts for free passage—than to fight them. Accordingly, Prince welcomed the chance for a negotiated settlement. On August 20, Prince sent a Lieutenant T. E. Powell to meet with the Comanches. During the ensuing council, the Comanches filled the lieutenant's ears with lies about their recent conduct. They asked Powell if they could henceforth settle peacefully on lands west of the Wichita village. Powell replied that this land had already been set aside for an Indian reserve and that the Comanches were welcome. He added that government surveyors would soon be marking the western boundary of the tract in question. The Comanches expressed delight. They promised not to attack the surveyors and to return the horses they had recently stolen from the Indian Territory. One chief told Powell that he would go visit the leaders of the various Comanche bands and return to Fort Arbuckle to continue the parley. Lieutenant Powell was well satisfied. In his mind he had tactfully conducted a difficult negotiation and brought it to a favorable conclusion. He had no idea that his efforts at making peace had just condemned some seventy Comanches to death.

Comanche scouts had tracked Van Dorn's approach march. When the troopers halted to boil coffee, two warriors watched from a nearby hill. When the cavalry formed up and resumed the march, a scout galloped back to camp to issue a warning. The Comanche leaders gathered in council. Prudence dictated that they pull up stakes and move off immediately. However, they had been living next to the Wichita village for more than a month without any interference from the army at Fort Arbuckle. They undoubtedly believed that they enjoyed a truce with the army. After conferring among themselves, the Comanche leaders consulted a female prophet to ascertain the intentions of Van Dorn's column. She examined the auguries and reported that the omens were good, the cavalry were friendly, peace would be preserved.[8] It was a disastrous prophecy. The Wichitas certainly knew what Van Dorn was up to. Warned by Nasthoe, most decamped before the battle.

Van Dorn organized his 225 troopers into four assault groups. Each company formed a two-man-wide column with hundred-yard intervals between companies. This allowed them space to deploy into line when the bugler sounded the signal. Normally the companies would have taken position according to alphabetical sequence. But Van Dorn knew that his Company A and Johnson's Company F detested each other. Their most recent dustup had come when a card game erupted into an enormous brawl. Accordingly, Van Dorn separated the feuding companies by inserting Company H between them. To avoid any confusion, the allied Indians tied on white armbands. Van Dorn instructed Ross to operate on the cavalry's right flank with the specific objective of securing the Comanches' horse herd. This would compel the enemy to engage on foot and prevent their escape. Officers would use hand signals to direct the cavalry until they sighted the Comanche camp. Van Dorn told his subordinates to trot their companies up the ridges. If the enemy lay on the far side, their buglers would call for the deployment and sound the charge. Otherwise, the cavalry would continue at a walk until reaching the base of the next ridge. They would continue with this trot-walk approach until contact.

The cavalry trotted up three successive ridges without seeing the enemy. As the sun rose over the horizon, they crested a fourth ridge. One of the left-hand columns spotted the enemy first. Its men saw the Comanche camp about 500 yards away. A line of tepees—a later count found 120—stretched along the bank of Wild Horse Creek. Mist rose from the water but there were no cooking fires. Comanche camp security was often lax, and so it was here. The camp appeared asleep. Not even the

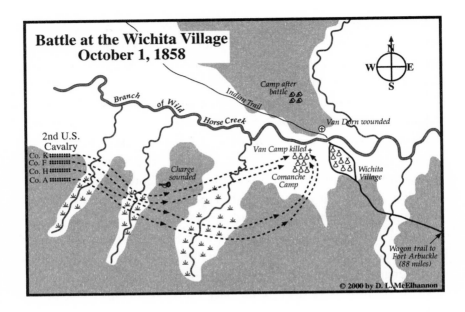

Battle at the Wichita Village
October 1, 1858

Camp after battle

Indian Trail

Branch of Wild

Horse Creek

Van Dorn wounded

2nd U.S. Cavalry
Co. K
Co. F
Co. H
Co. A

Charge sounded

Van Camp killed

Comanche Camp

Wichita Village

Wagon trail to Fort Arbuckle (88 miles)

© 2000 by D. L. McElhannon

dogs gave warning. Ross's Indians moved off to the south to capture the horse herd. The buglers gathered breath and sounded their instruments.

The two leftmost companies charged directly at the camp. They cantered down the ridge and across a marshy stream. The rough ground made it impossible to maintain a drill-book-style, hip-to-hip formation. Whiting's Company K was nearest Wild Horse Creek. Its troopers struggled through a series of dry ravines choked with fallen logs. Johnson's Company F found easier going. At the west end of the camp was an open glade surrounded by tall trees. Company F charged across the glade to meet the Indians. Meanwhile, Van Dorn led Companies H and A on a swing south so as to approach the camp's rear. He wanted to place the enemy between the two jaws of his fast-closing vise. Alerted by the bugle calls, the Comanche warriors rushed from their tepees to confront the rapidly approaching storm. At first contact, the fight degenerated into a series of individual, hand-to-hand combats. The cavalry had the tremendous tactical advantage of surprise and possessed superior firepower. The Comanches had courage alone. They fought desperately to cover their families' retreat. While the women, children, and elderly fled, the warriors prepared to die hard.

A tremendous din filled the air—the discharge of firearms, the shrieks and screams of wounded men and horses, bugle calls, troopers' cheers, Comanche war whoops. The Second Cavalry's officers led from the front. Wherever the fighting was most furious, the troopers saw Van Dorn spurring them on by personal example. Company H penetrated into the Comanche camp. Leading the way were Captain Evans and Second Lieutenant Charles W. Phifer. Each killed two Indians with their revolvers. No one surpassed the amazing Sergeant John Spangler. Exhibiting "cool courage" and "daring intrepidity," Spangler slew six warriors. Spearheaded by such killers, the cavalry methodically advanced. Individual warriors stood their ground to try to stop the cavalry surge. As had been the case in Hood's fight, some of their women remained behind them, calmly reloading the men's muskets. Yet a man on foot stood little chance against a Colt-armed, mounted fighter. Relentlessly, the cavalry pushed through the camp.

Caught in the squeeze between the cavalry's converging pincers, the Indians moved toward the creek. On the camp's northern edge Buffalo Hump rallied his men. For the first time the Indians enjoyed some kind of coherent fighting formation. Sheltered by the creek's ravine and its vegetation, the Indians launched a dangerous barrage of arrows that stopped the cavalry pursuit. Van Dorn directed mounted men to try to seal off the escape routes from the ravine. Another group of troopers dismounted and entered the underbrush on foot.

Now that the shock had worn off, the fight became more even since the Comanches lay concealed in the rough ground.

With no alternative except to root them out at close quarters, the cavalry engaged in a deadly, kill-or-be-killed hunt. During this action the cavalry absorbed most of its losses. After ninety minutes of stubborn, gallant resistance, the Comanche position collapsed. Having bought enough time to allow most of their people to escape, the warriors broke and ran themselves. Ruthlessly the cavalry hunted them down, killing the fleeing Comanches in ones and twos. Second Lieutenant James E. Harrison saw a score of warriors moving along a nearby ridge, driving a horse herd before them. He took a detachment of Company H men and galloped off in pursuit. A two-hour chase ensued, during which Harrison personally slew two Indians.

In a different sector, Van Dorn also became caught up in a chase. He saw two warriors riding double in a bid to escape. He spurred his mount in pursuit. Van Dorn was riding a small, nimble horse named Fink. Fink easily gained on the Indians but also outstripped his escort. Heedless of danger, Van Dorn splashed across the creek. Climbing the bank, he urged his mount onward. He entered close range and aimed his Colt. His shot killed the Indians' horse, throwing the riders onto the ground. Showing superb athletic skill, the Indians recovered, rolled onto their knees, and aimed their bows at Van Dorn. The Mississippian tried to shield himself with his hand. One arrow penetrated between his wrist bones and lodged against his left elbow. A second struck him with great force on his right side. It passed through his upper stomach, penetrated his left lung, and continued until the arrowhead protruded out his upper left rib cage. As he fell from the saddle, the captain managed to kill one of the Indians with his Colt. Van Dorn would have died at the hands of the surviving warrior had not a gallant man from his own Company A, Corporal Joseph P. Taylor, galloped onto the scene and interposed his horse between Van Dorn and the Comanche. The Indian fired again. His shot dangerously wounded Taylor. Van

Dorn lay on the ground, alone except for the loyal Fink. The captain's blood had splashed over Fink's withers and mane. Such blood smell would have driven most horses to stampede in fright. Instead, Fink stood over his fallen rider and lowered his head to probe the nature of his rider's distress. Up galloped additional troopers, who carried Van Dorn and Taylor to safety.

Like his commander, Second Lieutenant Cornelius Van Camp had been at the forefront of the fight, exhibiting a reckless disregard for his own safety. While fighting with the two companies who attacked the rear of the Comanche camp, he heard a voice shouting that some of the Indians were breaking free from the trap. It was Sul Ross. Ross called for help and set off. Van Camp spurred his horse in the direction Ross indicated. In the confusion only two men, Private Carroll C. Alexander and a Caddo scout, accompanied them. The four men were between the Comanche camp and the Wichita village, riding north toward Wild Horse Creek. The first people they encountered were a frightened group of women and children. Ross noticed that one dirty, ragged girl was white. He yelled to the Caddo scout to secure her. Preoccupied by this, no one saw a band of warriors approaching rapidly. The warriors carefully notched their arrows, drew back the bowstrings, aimed, and released.

One arrow drove into Van Camp's chest and pierced his heart. His comrades found him after the battle lying dead on his back, his saber still tied to his right wrist while his left hand clutched the arrow, having pulled it free during his death throes, the stain of his shameful conduct at the Brazos Agency washed clean with his own blood.

Another arrow seriously wounded Private Alexander while he was in the act of aiming his carbine.

Ross faced the Comanches and aimed his Sharps carbine. The percussion cap snapped but the weapon misfired. Then an arrow hit Ross hard in the shoulder. Nearby, a warrior seized

Alexander's carbine and ran toward Ross. Reeling in his saddle, Ross was defenseless. He looked down and recognized his assailant, a Comanche leader named Mohee whom he had known since childhood. Mohee discharged the carbine at point-blank range and knocked Ross to the ground. Stunned, his arm and side partially paralyzed, Ross struggled to draw his revolver. He saw Mohee draw his scalping knife and move toward him. Suddenly Second Lieutenant James P. Major galloped onto the scene. Major aimed his shotgun and squeezed the trigger. The blast struck Mohee between the shoulders. He was the third Comanche that Major killed this day.

With Van Dorn incapacitated, Whiting assumed command. He soon confronted an unexpected challenge. On the horizon appeared a large mounted party apparently moving to counterattack. Whiting ordered his buglers to sound the recall. He deployed a dismounted skirmish line to oppose the foe. Carbines at the ready, the weary troopers waited for the line to approach. To their relief it turned out to be Lieutenant Harrison and his detachment. Because they were herding eighty captured horses along with them, they had appeared to be a more numerous body.

While the Second Cavalry attacked through the Comanche camp, the allied Indians fought their own private war. After successfully stampeding most of the Comanche horse herd, numerous reserve Indians hunted their enemies through the hills and ravines surrounding the camp. Others joined the troopers in their push against Buffalo Hump's rearguard. Van Dorn particularly praised the allied Indians' contribution to the battle. Three allied Indians died. Two more received mortal wounds.

As the fight petered out, the cavalry policed the field, searching for dead and wounded comrades. Evans's Company H had borne the brunt of the fighting. From this company the men brought in the bodies of Privates Peter Major and Jacob Echard.

They never found Private Henry Howard. He was listed as missing and presumed killed. Troopers collected the wounded and brought them to assistant surgeon William Carswell. He had little hope for Company F's Sergeant James E. Garrison, who had received a grievous wound. It would indeed prove mortal. Carswell was not at all certain that either Van Dorn or Sul Ross would survive. But the latter had received skilled intervention from a Caddo scout. The Caddo had opened Ross's shirt to find two bullet wounds and four holes as well as the arrow wound to his shoulder. Probing the holes with a silk scrap wrapped onto a ramrod, the Caddo suspected that only one bullet had caused all the damage. It had entered the chest and exited Ross's back between his shoulder blades. The Caddo washed and dressed the wounds. Carswell so admired the job that he asked the Caddo what salve he had applied. The Indian refused to divulge his secret.

Van Dorn's fate was in the hands of white practitioners alone. At first they thought it likely that Van Dorn would die. Van Dorn later described his feelings to his wife using overwrought language utterly typical of the inner man: "When I pulled the arrows from me the blood followed as if weary of service and impatient to cheat me of life—spilling like red wine from a drunkard's tankard.

"It was sublime to stand thus on the brink of the dark abyss, and the contemplation was awful. . . . I had faced death before— I gasped in dreadful agony for several hours, but finally became easy."[9]

In fact, Carswell, not Van Dorn, extracted the arrow by carefully cutting off the arrowhead and then pulling out the shaft. Referring to the arrow's passage through the captain's body, the surgeon observed that if the command had taken time to eat before the battle and thus Van Dorn had entered battle with a full stomach, his stomach wound alone would have been fatal.

While Van Dorn lay gasping, Carswell attended to other injuries. Four troopers in addition to Van Dorn and Ross were severely wounded. Five troopers suffered light wounds. The intrepid sutler J. Ward had charged alongside Evans's Company H. He too received a grazing shot in the arm. Twenty of the regiment's horses had been killed or wounded in the fight.

Lacking an ambulance, Carswell did not want to move the seriously injured. Consequently, Captain Whiting sent an express to Fort Arbuckle requesting an ambulance and wagon along with four days' provisions. If the fort's doctor was available, Whiting asked that he come as well "and bring with him such medicines as are necessary for gun and arrow shot wounds."[10]

Meanwhile, the troopers gleaned the battlefield. They initially found forty-four dead Comanches, two of whom were women, along with two dead Wichitas, the latter innocent victims of war. They rounded up three hundred Comanche horses. After taking all usable ammunition, food, and forage, they fired the Comanche camp, burning 120 tepees, cooking utensils, clothing, and dressed skins. The Second Cavalry remained in a camp just north of Wild Horse Creek and across from the scene of the fight for five days. Not only were some of the wounded too hurt to move, but the men and horses were too worn from the arduous march and subsequent battle to depart any sooner. During this time they buried their fallen comrades. The next summer Lieutenant Van Camp's body would be exhumed and sent to his native Pennsylvania for reburial. On the battlefield, officers insisted on a body count of the enemy dead. This unpleasant duty arose because of General Twiggs's insistence that Indians did not take their slain from the field. Since it was simply a matter of counting, Twiggs prohibited the cavalry officers from reporting estimated enemy fatalities. However their superiors might dispute the best way to assess enemy losses, it fell to the enlisted men to perform what must have seemed to them to be an unnecessary exercise. The jaded troopers tromped through the rough terrain around the Wichita village and followed blood trails to find the victims. Over time the reported number of slain Comanches rose first to fifty-six and then to around seventy. The total included four prominent leaders. The Second Cavalry had delivered a punishing blow. However, Buffalo Hump and a substantial number of his warriors had managed to withdraw from the battle safely.

—— II. "Soldiers Worthy of the Name" ——

The express rider from Captain Whiting arrived at Fort Arbuckle about twenty-four hours after the battle. He delivered the news of the victory and the request for help. The fort's commander responded handsomely. He hired a wagon and sent a detachment to escort it and an ambulance loaded with medical supplies. The fort's doctor went along. He also sent a warning. He knew this territory better than Van Dorn and Whiting. There were so many hostile Indians nearby who particularly hated the army units stationed in Texas that he feared the recent battle would inflame them to revenge. The isolated garrison at Camp Radziminski might be a particular target.

Back at the Wichita village, Van Dorn and Whiting welcomed the arrival of help. They ignored the warning, although in this case their confidence was not misplaced. By October 5, Van Dorn recovered well enough to dictate his official report. It was uncharacteristically modest in style. Perhaps he understood that the result would speak for itself, or possibly he was too weak from his wound to employ the same style of lurid metaphors he used to communicate with his wife. He sincerely mourned the loss of Van Camp, "one of the most promising and gallant young officers of our regiment." He praised the conduct of the men under his command. "They proved themselves," he wrote, "to be soldiers worthy of the name."[11]

After Surgeon Carswell judged that the wounded could be moved, Whiting split the command. He sent forty-two men to escort the ambulance and wagon carrying the wounded to Fort Arbuckle. Whiting took the others back to Camp Radziminski. Van Dorn chose to accompany Whiting. Troopers suspended a litter between a pair of mules and loaded Van Dorn into it. By the time the command returned to base, Van Dorn was sufficiently recovered to sit upright unaided. He had had time to think further about the battle. He knew it would create a big sensation. Reveling in the attention, both immediate and anticipated, he again wrote his wife, to ask, "Don't you feel proud of me?"[12]

Meanwhile, the allied Indians carried Sul Ross back home. Along the way his wounds became infected and his suffering grew so intense that the young man begged the Indians to kill him. Yet he survived the journey. The reserve's schoolteacher saw him arrive at the Brazos Agency looking "verry [sic] much wasted by fatigue and his wound" but still "full of life and fun."[13] The twenty-year-old man had so impressed the officers in the Second Cavalry that they recommended him to the commanding general of the army. Winfield Scott, in turn, offered Ross a direct commission in the army. Although Ross had enjoyed the campaign—he judged that his growing fame made up for the wound—he resolved to return to Alabama to complete his senior year at the university. He could not know that four of the Second Cavalry officers with whom he had served—Van Dorn, Evans, James Major, and Charles Phifer—would become Confederate generals with whom he would serve again.

The army called Van Dorn's fight "the battle at the Wichita village." The Second Cavalry was well satisfied with itself. Although the victorious troopers mourned their losses, particu-

larly the death of the popular Van Camp, they consoled themselves with the knowledge that in the regiment's severest combat to date, they had completely whipped the Indians. Fearing
that the Comanches would certainly blame them this time, the
Wichitas themselves abandoned their village and fled for safety
to Fort Arbuckle.

News of the battle spread quickly. On October 25 a brief
account reached New Orleans and was sent by telegraph to the
War Department. Scott commended Van Dorn's entire command,
calling the battle a brilliant success. He particularly praised the
officers who had killed Indians in hand-to-hand combat. At West
Point the commandant of cadets received the news with great
satisfaction. Major Hardee had trained many of the cavalrymen
involved in the fight. In a letter to Van Dorn, Hardee called
it "the handsomest affair with the savages" of which he had
ever heard.[14]

At district headquarters, Twiggs learned of the battle on
October 5. After receiving full reports, he described it as "a victory more decisive and complete than any recorded in the history
of our Indian warfare." Twiggs judged that the battle at the
Wichita village vindicated his strategy. Victory convinced him
that it was wise to "abandon the defensive system" that had scattered the Second Cavalry all over west Texas. However, he knew
that his forces remained stretched terribly thin just at a time when
affairs on the frontier were approaching a crisis. He asked for
reinforcements to sustain his offensive and thoroughly "chastise"
the Indians. Otherwise, the Second Cavalry's sacrifices would
have been in vain.[15] In lieu of any accretion to his force, Twiggs
still resolved to reinforce success as best he could. He ordered
Captain Oakes to lead two more companies north to Van Dorn.

Two days after hearing about the victory, Twiggs received
upsetting news that tainted the entire affair. Somehow the *Washington Star* had obtained and published Lieutenant Powell's

letter describing his parleys with the Comanches before the battle. The article was the first time Twiggs had heard of Powell's effort. He now understood that during the very time he was busily preparing Van Dorn's expedition, Powell was negotiating a treaty. Twiggs sensed a major embarrassment or worse. He immediately fired off a dispatch to army headquarters in Washington. He stated the obvious: "There ought to be some concert of action." Twiggs candidly wrote, "One of us has made a serious blunder—he in making a treaty, or I in sending out a party after them."[16] Admittedly the army's left hand at Fort Belknap did not know what the right hand at Fort Arbuckle was doing. It took three days for a dispatch rider to deliver a message from one post to the other. When dealing with a fluid environment, this alone made coordination difficult. Captain Prince at Fort Arbuckle warned Twiggs about the Indian concentration north of the Red River on August 9. Lieutenant Powell returned from his parley at the Wichita village on August 25 or 26. If Prince had immediately sent a rider to Texas, the message would not have reached Van Dorn, since he was already across the Red River. Still, for the honor of the army it would have been nice if Prince had at least tried to warn the Second Cavalry that the Comanches were living under what amounted to a flag of truce.

Department of the Interior officials cared not one whit for the realities of army communication on the frontier. They picked up on the blunder and used it in the ongoing turf war with the army. Likewise, eastern newspapers used the incident for political ammunition to attack the Pierce administration. The *New York Weekly Times* claimed the peace could have easily been preserved if friendly Indians had not been victims of an unprovoked attack. The paper warned direly, "War has now begun in earnest, and there is no saying where it will terminate."[17] After its first glowing reports of a creditable victory, the army had too much prestige invested to pursue an investigation. It waited for the controversy to die down, knowing that the Second Cavalry's gallant conduct would overshadow awkward additional questions about a violation of a truce. On November 10, the army published a general order describing the action as "a most decisive and important victory."[18]

Twiggs and the officers in the Second Cavalry read about the controversy surrounding the battle with anger. Twiggs complained that the troopers had endured two years of hardship, privation, and danger, only to be attacked in print by eastern publications. Twiggs asserted that Van Dorn's battle was an unadorned success. His only worry was that authorities might make peace before the cavalry could complete the job. He urged the War Department not to negotiate with the Comanches since they never observed any treaty stipulations. Rather, he recommended that the Comanches "must be made to feel the power of the United States. Three or four such drubbings as Major Van Dorn gave them might bring them to submit to the United States."[19]

For a brief time, Earl Van Dorn was the most celebrated officer in the country. He enjoyed every minute of it. Upon his return to Mississippi on sick leave, he continued to receive accolades. His friends had already presented him with handsome sabers to honor his Mexican War feats. This time they gave him a splendid silver service. The much-caressed captain particularly enjoyed reading glowing accounts of his recent exploit in the *Natchez Democrat* and the *Southern Reveille*. His sister was an accomplished musician. She entered into the proper spirit of the day by composing a martial tune and dedicating it to the hero. The "Wichita March" became a regimental favorite and a mainstay of the regimental band's inventory. Showing remarkable recuperative powers, Van Dorn returned to Camp Radziminski after just a five-week absence.

*　　*　　*

Van Dorn's victories at the Wichita village did little to reduce the frequency of Comanche raids against the Texas frontier settlements. (National Archives)

UNNOTICED AMID the martial celebration in Mississippi and Washington was the fact that the battle at the Wichita village did nothing to reduce the frequency and intensity of Indian raids against the Texas frontier. In Palo Pinto County, ten days after the battle, the Reverend Webb Slaughter lost thirty horses to Indians. The raiders continued eastward into Parker County and stole fifty more from Oliver Loving and his neighbors. Unabated theft and murder prompted citizens to send a petition to Governor Runnels asking that something be done before they were driven from their homes. In familiar fashion Runnels, in turn, forwarded the information and petition to Secretary of War Floyd, who relayed it back to Twiggs in Texas. In spite of such incidents, Twiggs remained confident that his strategy was sound. He resisted the forces trying to pull apart the concentration of force he had created at Camp Radziminski. The Second Cavalry would simply have to press the advantage and continue to take the war to the enemy in his home.[20]

So it was that Van Dorn's victory pleased the regiment, the public, and the authorities in Washington but actually made little difference to citizens living along the Texas frontier. On peril of their life they had to remain perpetually vigilant. Since no action by the regular army or their beloved Texas Rangers seemed to reduce the border violence, they turned their anger against those Indians nearest at hand, the people living on the two Indian reserves. One of many demonstrations of frontier enmity came when a band of citizens set out from Burnet to pursue marauding Indians. Among them was thirteen-year-old Billy McGill. While his elders skirmished, Billy rode up, took aim, and fired. An Indian fell, but it proved to be a squaw. A participant recalls, "Billy, however, was after Indians, and he was not particular about the sex."[21] The next day the citizens chased a wounded Indian. They found him trying to stanch his blood flow in a pool of mud. They shot him sixteen times before killing him. Clearly they meant to torment.

Such vigilantism was no more effective than the efforts of the Second Cavalry at providing real security. So the panic spread, rumor feeding upon rumor. In Denton, Montague, and Jack Counties, in settlements along the Llano, talebearing riders appeared during the day to broadcast alarm, only to "depart all by night."[22] People fled their homes to fort up for safety. Among those driven into hastily rebuilt fortifications were citizens on the upper Pecan Bayou. One settler whose ranch lay exposed to raids rode to the nearest cavalry camp to request help: "I found Lt. Hood to be a most perfect gentleman and anxious to do all he can." But Hood had his own problems. He told the settler that he had only thirty able-bodied troopers; the rest were on the sick list. His able-bodied men had to build shelters for the impending winter and he could not keep out scouts. The settler concluded that while everyone thought very highly of the lieutenant and believed that he did everything within his powers for their protection, it simply was not enough.[23]

A rancher living eighteen miles north of Fort Mason was the victim of repeated Indian raids. When he sent his son to complain to the army at Fort Mason, the cavalry lieutenant responded with the claim that the raiders were white bandits and therefore outside the army's jurisdiction. Yet three days later troopers recaptured some of his stock and found them wearing saddle blankets of the type the Indian agents on the reserve distributed. Besides converting one more Texan to the swelling ranks of those opposed to the reserve Indians, the experience persuaded the rancher that it was useless to complain to the army. So this man was left to live a life of extreme anxiety: "I dare not to leave my house to go one mile on aney buisness for fear my familey is murde before I can get back" [sic]. Settlers had eagerly waited to see how effective Van Dorn's campaign would be, but as far as they could tell it simply deprived Indians of horses and compelled them to intensify their raids.[24]

Around this time, the number of Indians residing on the reservation increased. In December 1858 a band of Comanches who had survived Rip Ford's attacks straggled into the Comanche reserve in hopes of at least eking out the winter in peace. It proved a vain hope. Picking a time when Major Neighbors was at home in San Antonio for the Christmas season and agent Shapley Ross was in Austin, the enemies of the reserve program attacked a peaceful band of Indians who were hunting near the Brazos reserve. The Indians were relatives or friends of Choctaw Tom, a man who enjoyed the confidence of most whites and had once served as an interpreter for Sam Houston. Choctaw Tom had secured permission to take his party below the reservation where there was superior grazing. Among his party were two young men who had just returned from Van Dorn's Wichita expedition, where they had served with Sul Ross. These men's horses were thin and jaded as a result of the strenuous campaign. They wanted to restore their horses so they could rejoin Van Dorn in the spring.

None of this mattered to Peter Garland and his gang when they entered Golconda on the evening of December 26. The whites openly boasted about their plan to attack Choctaw Tom's party, and although most citizens disapproved, none did anything to stop them. The next morning Garland's gang struck. One of the first whites on the scene stated: "A more horrible sight I never expect to see. There, on their beds, lay the bodies of seven of the best and most inoffensive Indians on the reserve, their bodies pierced by buck shot and rifle balls."[25] Among the killed were three women; among the wounded, three children.

After the massacre, the adjacent white communities feared retaliation. The communities raised an armed mob, nominally embodying them as militia, and sent them against the reserve. Matters came to a head when Sheriff R. King and some fifty armed men stormed onto the Comanche reserve with the determination to arrest a suspect. The Indians, in turn, fled to the agency buildings for protection while the agent appealed to Major Thomas for help. Thomas sent Captain Innis Palmer with a detachment of troopers belonging to Company D. Palmer's troopers and the militia glared at each other at point-blank range. The troopers' disciplined demeanor cooled the mob's ardor. Then, in an astonishing display of self-assurance, Neighbors stood next to the cavalry and read aloud the act of the Texas legislature granting the reserve to the federal government. Neighbors reached his succinct conclusion: it was Sheriff King who was in the wrong and acting illegally. King and his men gave up, undoubtedly more influenced by Palmer's grizzled troopers than Neighbors's legal allocution.

Without having to resort to outright combat, Palmer had won a small but important battle. He had changed the environment from fighting to talking. The local citizens sent emissaries who told Palmer that the militia had no intention of attacking the reserve. Palmer well knew that this was an outright lie. What they wanted, the citizens said, was assurances that the Indians would not seek revenge. Working closely with the Indian agent, Palmer was able to provide the necessary assurances, and the mob dispersed. Confronting a difficult situation outside of his training, Palmer had performed admirably in a peacekeeping role more familiar to the army 140 years in the future than to the frontier army of 1858.

In Neighbors's view, the coldblooded murder of women and children by Peter Garland and his gang exceeded the Comanches' worst atrocities. Governor Runnels may not have concurred entirely, but he did order all the commanders of Texas State troops to assist in the arrest of the murderers. A Waco judge, in turn, directed Captain Ford and his Ranger company to serve the warrants and bring the prisoners in. Ford flatly refused. No sheriff willing to undertake the duty could be found. Emboldened by the public's response, Garland and his men published a statement to justify their actions. It concluded, "We have no apology to offer for what we have done."[26] Likewise, a grand jury in Palo Pinto County not only refused to indict them but praised their public service. The *Northern Standard* cried out for more of the same, advocating a war "to the knife."[27]

So it was that Texas law did not touch the Garland gang. In spite of the murders and in spite of Rip Ford's unwillingness to arrest the man who everyone knew had committed the crime, in February of the following year thirty reserve Indians joined Ford's Texas Rangers on a scout against the Comanches. Then came a message from Van Dorn. The Mississippian was planning another campaign. Would the reserve Indians help? Two expert Indian scouts immediately set off to join Van Dorn. Shortly thereafter followed Ford and his men, white and red alike. Their shared hatred of the Comanches superseded all else. Together they rode north to join forces with the cavalry and with a leader who had proved he possessed the talent to kill Comanches in large numbers.

8

"Near to Death's Door"

I can now scarcely realize that I have passed through such a severe ordeal—Indian warfare is not the most glorious in the world, hard fighting after riding miles and miles through the hot sun, often suffering for the want of water and sometimes food, exposed alternately to the heat of the sun and the rains and getting but little if any glory.

—Fitzhugh Lee, 1859 (in Lee to A. M. Fitzhugh, September 1, 1859, Papers of Fitzhugh Lee, University of Virginia)

I. "The Rough Service of the Horse"

Except for the forty-two-man detachment assigned to escort the wounded to Fort Arbuckle, Van Dorn's cavalry returned to Camp Radziminski on October 10. The forced march and fight at the Wichita village had drained the horses. To support active service, each horse required twelve pounds of grain and fourteen of hay per day. Whenever a patrol left its wagons behind, the horses began to lose weight and condition. Weight loss caused saddles to fit poorly, producing saddle sores. Sore-backed, malnourished horses could not carry riders at the pace required to catch Comanches. Consequently, the command remained in camp for the next seventeen days so the horses could partially recover. Their recovery was incomplete because Camp Radziminski was at the end of the regiment's logistical tether. Wagons bringing grain from the settlements along the Brazos River followed Van Dorn's original line of march. It was a primitive track of the worst sort. When Twiggs sent three more companies north to Camp Radziminski, the wagons moving along this track had to supply 70 percent of the regiment. The supply line could barely sustain the regiment. At Camp Radziminski, the Second Cavalry learned that in a semidesert environment, a man recovered from extended exertion faster than a horse.

While Van Dorn was recuperating in Mississippi, Captain Whiting conducted an ill-considered, extended search for the enemy that further depleted the cavalry. Without the allied Indians to perform scouting duties, no one knew the whereabouts of the Comanches. After the fight at the Wichita village, rumor variously placed the Comanches along the Brazos, Colorado, or Arkansas River. Some reports claimed they had fled to Mexico. Whiting's expedition scoured the country around the Antelope Hills for two weeks and found nothing. They marched nearly three hundred miles during this futile exercise. When Van Dorn returned in mid-November, he too proved foolishly eager to resume the hunt. The arrival of Captain Oakes with two more companies reinforced Van Dorn's zeal. Even though Oakes's Company C had just completed a grueling fourteen-day march from Fort Clark, nearly four hundred miles southwest on the Rio Grande, Van Dorn organized a force built around Oakes's men and the newly arrived Company B. He added Shanks Evans's company, selecting it because it had the least-worn horses, and sent them to the edge of the Staked Plain. Simultaneously, Whiting led the three other companies to search the valleys feeding into the Red River. These efforts also failed to find the enemy. Puzzled by the lack of contact, Van Dorn reported that the

The shortage of potable water curtailed numerous expeditions. The finely bred eastern horses proved less suited for Texas conditions than the locally procured mounts. (National Archives)

Comanches had "disappeared as a mist."[1] This second failure proved costly. Twenty-one horses and six mules had perished.

Even Van Dorn recognized that his command needed to rest before it broke down completely. Since July 1 the majority of his companies had marched at least twleve hundred miles. The hard service had exhausted the horses. The men too were showing the strain, and none more than James Oakes. He had led his squadron north while carrying the seeds of a ravaging tuberculosis in his body. Oakes was a seasoned combat veteran who had earned two brevets for gallantry in Mexico, but campaign exposure at Camp Radziminski proved too much. He applied for sick leave and turned command of Company C over to First Lieutenant William B. Royall. It was time to go into winter quarters. But what poor quarters they were; conical Sibley tents surrounded by a low, crude, turf-and-stone wall. They would fail to turn away the cold northers that were certain to strike.

The winter on Otter Creek indeed proved miserable. A succession of blizzards came howling down from the north, pinning the regiment to its camp. In an effort to stay warm, two men burned to death in their tents one night. Three others died from disease. The grain ration for the horses was inadequate, compelling the suffering beasts to subsist on buffalo, grama, and mesquite grasses. When heavy snow covered even this inadequate graze, soldiers cut down cottonwoods so the horses and mules could feed on bark and twig. Twice during thaws Van Dorn ordered the camp relocated so the horses could find better graze and the troopers drink uncontaminated water. The third site was the best of all: a cove sheltered from the northers with plenty of nearby grass and timber. Still, exposure killed numerous horses and invalided many men back to Fort Belknap. During the bleak months, Van Dorn remained a strict disciplinarian. The regiment had absorbed a large influx of new recruits. Whenever the weather permitted, officers conducted individual and unit drill. Even the horses were taught to gallop from their sparse pastures back to the corral upon hearing the warning signal. Van Dorn reckoned that this equine drill might be useful should Indian horse thieves strike. To eke out rations and break the monotony, officers led hunting parties into the hills above Otter Creek. The hunters usually returned bearing elk, bighorn sheep, and deer for the camp mess. Because bison commonly took shelter in the ravines near Otter Creek, at times the officers led buffalo-hunting patrols. Through it all, the irrepressible young officers made the best of it. Long afterward historians would find broken champagne bottles and marble poker chips littering the cavalry camps at Camp Radziminski.

No one enjoyed himself more than Second Lieutenant Fitz-hugh Lee. Fitz Lee was a blithe spirit not overly oppressed by family tradition. Whereas his uncle Robert's reading list during his cadet days encompassed learned works on military science and engineering, Fitzhugh preferred novels and poetry. His wild pranks—dancing across the parade ground, dancing in front of the guard tent, absence from quarters between 11:40 P.M. and 5:20 A.M.—almost saw him dismissed from West Point at a time when his uncle was superintendent. He tried to better himself but often found life too full of enjoyable diversions. "I entered this Academy a wild, careless, and inexperienced youth," he wrote his godmother; "I shall leave it a wiser and I hope a better man." He trained recruits at Carlisle Barracks until finally joining his regiment in the spring of 1858. During the time Van Dorn was campaigning in the north, Lee was leading a lonely life back at Fort Mason. His captain, Kirby Smith, was on leave in France. Both the first lieutenant and the surgeon were on leave as well. In the absence of fellow officers, Lee idled away his time play-ing billiards, reading, riding, and hunting. There were occasional patrols, which Lee described as "the rough service of the horse." Wearing a blue flannel shirt, top boots, and soldier's pants, with a mule to carry his provisions, he would set out in no particular direction, hoping to come on an Indian trail and then follow it. The expeditions proved fruitless. Because he was a healthy, brawny twenty-three-year-old, Fitz endured these tedious scouts little the worse for wear except more tanned, his beard shaded a deeper brown.[2] The second lieutenant welcomed his company's mid-November transfer to Camp Radziminski. He had yet to see combat and knew that service with Van Dorn was the most likely way to meet the Indians.

While Fitz Lee and his fellow junior officers hunted, gam-bled, and raced horses, Van Dorn contemplated strategy. He learned that although the Second Cavalry had been unable to locate them, the Comanches were present in force. While his troopers had futilely searched west all the way to the Staked Plain, most of the hostile Indians assembled along the Arkansas River to the north and east. However, for the first time the War Department was successfully coordinating the efforts of its two cavalry regiments. Two squadrons of the First Cavalry had marched from Kansas to Fort Arbuckle and Fort Washita. During the winter, the First Cavalry's aggressive patrolling drove the Comanches back within striking range of Camp Radziminski. Thus did General Twiggs's aggressive strategy bear fruit.

Also while in winter camp, Van Dorn's conscience began to disturb him. Newspaper criticism of his attack against Indians who were peacefully negotiating with the commander at Fort Arbuckle bothered him. In his view, the battle at the Wichita village had severely punished the Comanches by driving them from their homes. He wanted to pursue his mission to completion by attacking and killing Indians wherever found between the Rocky Mountains and the Rio Grande, until they learned that there was no refuge for them as long as they continued to murder and steal. Even while advocating this bloody-minded strategy, Van Dorn said that it could not be reasonably expected that the Comanches retire to the Indian reserves as they currently existed: "If something better is not offered them, as the boon of peace and friendship, I am afraid our difficulties with them will be resolved into a war of extermination, which would hardly be in accordance with the dictates of humanity."[3] Back in Texas, supervising agent Neighbors had reached a similar conclusion. However, neither General Twiggs in Texas nor the War Department in Washington was overly concerned with Van Dorn's worries about "the dictates of humanity." Twiggs's efforts focused on receiving an unequivocal order from the War Department to permit the cavalry to kill any Indian found outside the designated reserves. The War Department responded with a carefully shaded set of instructions that let the commander on the ground do the killing while the War Department escaped any criticism in case "friendly" Indians were among the dead.

Van Dorn's campaign was the first time that Twiggs thought he had the authority to carry the battle to the enemy in the style that he had been requesting for some time. Having gambled once and won out, Twiggs stripped more men from his line of communication. Now the chorus of protests included the howls of the agents for the Overland Mail Company. They told Twiggs that it would be impossible for the company to continue unless the army provided more protection. Twiggs well knew that the enemy infested his rear. Even army convoys moving north of San Antonio had to fort up until an armed escort could accompany them. Convinced that an offensive against the Indians in their base areas was the only way to provide security for Texas, Twiggs ignored secondary concerns and instead strained every nerve to strengthen Van Dorn's force.

IN A HARD WINTER, March proved the worst. Rip Ford visited Camp Radziminski on March 1 and found the troopers huddled in their tents enduring a blizzard. Ford wanted to cooperate with the cavalry in another offensive. Van Dorn considered the notion until yet another norther struck on March 6 and 7. The continual cold forced Van Dorn to postpone any movement. An infantry lieutenant arrived in the middle of March and was dismayed at what he found: "Things are in rather a bad state up here. Since I left, more than a hundred horses have died and about fifty mules; the rest look as if they might go at any time. There has been no rain since I left but a good deal of snow."[4] So many equines perished that large wolf packs gathered on the camp's fringe to feast on the carrion.

Also troubling for Van Dorn was the large influx of inexperienced officers and recruits. He partially had himself to blame for this. At one point Indian depredations back in Texas compelled him to relinquish one of his companies. He was supposed to send the company whose horses were in the worst condition. He selected Whiting's Company K and was glad to be rid of that outspoken abolitionist. The loss subtracted seventy-one combat veterans from his command as well as one of his most senior captains. In February, Captain Evans departed on a yearlong leave. The absence of Whiting and Evans meant that five of six companies would be led by lieutenants. Of course, Major Thomas remained languishing at regimental headquarters, but Van Dorn knew better than to interfere in Twiggs's vendetta against Thomas. Besides, if Thomas joined the expedition he would be the senior officer, and this surely did not congrue with Van Dorn's Napoleonic visions.

As he examined his command, Van Dorn anticipated that the sixty-four troopers of his cherished Mobile Grays would be in good hands because Lieutenant George B. Cosby had returned to camp, bringing with him eleven veterans. Cosby had been on detached duty escorting an engineer officer named John Pope on a mission to assess the practicality of boring a string of artesian wells along the thirty-second parallel. Cosby was a veteran of the Mounted Rifles and had been severely wounded in combat against the Comanches in 1854. Cosby remembered this experience when he served as an instructor at West Point. He developed a set of training exercises in hand-to-hand combat. Much like a modern martial arts teacher, Cosby demonstrated to his class using two cadets, Fitzhugh Lee and Manning Kimmel, as dummies. Cosby taught saber thrusts, use of a revolver as a club, and wrestling holds. Within the coming year his instruction was to save Lee's life.

Captain Edmund Kirby Smith thoroughly enjoyed his service in Texas in spite of his wound at Crooked Creek. Few could have imagined that he would rise to full general in the Confederate Army and command the Trans-Mississippi, a region that became known as Kirby Smithdom. (National Archives)

Van Dorn also had no concerns about the seventy-three troopers of Company B once Captain Kirby Smith returned from a long leave of absence. Smith had fulfilled a life's ambition by touring Europe, only to find the experience disappointing. He learned that he did not much care for foreigners. The English were "rude, surly, disagreeable," while coexisting with the peculiar tastes of the Germans and French required "an exercise of great self denial."[5] Smith brought his servant with him when he rejoined the regiment. Presumably the slave would provide some familiar comforts to help Smith forget the horrors of Europe and to ease his transition from tourist to frontier fighter. Smith was Van Dorn's second in command.

First Lieutenant William B. Royall returned from recruiting duty in Philadelphia and training duty at the cavalry barracks in Carlisle, Pennsylvania, to assume command of the sixty-nine troopers in Company C. Although the lung-sick James Oakes would be missed, Royall was another officer who could be trusted in a tight spot. A decade ago he had helped stand off three hundred Comanches who attacked his wagon train. Not content with merely defending his wagons, ignoring the odds of ten to one against, Royall had taken thirty-four picked men in pursuit! Royall shepherded fifty-six raw recruits to Camp Radziminski. Van Dorn set him to drilling the greenhorns as thoroughly as possible.

Michigan-born Second Lieutenant James B. Witherell had been one of the officers appointed from civilian life to the regiment. He had been with the patrol that fought three separate combats on the same day back in 1856, and he had seen much action since that time. Witherell commanded the strongest element in Van Dorn's force, the seventy-six troopers of Company F.

Company G was also in the hands of a junior officer, but this was because of a scandal the previous summer. One morning, Captain William R. Bradfute, the commander of Company G, issued an order to a Company K private named William Murray. Because Murray was in a different company and in recent times Bradfute had been absent on leave, the two men did not know each other; but orders were orders, and Murray was compelled to obey. Perhaps Murray was hungover, or perhaps something in Bradfute's tone deeply offended the private. He reacted by punching the captain in the face. It was the last mistake he made. Staggered by the blow, Bradfute drew his revolver. Veterans who had served with Bradfute knew him to be hotheaded and a crack marksman. At this range, with this weapon, the outcome was certain. Horrified by his own action after shooting Murray dead, the captain went to nearby Fort Belknap to surrender himself to Thomas.

Thomas convened a long and searching court of inquiry that exonerated Bradfute. Civilians living around Fort Belknap sensed a deep miscarriage of justice. They contrived a warrant for Bradfute's arrest. Somehow Texas law permitted a marshal to transfer the bewildered captain from military to civilian authorities. Thomas had no choice but to relieve Bradfute of command pending a trial. Although Bradfute was released on bail, the trial never occurred. For the next two and a half years Bradfute lived in limbo, a nominal civilian prisoner, unable to return to the regiment. He did not return to active service until March 1861, when he resigned his commission to join the Confederacy.

At Camp Radziminski, with Bradfute facing trial for murder and First Lieutenant Kenner Garrard off recruiting, the former training dummy Second Lieutenant Manning M. Kimmel took over command of the seventy-two troopers in Company G. He was the son of the governor of Missouri and a high-spirited young man. However, Kimmel had never seen combat before. History would not record any particularly notable exploit by Kimmel in Texas. His son, Admiral Husband E. Kimmel, would have the misfortune to be in command at Pearl Harbor on December 7, 1941.

New York–born Lieutenant Robert N. Eagle replaced Evans at the head of the sixty-four troopers of Company H. Eagle had recently returned from an extended sick leave, followed by a stint as instructor at Carlisle. He too was inexperienced. However, his subordinate, Second Lieutenant James Harrison, was one of the regiment's outstanding fighters. Among officers of diverse background, Harrison was particularly noteworthy. In 1855 he had been an officer in the revenue service stationed in the Pacific. Bored, he volunteered for an expedition against the Indians in Washington Territory. When Indians killed the expedition's commander, Harrison led it to safety and so distinguished himself that he received a citation for gallantry. This brought him to the attention of Jeff Davis, who appointed him to the Second Cavalry. In keeping with his reputation for bravery, Harrison had killed two Comanches in close combat during the fight at the Wichita village.

In total, Van Dorn took eleven officers and 418 enlisted men into the field for his second campaign. They were an amalgam of combat veterans and greenhorns. By now the Second Cavalry had established a morale ascendancy over the Indians, and Van Dorn had little fear for the result of any encounter. His staff comprised four men, including Lieutenant Fitz Lee. It annoyed Lee that his friend Kimmel, who had graduated one year later than himself, should be at the head of a company while he served in a paper-pushing position. However, Van Dorn needed someone to perform as his adjutant and already had enough inexperienced men in important company-leadership positions. Since Lee evidently possessed a boisterous spirit but had never seen combat, Van Dorn figured he would ease him into the regiment by assigning him a staff position.

Finally the terrible winter broke. The snows disappeared from the Otter Creek valley and gradually receded up the adjacent heights. Nourished by a wet winter, the first blades of grass pushed through the overgrazed pastures around Camp Radziminski. A "delightful spring" ensued, bringing thick grass dotted with colorful wildflowers.[6] The depleted horses stopped losing weight and then slowly began to regain condition. Having wisely waited for the grass to green up nicely, on April 29, 1859, Van Dorn issued his order: the expedition would depart at sunrise tomorrow!

—— II. The Fight on Crooked Creek ——

The bugles sounded "Boots and Saddles" at first light on April 30. Because Van Dorn intended to conduct a sustained campaign, a large train carrying food and forage accompanied the column. Thus, the pace was far slower than last September's killing speed march to the Wichita village. Complete with its wagons and pack mules, the column extended across a mile of prairie. Led by Indian guides, it marched northwest to Elk Creek, a tributary of the Red River, and then followed the creek upstream. After traversing about twenty-one miles, the troopers made camp. In order to keep the train as light as possible, tents had been left behind. Likewise the pack mules carried only the most basic rations: pork, flour, coffee, sugar, salt.[7] Consequently, the troopers ate a crude dinner and slept in the open beneath a single blanket.

The march continued for two more days and forty-five miles along Elk Creek. The rainy spring had filled the creek, so for a change, water, albeit opaque with mud, was not in short supply. On May 2 the cavalry encountered a tremendous bison herd. Like a wave parted by contact with land, the herd divided onto either side of the regiment. For thirty miles the troopers marched through this living sea. For dinner that night everyone enjoyed roasted buffalo steaks.

During Van Dorn's first campaign, the allied Indians had made a tremendous contribution. Consequently, Van Dorn applied to Shapley Ross for a contingent to join him for his second campaign. Fifty-eight Caddos, Keechis, Tonkawas, Delawares, and Shawnees joined him at Camp Radziminski. Most had not previously served with the cavalry. They were young men eager to prove themselves. They came without Sul Ross, who was back in Alabama completing his senior year at the university, and Ross's absence made a difference. When the expedition got under way, the warriors were full of confidence. They dressed in war paint and bonnets and boasted about their impending exploits. At first they scouted up to ten miles in front of the cavalry. But each step north took them farther into territory that had been dominated by the lords of the plains for a span beyond living memory. The allied Indians grew cautious. Cavalry officers grumbled that they seemed unwilling to venture beyond gunshot range of the blue-clad troopers. So it was that cavalry scouts and not the allied Indians first encountered the enemy.

This enemy was not particularly threatening—Comanche scouts detected watching the column from a nearby ridge. Van Dorn had anticipated that the enemy would try to track his men's march. To deceive them, each evening he assembled his men as if preparing to make camp and then, under cover of darkness, shifted position a mile or two before resting for the night. During the day he organized a counterreconnaissance screen by placing cavalry vedettes in front, flank, and rear. It was the thrusting Lieutenant Harrison, in command of a party of flankers, who pursued the enemy scouts and managed to capture one of them. He was a mere boy, possibly out on the first expedition of his life. With Van Dorn's approval, Harrison turned him over to Shawnee Jim, the experienced guide and translator.

All accounts gloss over how Shawnee Jim extracted the intelligence from the boy, but there is little doubt that the interrogation was not gentle. The boy divulged that he was one of three warriors riding south to scout Camp Radziminski. He said that five days' ride to the north, adjacent to a large salt creek, were two camps, one nearly ten miles long, sheltering sixteen hundred lodges, and another with about two hundred lodges. Van Dorn knew that his previous campaign, coupled with the aggressive efforts of the First Cavalry, had pushed the Comanches away from their favored wintering grounds along the North Fork of the Red River, an area featuring mild winters and a good supply of forage, wood, and water. Reports suggested that the Indians had retired deep into their domain near the Arkansas River. The boy's story seemed to confirm this notion.

Convinced that the prisoner was telling the truth, Van Dorn conferred with his second in command. If there were five people per lodge, than there must be nine to ten thousand Indians present, a total that must represent nearly the entire population of "wild" Comanches and their Kiowa comrades. Perhaps one in five were warriors. Odds of four to one or worse no more fazed Van Dorn than they had restrained Hood in his fight at Devil's River. Albeit the stakes were vastly larger: Hood had commanded a small detachment; Van Dorn commanded 60 percent of the regiment. He could not expect to achieve another surprise, since the boy's two companions must be galloping north to alert the camps. Still, neither Captain Smith nor anyone else doubted what Van Dorn would do. Smith wrote that after the interrogation, the "excitement became general," for "our little major" resolved to push on.[8]

The cavalry set out on May 4 with firmness of step. The objective was no longer an ephemeral foe but rather the largest concentration of Indians ever detected by the regiment. Van Dorn personally threatened the prisoner: lead the cavalry to the Indian camp or he would order the boy shot. Van Dorn's allied Indians certainly added their own gruesome threats. Whereas an adult warrior would have chosen death, the terrified boy decided to betray his people.

Yet it seemed that the gods were against the Second Cavalry. Persistent rains slowed progress to a mere twelve miles that day. The draft animals could barely pull the wagons up muddy slopes and across rough, broken terrain. It was worse the next day. Van Dorn ordered a halt in midafternoon to rest the command. He assembled his officers to explain his plan. He intended a repeat of his strike at the Wichita village. They would force-march through the night and attack the larger village at dawn. Depending upon enemy resistance, they would exploit any success and charge the smaller village in a follow-up effort.

By the time the troopers mounted, the steady rain had turned to violent thunderstorms of the type unique to the Great Plains. Impenetrable darkness shrouded the column. A wind-whipped rain blinded rider and horse, while overhead jagged streaks of lightning leaped from cloud to ground. The terrain became more broken still, full of hills, ravines, and rocky cliff edges. In spite of everyone's best efforts, progress reduced to a snail's pace. At dawn on May 6 the storm subsided. Before the cavalry was the flooded South Fork of the Canadian River, its normally placid trickle a roaring, half-mile-wide torrent. There was no alternative but to halt. Van Dorn summoned the prisoner. Where was the Indian camp? he demanded. The boy answered that it was still three days' ride north.

Why his response surprised Van Dorn is unclear. The boy had always maintained that the distance was a five-day ride. The cavalry had marched for part of two days and one night, all the while slowed by the plodding wagon train and the cloying mud. Somehow, Van Dorn had miscalculated. However, he recovered to devise a new plan. Rather than continue north with the train, as had been his original plan, he would leave it here. He ordered his officers to select a guard detail based on those whose horses were least fit. They would circle the wagons, construct a corral, and remain behind. This would serve as a base of operations. With the balance of the command including the pack mules, Van Dorn would continue as soon as the waters receded.

When the waterlogged command awoke on May 7, troopers saw that the South Fork had dropped as quickly as it had risen. The next three days featured marches of 22, 25, and 17 miles, thereby bringing the column to the banks of the Cimarron River. It marked the boundary of the Kansas Territory. The cavalry crossed the Cimarron and went into camp. On the afternoon of May 10, the allied Indians detected Comanche scouts and gave chase. They killed one Comanche but at least four others fled into the broken country to the west and north. This contact suggested that the great Indian camp was near, a fact confirmed when Van Dorn again interrogated the prisoner. In order to move light and fast, Van Dorn ordered supplies cached for later retrieval and instructed his subordinates to prepare for a dawn approach march.

Guided by the prisoner, on May 11 the cavalry marched north of the Cimarron and then turned northwest to parallel a small stream known as Big Sandy Creek. The track followed an old Indian trail. The approaching hills suggested an even more rugged country ahead. The Indian scouts reported that the next decent campsite was quite a lot farther ahead. Accordingly, Van Dorn ordered a halt even though the day's march had spanned only fourteen or so miles. He must have worried about keeping a fighting edge on his men. Twice now he had predicted that combat was imminent, and twice he had been wrong. With scouts questing ahead and flankers protecting the column against ambush, the cavalry marched cautiously on May 12 in the belief that the enemy camp would be over the next hill.

They came to the valley of Crooked Creek. The scene presented a very different sight from the arid semidesert through which they had been marching. Crooked Creek cut a green swath through a brown, barren upland. Nourished by Spring Creek, Crooked Creek provided a consistent enough flow to support a fine stand of mixed grasses as well as scattered cottonwoods and scrub trees. Strung across this oasis were two long series of circles, formed by holes in the ground, with a dark depression in the center of each circle. The veterans instantly recognized lodge circles, formed by the poles supporting the tepees, and the central fire pits used for heating and cooking. The prisoner had not deceived. The abandoned village extended for miles along both banks of Crooked Creek. Clearly the Indians had learned of the cavalry's presence—probably it had been the companions of the boy prisoner who had provided the warning—and broken camp and moved on.

Van Dorn had urged the unrelenting pursuit of the wild Indians from the Rio Grande to the Rocky Mountains. Having penetrated deeper into Comanche country than any prior punitive expedition, he now stood less than three hundred miles from the Rockies. But he had yet to find his enemies. His command was well beyond its temporary supply base back on the South Fork of the Canadian River. The tracks showing the Comanches' exodus from the Crooked Creek village pointed north, northwest, and northeast. This was the time-honored tactic of a guerrilla force facing detection: disperse in multiple directions to frustrate pursuit by the heavier enemy force until that force turned back for lack of supplies. Late in the day, as he considered how to proceed, his Indian scouts reported the discovery of a large, fresh trail four miles away. Van Dorn decided to continue the hunt. After a moist, dreary day, the troopers bedded down beneath yet another set of showers, wet blankets pressed against soaked wool.

May 13 dawned with more of the same. The Indian scouts guided the cavalry along the fresh trail for over twenty miles. A cold north wind, rain, and intermittent hail made this day the worst so far. Van Dorn called a halt around 2 P.M. so the leg-weary animals would have an opportunity to graze. Thirty minutes later one of the herd guards sighted three Indians apparently stalking the herd in hopes of stampeding them. The guards sounded the alarm. The cavalry horses performed as they had been trained the previous winter. They galloped back to the safety of camp. Van Dorn ordered Lieutenant Royall to take a thirty-man detachment and chase the Indians. Setting off, Royall's troopers climbed a nearby height and spotted the Indians fleeing in the distance.

The troopers spurred their mounts hard until they climbed another rise. Here one of the men noticed a large horse herd sheltered in an adjacent valley. Because he was an experienced campaigner, Royall knew that the owners had to be nearby. He led a stealthy approach and saw that overwatching the horses were a few not very vigilant herdsmen. Farther away, just beyond a tree line, loomed the protruding poles of a small village.

In Indian warfare, any time spent reconnoitering increased the likelihood of being detected oneself. The cavalry had learned repeatedly that audacity was everything. Royall sent a courier galloping back to Van Dorn to inform him that there was an Indian village in a ravine a mere three miles to the east of the cavalry camp. Royall told Van Dorn that he would attack at once in an effort to stampede the horse herd and thus keep the enemy at bay until the cavalry arrived.

George Custer would become the most notable example of the perils of charging an Indian village of unknown size. In this case, fortune smiled upon William Royall. He deployed his twenty-nine troopers into line and charged at a gallop directly toward the horse herd. The surprise was complete. By firing their pistols and shouting, the cavalry panicked the herd. The Indian horses scattered beyond immediate recall. Having taken away their means to escape, Royall deployed two firing teams in the creek bed above and below the village and stationed his remaining men just beyond effective range south of the village. Royall's dispositions effectively sealed off the village.

The eighty-odd men and women inside the village were astonished at the sudden appearance of the Second Cavalry. At the time Royall's troopers stampeded their horses, most of the warriors were inside their shelters to escape from a heavy downpour. Historically, Comanche camp security had been lax, but this incident is difficult to fathom. The most likely supposition is that the camp contained a hunting party—otherwise there would have been children present with the women—who were not connected with the inhabitants of the recently abandoned large village. At any rate, they belonged to Buffalo Hump's band, although that leader was not present. By now all Comanches well knew that Buffalo Hump was among the cavalry's most sought after foe. The Comanches customarily kept a rearguard lookout. Probably the Indians who were first spotted by the cavalry's herd guards belonged to such a rearguard. Possibly they allowed themselves to be seen and then deliberately led the cavalry toward the unwitting hunting village in the hopes that the bluecoats would be satisfied with destroying Buffalo Hump's band and leave their own bands alone to continue their flight.

As soon as Van Dorn received Royall's message, he ordered his chief bugler to sound "to horse." Amid a pelting rain, the Mississippian led the command at a foxhunting pace across the prairie toward the Comanche village. Private Willis Burroughs lagged behind his comrades in Company G. Whereas many men joined the cavalry to receive free transport to Texas and then deserted, Burroughs had traveled on his own from his native Tennessee to Texas and then enlisted. He had the misfortune to ride a "stump-sucking" nag, whose lung ailments prevented him from keeping up with the rest of the company. The horse could not endure the three-mile gallop and came to a gasping halt. Rather than return to camp, Burroughs dismounted and used his own legs to run to rejoin his unit. It was not a dignified way for a cavalry trooper to enter combat. His incomparable zeal well represents the Second Cavalry.

At the head of his men, Van Dorn saw Royall's troopers poised at the ready on the south bank of Crooked Creek. Royall quickly apprised Van Dorn of the situation: the Indians' horse herd was safely secured, the Indians themselves trapped somewhere below, hidden amid the trees and bushes that lined the streambed. Van Dorn immediately perceived the strength of the enemy's position: "a deep ravine, densely covered with a stunted growth of timber and brambles, through which a small stream, with abrupt banks, meandered from bluff to bluff on either side."[9] Kirby Smith's Company B was the nearest unit at hand. Van Dorn ordered it to dismount and probe the position. He directed the next available company to take position upstream and drive the Indians toward Smith's men.

Kirby Smith was notoriously nearsighted. In the rainy weather, the heat from his excited brow caused his glasses to fog over. He never saw the Indian who shot him until too late. Fired from point-blank range, the musket ball struck him full force in the thigh, missing only fractionally his femoral artery. Staggered, Smith carried on, motioning for his men to follow.

The dimensions of the Second Cavalry's tactical problem now became apparent. The Comanches knew that without their horses flight was not an option. Few doubted that they were doomed. As with the Japanese in the Second World War, the thought of surrender was not part of their warrior ethic. They neither asked for nor granted quarter. They concealed themselves in the streambed, hiding behind fallen logs, using bushes and clumps of tall grass as camouflage. Some scraped firing pits into the sandy soil to provide partial protection. As Captain Smith had learned, a few of the Indians possessed trading post muskets or plundered rifles. The majority notched their bows and prepared to die hard. The lowering clouds reduced visibility. Thus, the first indication that the enemy was present was too often the sound of an arrow in flight. The arrows seemed to rise out of the ground, fired by unseen foes. Only later would the cavalry come to realize that the overcast skies and rainy conditions that limited their visibility also slackened the Indians' bowstrings. This reduced the arrow's velocity.

It did nothing to slow the speed of flying bullets, a fact that the dismounted troopers in the ravine and their commander quickly appreciated. The troopers slipped and slid over the rain-soaked, uneven terrain of Crooked Creek. As the pincers closed, the troopers inadvertently faced one another from opposite sides of the ravine. Their wild shots began striking within friendly lines. To prevent self-slaughter, Van Dorn ordered his bugler to sound the rally. It was a commendable decision by which Van Dorn demonstrated that he was no mere hothead, an unthinking gallant whose only notion of duty was to press the issue hard.

While the noncommissioned officers sorted the men back into formation, Van Dorn explained his plan to the officers. He placed one squadron apiece on either side of the stream. They remained mounted, ready to slaughter any foes who emerged onto the open ground. Van Dorn ordered his remaining squadron to dismount, disperse into skirmish line, and push through the ravine. Since one man in four had to remain behind to hold the horses, this meant that about ninety cavalrymen advanced into the streambed. Absent from the force was Kirby Smith. His leg wound was bleeding so badly that Van Dorn ordered him to the rear for medical assistance. In his place stepped two other notable men: Fitz Lee and Willis Burroughs. With Smith incapacitated and Company B short one officer, it was natural that Lee, who served in Smith's company, should ask to rejoin his men. Moreover, Lee was eager to experience combat. Van Dorn sent his adjutant to join the skirmish line. About the same time, Private Burroughs completed his cross-country run to also take his place with his dismounted comrades. Then the skirmishers advanced.

Those two fire-eaters, Lieutenants Harrison and Lee, led an advance force into the creek bed. They moved along the stream's north bank until they encountered what appeared to be a log breastworks. In fact it was a tangle of fallen trees piled into a snag by periodic floods. Protruding above the logs were the heads of the Indians. Instead of charging ahead foolishly, the

Second Lieutenant Fitzhugh Lee, wearing his cavalry uniform, was another officer who enjoyed the blood sport of hunting Indians. (Kansas State Historical Society)

Virginians retired to report the apparent location of the enemy's main line of resistance to Van Dorn.

Having a clearer notion of what his men confronted, the captain issued final instructions. Lieutenant Lee, joined by his friend Lieutenant Kimmel, would lead the way toward the breastworks. Lieutenants Cosby and Eagle would follow with their companies. Depending upon developments, Van Dorn would add additional strength. Until now, the allied Indians had taken no part in the fight. Impatient with the lack of action, one of their leaders, a respected Delaware guide whom the whites called Jack Harry, appealed to Van Dorn. The captain denied his request in spite of Jack Harry's angry assertion that he and his men could not return home having taken no part in the fight. Probably Van Dorn did not want to create any chance of a mistaken identity during the forthcoming close-range fighting in the "thick jungle"—Van Dorn's word choice to describe the terrain—below. Jack Harry returned to his men. He consulted with Shawnee Jim, who had been serving with the whites since the days of the Texas Revolution, and the two leaders decided to ignore Van Dorn. The allied Indians put on white headbands so they could be distinguished from the Comanches, and with a whoop charged toward the fray.

Led by Kimmel and Lee, the cavalry entered the ravine. Hoping to unnerve their foes, the troopers shouted while firing rapidly regardless of whether they saw a target. The Comanches were far too experienced to be bothered by the wild shooting or the shouts. They waited until the cavalry presented a clear, close-range target before rising to fire. Contact was sudden and usually at point-blank range. Lee's detachment saw a group of women hiding in a thicket. They captured them without resistance and escorted them to the rear. Returning to the fight, Lee led a charge into a dense thicket. He saw a warrior crouching behind a log. He killed him with his Colt. Alerted by the report, another Indian rose to fire at Lee. Lee leveled his revolver and aimed carefully. It was bow versus Colt at twelve yards' range, "he shooting and I shooting, a sort of duel." The lieutenant fired twice, felling the Indian with a shot to the chest. Ten yards to Lee's side, a third Indian appeared. Lee was intent on finishing off the fallen warrior and did not react to this newest threat. He was firing a third shot when the warrior's arrow struck him beneath his upraised right arm, penetrated his lung, and emerged out his back beneath the shoulder blade. The blow staggered Lee. He fell backward against a tree, scarcely able to breathe because blood was rising in his throat and mouth.

His former martial arts instructor, George Cosby, ran to Lee. He pulled the shaft of the arrow from the lieutenant's chest and summoned help from nearby troopers. As they carried Lee back to the surgeons, Cosby presumed the wound was mortal.

Nearby, although unremarked at the time, another Comanche aimed at a blue-clad trooper charging through the brush. He released the arrow and had the satisfaction of seeing he had hit his target. Private Willis Burroughs fell dead. Sergeant William P. Leverett was also at the forefront of the fight. He was a career soldier, a classic example of the invaluable noncommissioned officer whose leadership bonded the regiment together. As he had done in past battles, he exposed himself recklessly in order to inspire those recruits facing combat for the first time. His battle frenzy subsided only after he received multiple wounds.

The relentless struggle continued, pitting carbine-and-revolver-armed troopers and their Indian allies against bow-armed Comanches. Everything was against the defenders. The heavy rain loosened the bowstrings, causing the arrows to fly wild and with reduced velocity. The cavalry outnumbered the Indians nearly tenfold. If the warrior's first shot did not fell his opponent, he found himself the target of a growing volume of return fire. After being shot at, the trooper returned fire with his own weapon. By so doing he pinpointed the target area for nearby comrades. Soon the warrior found himself deluged by overwhelming carbine and revolver fire. To reveal himself in order to aim his bow, he courted near-certain death. Pinned to his position, all the man could do was die gamely. Methodically the cavalry exploited their advantages, killing the Comanches in ones and twos. In about an hour the cavalry and their allied Indians had wiped out all resistance. The victors counted forty-one dead warriors. In the confusion of battle, eight women had also been killed. All died within about a hundred-yard stretch of creek bed. The cavalry secured thirty-seven prisoners, including five males who were incapacitated by their wounds.

Surgeon James Simons and his assistant, W. H. Babcock, provided a gesture of humanity that slightly relieved the slaughter. One of the female prisoners had a serious thigh wound. The surgeons administered an anesthetic, probably laudanum, removed the bullet, and dressed the wound. When the woman awoke, she was amazed. She told her fellow prisoners that these white men possessed powerful medicine. They were true healers. Her report gave all the prisoners hope that they too might survive.

A search of the battlefield found only one dead cavalryman, the eager recruit Private Burroughs. Surgeons Simons and Babcock had thirteen wounded cavalrymen to attend to. Five of them had serious injuries. The surgeons correctly suspected that Sergeant Leverett's dangerous wound would prove mortal. He would be buried alongside Burroughs on a rise overlooking the battlefield. Private Patrick Ninevane had two severe wounds but would survive. First Sergeant John Spangler, who had slain six Comanches at the Wichita village, continued to build upon his heroic reputation. He was among the six troopers who received light wounds. Van Dorn would claim that only two allied Indians received wounds. The Indians maintained that they lost two killed on the field while two others received mortal wounds. In total, fourteen cavalrymen had been hit. Such was the nature of the regiment's frontline style of leadership that five noncommissioned and two commissioned officers were among this total. Of the two wounded officers, the surgeons were confident, barring the always unpredictable onset of infection, that Captain Smith would recover. They were also fairly certain that Fitzhugh Lee would not.

When troopers deposited Lee at the aid station, blood was streaming from his mouth. He lay propped on the lap of his sixteen-year-old bugler, Edward M. "Jack" Hayes. Surprisingly, his chest wound seemed not to be bleeding. One of the surgeons forced salt water into Lee's gasping mouth. The blood flow subsided. The surgeons suspected that the arrowhead still lay lodged somewhere within Lee's chest. Van Dorn sent Cosby to search the site where he had removed the arrow from the lieutenant. Cosby returned with a number of bloody arrows. Some still had their points, some did not. This left the surgeons with an open question whether the arrowhead had passed completely through Lee's body or remained lodged inside his chest cavity. They doubted that it mattered greatly. Since Lee remained lucid, they suggested he dictate any last wishes. Lee delivered what he believed was his dying message to his parents. Then surgeons ordered the crowd of concerned friends to disperse.

Lee's good friend Manning Kimmel had almost suffered Lee's fate. A bullet had passed through Kimmel's Hardee hat. This, coupled with the general excitement of having participated in his first battle, left Kimmel a bit off balance. When he learned of his friend's mortal wound, he ran to the aid station and sat down next to Lee. Somewhat at random, he pointed to the hole in his hat. Lee managed a faint smile and spoke: "Kimmel, do you want me to believe that an Indian shot that hole through your hat? Now, old man, acknowledge the corn—didn't you go behind a tree and shoot that hole yourself?"[10] Encouraged by his leader's attempt at a characteristic witticism, Bugler Hayes spoke up. He told Kimmel to fear not, Lee would recover.

AFTER SEEING THAT the wounded were receiving every possible attention, Captain Van Dorn recalled his pack train and ordered his command to camp for the night in the Comanche village. He retired inside a tepee to escape the rain and wrote a brief account to General Twiggs. It tabulated the losses for both sides and reported that his command was "crippled" because it had to care for its wounded and prisoners. This is a surprising assertion. For nearly a year, every decision and every effort within the Department of Texas had pointed toward supporting an expedition deep into Comanche territory. Van Dorn had enthusiastically concurred with Twiggs's strategy. Yet here he was—having engaged (as he well knew, since he had marched through the large Comanche village only yesterday) a small portion of the enemy force operating in this region, and having lost one killed and thirteen wounded (a casualty rate of 3 percent)—claiming that his command was crippled. Perhaps the shock of seeing Kirby Smith seriously wounded and Fitz Lee mortally wounded unbalanced Van Dorn. At any rate he concluded that he was "compelled to return at once to Camp Radziminski."[11]

Van Dorn divided his command. Part of Company A and all of Company B remained on the battlefield until the wounded recovered sufficiently to endure the trip back to Camp Radziminski. When they departed they were to destroy the village and all the Comanches' possessions that they themselves could not use. Meanwhile, Van Dorn led the rest of his force on a circuitous return route to permit them to scout the Antelope Hills. This was a traditional staging area for raids into Texas. But the Indians were well aware of the cavalry's presence and there was no contact. Van Dorn himself seemed in a great hurry to return. He took about a hundred troopers and speed-marched ahead, arriving at Camp Radziminski on May 26, four days before the balance of his command. Perhaps the desire to broadcast his accomplishment accounts for his haste. The march of the wounded and the prisoners proved slower and more difficult. The death of Sergeant Leverett two days after the battle relieved the surgeons of their gravest case. To transport the other seriously injured, the troopers fashioned litters from the dismantled tepees and buffalo hides. A thick layer of grass and leaves provided cushioning. A saddle blanket was placed atop this cushion and the ends of the litter suspended between a pair of pack mules. Captain Smith gallantly declined a litter, giving his place to a more seriously wounded enlisted man. He stiffly climbed into his saddle and rode the two hundred miles back to base. Amazingly, by the time he reached Camp Radziminski his wound had completely healed.

Fitz Lee found the trip much more uncomfortable. Early in the trip, while securing his litter to the mule, surgeon James Simons thoughtlessly slapped at a large horsefly with the flat of his saber. The startled mule took off running, dragging the suffering lieutenant. The jolting reopened his wound. The devoted nursing from Bugler Hayes and Lee's eternal sense of humor helped pull him through. At one point the jostling over rough ground proved extremely painful. Rather than complain, he sent for his former teacher Lieutenant Cosby. "Cosby, I wish you would have these mules changed and put the old gray in front. Every step he takes his muzzle comes within a few inches of my face and he flaps his long ear in a way that I don't like. 'Familiarity breeds contempt,' you know, and probably the mule feels that way about it, too."[12] Laughing, reassured by Lee's joking, troopers switched the pack mules and the march continued. Retracing its steps, the column gathered in the supplies that had been cached and later absorbed the supply train stationed on the South Fork of the Canadian River. They reached Camp Radziminski without incident.

Although the camp had only a makeshift tent hospital, Lee and the other wounded recovered rapidly. On June 3, a hospital steward propped Lee up on his pillows so he could write home. It was an entirely different communication from the letter he had dictated when he believed he was dying. He assured his parents that he had recovered, contrary to everyone's expectation. He felt fortunate. The arrow that hit him had done fearful damage, yet because the rain had caused the bowstrings to slacken, it lacked the usual force. Still, his letter contained a sober reflection: "I have been as near to death's door as it falls to the lot of a mortal to be, and still not enter."[13]

On May 31, Van Dorn completed a detailed report of the battle he called the fight on Crooked Creek. During the campaign, it had rained on half the days. Although the troopers slept without shelter, there were few complaints and no despondency. When confronting an unseen foe at the bottom of a dark ravine, the troopers had not hesitated to charge. Van Dorn paid fulsome homage to his men's "unflinching courage" against a "desperate and skillful foe." The Comanches had also gained Van Dorn's grudging respect. He wrote that they "fought without giving or asking quarter, until there was no one left to wield a bow."[14] In keeping with most whites, who thought that only a thorough "chastisement" could bring the Comanches to their senses, Kirby Smith hoped the punitive campaign would give pause to the Indians and cause them to reflect that there was no place safe for them.

The nation was undergoing a frenzy of telegraph construction. Communication was improving so rapidly that Twiggs's report of Van Dorn's battle reached the War Department just five days after Twiggs wrote it. Predictably, Van Dorn's second expedition received much praise. But it was very much the exception, a welcome "big" battle only partially offsetting repeated futile chases. Indeed, the offensive activities of the cavalry alongside those of the Texas Rangers gave little relief to the frontier. These offensives broke up large encampments, which had the effect of dispersing the raiders into small groups, numbering a handful of warriors. In 1858 and 1859, they continued to attack isolated ranches along the north Texas frontier, stealing hundreds of horses and killing the unwary or unlucky. And the cavalry could not prevent it.

___ III. The Reservation War ___

The situation on the Texas frontier depended entirely upon one's perspective. The cavalry troopers patrolled ceaselessly and seldom contacted any Indians. For them the Comanches were usually a remote peril. From the frontiersmen's viewpoint, the presence of the cavalry had changed very little. Their livelihood depended upon their cattle and horses. Uneventful months provided a false sense of security and their herds grew. Then a morning's ride of awful discovery: cattle down, riddled with arrows, bellowing in pain and fear; horses missing, the paddock imprinted with moccasined feet, horse tracks leading to the wild hinterlands. If unarmed or unwary, the rancher himself became the target of Comanche ambush. Stories of women and children murdered—much exaggerated in the retelling—and livestock stolen struck at Texans' deepest emotions. Citizens petitioned the governor for protection, their letters a tabulation of loss and woe. Since neither the cavalry nor the Texas Rangers could prevent the raids, they demanded permission to form militia groups to defend themselves. They also became convinced that the Indians living on the reserves were complicit in the crimes.

Indians who tried to eke out an existence on the reservations were confined to a barren island sanctuary in a sea of temptation and danger. Earnest, well-intentioned agents such as Robert Neighbors tried to make the reservation life a success, but inexorably the tide of white hatred gathered force. Quite simply, the whites who lived near the Brazos reserve regarded a handful of tribes as "friendly & reliable," whereas the inhabitants of the Comanche reserve were "looked upon with distrust & regarded as vindictive & treacherous."[15] Texans who lived farther away from the reserves made no such distinctions.

The veteran Texas Ranger Rip Ford had seen a great deal of trouble since the dawn of the Texas Republic. But he reported that the bad situation in the spring of 1859 was unprecedented. The settlers' feeling of insecurity approached hysteria, and it spread rapidly along the frontier. Recent settlers had come from the East, where they had no experience of Indian conflict. All they understood was that neither the army nor their own militia provided peace. Not knowing where else to turn, they focused on the Indians living among them. They ignored the faithfulness and valor of the allied Indians who accompanied the Second Cavalry and the Texas Rangers. All they heard was "the mad clamor that Texas must expel all Indians, whether friendly or wild."[16]

Amid the hysteria, there were real problems. Ranchers often found their stolen stock in the hands of the reserve Indians. On the Comanche reserve, the Indians routinely accounted for their stock by saying that they had met some Kiowas, whipped them, and seized their animals before returning to the reserve. It did little to mollify the ranchers when the government agents explained that the reserve Indians were doing the ranchers a favor by recapturing their stolen stock and returning it for $10 a head. In the words of a Bosque County rancher: "However, after Fred Gentry's horse had been found on the upper reserve, in possession of the Comanches, and four of the reserve Indians were killed by Captain Preston and his neighbors, when in the act of driving off a number of stolen horses, we were pretty satisfied that these reserve Indians were leagued with the wild tribes in raiding on the settlements."[17]

In fact, what was typically taking place was that the Comanches and Kiowas living to the north made a habit of passing near the reserves while returning from raids. They did this both to steal horses from the reserve and to direct the attention of the pursuers toward the reserve. White outlaws also used this ploy. Captain Ford, the *Dallas Herald*, and the *Waco Southern Democrat* shared the belief that there was an active gang of white outlaws operating with the Indians. Among them were the "mustangers," the wild-horse hunters who haunted the chaparral wilderness to collect mustangs for sale to both Texans and Mexicans. They tended to be a shiftless, lawless bunch. Capturing wild mustangs required determination and patience and usually involved hardship. Some found trading with the Comanches preferable; others decided that stealing horses from the settlers was easier still. They left at the crime scene a few arrowheads and moccasin prints, and the deed was done.

Into this charged environment came an incendiary Indian hater. Since his dismissal at the hands of Robert Neighbors, John Baylor, the former Comanche agent, had plotted revenge. He orchestrated a campaign that blamed the reserve Indians for committing depredations throughout Texas. John Baylor and his cronies used the pages of sympathetic newspapers like Weatherford's *Frontier News* and Waco's *Southern Democrat* to inflame the frontier settlers against the reserve Indians. Baylor was also a charismatic speaker and frequently addressed mass meetings. Won over, his adherents sent petitions to Austin and Washington demanding the Indians' removal. They also began to kill indiscriminately any Indians found off the reserve. It did not matter that their victims included some of the men who had served the Rangers and the cavalry most loyally. When they encountered an Indian carrying government dispatches from Fort Arbuckle to Fort Belknap, they killed and scalped him just as if he had been caught in the act of stealing their horses. The Baylor men, as his partisans were known, also conceived that the cavalry made the situation worse. John Baylor's younger brother George recalled this attitude: "The Comanches had been run out of this country on account of the many bloody murders committed by them on innocent women and children, and the United States troops had taken the part of the Indians."[18] The killing of the Mason and Cameron families fanned to fever heat the settlers' hatred of the reserve Indians.

William Cameron was a cautious man. For mutual security he built his farm near that of another family, named Mason. The nearest town, Jacksboro, was ten miles distant. For a very long time the two families maintained their vigilance, but eventually the absence of Indian signs caused them to relax their guard. In the spring of 1859, Cameron and his teenage son were working in the fields some three hundred yards from the house. They did not carry any weapons. When a large party of Indians attacked, they tried to run back to the cabin. The Indians apparently shot them down. Mrs. Cameron seized a revolver and her baby with the intention of trying to help her husband. Finding the weapon unloaded, she hid in the cow lot. There the Indians found her and split her head open with an axe. Cameron's other son, a young boy, ran screaming toward the Mason home. Alerted, Mason took his gun and ran to meet the boy. The Indians speared the boy and left him for dead. Mason tried to fire but his gun failed. Mrs. Mason ran outside to bring a fresh supply of percussion caps. Before she arrived the Indians killed and scalped him. The Indians then killed Mrs. Mason and her two-year-old child.

When local citizens investigated, it was unclear to them exactly what had taken place. Cameron was known to keep $1,200 in his home. Money was never a motive for an Indian raid, but the money was missing. The locals conjectured that another neighbor, of unsavory reputation, had persuaded the Comanches to commit the crimes. Indeed, but for the chance survival of an eyewitness, the eight-year-old Cameron girl, the crime would not have been solved. A white man had masterminded the crime and actually killed Cameron, although the

Comanches had done the rest of the killing. The white man then rifled Cameron's trunks for the money.

Rumor quickly exaggerated what had taken place. Reputedly, the first white on the scene found Mrs. Mason's body in the corral, her babe still in her arms nursing its dead mother. An experienced local rancher recalled, "Since this was the first bad Indian murder that had occurred on that frontier for many years, it created an unusual excitement because those settlers were not originally frontier people. They were then not accustomed to such horrible occurrences."[19] The inexperienced, panic-stricken settlers were unable to separate rumor from fact and stampeded on the most frivolous of alarms. They were easy prey for the demagogues.

John R. Baylor publicly circulated charges that the reserve Comanches were committing the depredations and that Neighbors was shielding them in order to preserve his salary. Cavalry captain George Stoneman, still smarting from his quarrel with Neighbors, which had led to the humiliation of his transfer from Camp Cooper, covertly provided support for the Baylor faction. In turn, Neighbors refused to engage in a public debate, but he began to travel armed because he was aware that he was becoming one of the most detested white men in Texas.

FOR MORE THAN a year, Major Neighbors had been resigned to his conclusion that the establishment of Indian reserves in Texas, his pet project, toward which he had devoted so much effort, had failed. Peter Garland's massacre and his subsequent success at evading justice simply confirmed Neighbors's opinion that the reserves should be abandoned for the safety of the Indians themselves. In mid-April 1859, Neighbors received authorization from the commissioner of Indian Affairs to move the Indians somewhere to protect them from lawless violence. Neighbors knew that that somewhere could not be in Texas. The commissioner recommended making the move in the fall, after the Indians had harvested their crops. The bureaucrats in Washington did not realize that events were speeding beyond their control. Ranger Buck Barry recalled, "The citizens asked the government . . . to move all the Indians out of Texas so that we might know that when we saw an Indian he was our enemy."[20] When the political authorities seemed slow to respond, the mob gathered in May of 1859.

The Second Cavalry was supposed to be protecting the reserves. But with so much strength concentrated in the north to participate in Van Dorn's campaign, the remaining troopers were stretched very thin. Had a trooper been present in Jacksboro, some thirty-five miles east of Fort Belknap, he would have witnessed an ugly scene. Five hundred men mustered under the leadership of John Baylor and Peter Garland. The town's women presented them with a flag that carried the inscription "Necessity knows no law."[21] A preacher blessed the mob, likening their projected attack on the reserves to a righteous crusade. Baylor had big plans. He deployed his men on several missions: to attack Fort Cooper and capture the artillery; to intercept and destroy the Indians returning from Van Dorn's campaign; and perhaps to make a diversionary demonstration against the Comanche reserve.

Pledging to take no prisoners and to hang any federal troopers who defended the reserve, Baylor led the mob against the Brazos reserve. Defending the reserve was a detachment of regular army infantry. When the mob confronted them, and saw that they were backed by numerous mounted warriors who lived on the reserve, they recoiled. While Baylor equivocated—it was one thing to attack defenseless old men, women, and children, and quite another to face U.S. regulars, even if the odds were something like ten to one in his favor—some of his men grew impatient. They turned on an elderly Indian, killing him and his wife and family. As one member of the mob recalls, it was "a dirty piece of business. They just wanted to be killing some Indians."[22] Driven beyond endurance, the reserve Indians counterattacked.

A running battle battle ensued over the next several hours. Both sets of combatants fought in "savage style . . . each putting to death all the prisoners taken."[23] The Indians then returned to the Brazos reserve. The old Tonkawa leader Placedo, who had served with the Texans ever since 1839, told an officer that this day marked the first time he had fought against the whites. Reflecting upon the day's events, an infantry officer wrote his father, "The fools in this country have opened a sore that will bleed for years."[24]

The Indians serving with Van Dorn had already been warned about the impending conflict and were hurrying to return home. Simultaneously, Neighbors sent a plea for help to the Second Cavalry. Major George Thomas reported that "all civil authority seems to be at an end."[25] He sent an express to Camp Radziminski to recall the cavalry. In response, Lieutenant Robert Eagle led a forced march with sixty troopers to the Comanche reserve. By the time he arrived, tension had ebbed.

The May battle left no doubt that the reserve Indians would have to abandon their homes immediately. Since he had missed participating in Van Dorn's campaign, it fell to Thomas to command the military escort for the Indian removal. On August 1 the Indian exodus from Texas began. A total of 1,112 Indians departed the Brazos reserve, while 384 people left the Comanche reserve. Ironically, they followed the Van Dorn trail north from Fort Belknap, the same track that had been originally laid out by Van Dorn's allied Indians. The Second Cavalry's Companies G and H, along with two infantry companies, provided the escort. The plan was to settle the Indians on the Washita River in present-day Caddo County, Oklahoma. The fear was that during the march Baylor and his mob would attack.

Thomas found himself responding to a bewildering set of civilian-military conflicts of the type the army would again encounter during its peacekeeping deployments in places like Somalia, Haiti, and the Balkans, about a century and a quarter in the future. Local citizens along the line of march claimed that the Indians were taking their cattle and demanded that all brands be carefully inspected. Thomas replied that his troopers were diligently keeping the Indians on the march route so they could not steal livestock. Such harassment made Thomas's life miserable, particularly when he well knew that instead of protecting peaceful Indians from attack by whites, he and his men should have been protecting white settlers against attack from the wild, northern Indians. Thomas was not displeased to receive an order on August 15 to return immediately to Camp Cooper. It marked the formal end of the regiment's association with the Indian reserves. From the time that they first came to Texas, no cavalryman had enjoyed protecting the Indian reserves. The regiment's performance of this duty did not live up to its high standards. A prominent Texas historian concluded, "It must be said that during much of the four years of the reservation's history, the United States Army did not give the protection which even its limited means might have permitted."[26]

Less than a month later Thomas learned that Neighbors had left the Indians in their new home and returned to Texas. However, Neighbors had been foiled in his attempt to reach Camp Cooper by the high waters of the flooded Brazos River. He had camped nearby for the night. Thomas had gotten to know the architect of the Texas Indian reserves better during their time together, and with knowledge came esteem. Thomas learned that Neighbors intended to visit the nearby village of Belknap. Because Thomas had heard many Texans make threatening comments about Neighbors, he passed on this information and offered a cavalry escort. Neighbors had confronted danger too often to believe that he required an armed guard and declined.

After concluding some business in a clerk's office, Neighbors stepped into the street, where an armed man accosted him. The man, a certain Patrick Murphy, spoke: "Neighbors, I understand that you have said that I am a horse-thief. Is it so?"[27]

Neighbors was making a reply when one of Murphy's confederates approached from behind, put his double-barreled shotgun against Neighbors's back, and pulled the trigger. Since it was a civil affair, the assassination fell outside of Thomas's jurisdiction. It is unlikely he could have done anything anyway, since in the event the assassin, although well known and positively identified, escaped arrest. There is little doubt that the killer was part of the group who violently opposed Neighbors's Indian policies.

During the years 1858 and 1859, the Second Cavalry and the Texas militia, both assisted by Indian allies, had shown that they could penetrate the hinterland with large enough force to destroy the Comanches wherever they tried to establish their lodges. The end of 1859 found the Comanches huddled for protection near the Indian agency on the Arkansas River. Around their sanctuary flowed a tremendous emigrant wave moving west in response to the discovery of gold in Colorado. An Indian agent observed that it was a movement "constantly swelling and incapable of control or restraint by the government."[28] Yet events soon proved that the Texas Indian reserves had acted as a buffer between the wild Indians and the settlements. Without their invaluable Indian guides, whites found it exceptionally difficult to anticipate Indian raids or to track the raiders after they struck. So, from their sanctuary on the Arkansas River, young Comanche men still waited for the waxing moon and set out to attack the frontier settlements. It was a situation that could not have endured. The white man would have destroyed the Indians in their homes, but instead the whites turned to destroying one another.

9

Crisis on the Rio Grande

I have been directed by the Honble. Sec'y of War of the U.S., to notify the Mexican authorities on the Rio Grande, that they must break up and disperse the bands of banditti concerned in the outrages against the persons and property of American citizens.

—Robert Lee, 1860 (Lee to Garcia, April 12, 1860, in John William Jones, *The Life and Letters of Robert E. Lee: Soldier and Man*)

___ I. A Rogue Named Cortina ___

The Second Cavalry was falling into a routine, and not all of its habits were good. Because so many officers were so often absent, corporals and sergeants frequently led patrols. This was asking a great deal, and some were unequal to the demand. A settler went to Fort Mason to report that Indians had attacked his ranch and wounded his son. He asked Major Thomas to send a patrol. Thomas promised that the cavalry would be at his house at sunrise. Instead, according to the settler, a sergeant and ten troopers appeared at noon. They "fished and wallowed about" until past 2 P.M., at which time they began to scout. At the place where the attack had occurred they found three arrows and moccasin and horse tracks. They followed the trail for about two miles and then encamped at 4 P.M. At sunrise they continued the "pursuit" and followed the trail for another three miles until it began to rain. The sergeant ended the patrol and returned to the fort, apparently claiming that he had followed the trail for fifteen miles until the rain "destroyed the trail."

When the cavalry had lived near the Indian reserves, troopers got in trouble selling liquor to the Indians. Now that the Indians were gone, some found other illegal activities. The troopers' Colt revolvers were a valuable commodity. Something of a black market developed, with men selling them and then claiming that they had lost them. As early as 1856 Robert Lee had presided over an inquiry into the theft of pistols from Company E. By 1859 the situation had gotten so out of hand that the Adjutant General's Office issued an order stating that a soldier who lost his revolver would be fined $40.[1]

The practice of awarding prize money for the resale of captured horses opened the eyes of unscrupulous troopers to another moneymaking enterprise. Troopers who had risked much but accumulated little wanted something tangible to show for their effort. They, as well as civilian sutlers, knew that there was always a market for stolen horses and mules. It was also widely known that merchants of otherwise fair standing were not above purchasing a quality animal without attending too closely to its origins. Thus the complete business was there for the willing: troopers could obtain, one way or another, horses; sutlers could act as distributors, the essential go-betweens linking the suppliers with the buyers; nearby businessmen provided a ready market for stolen property.

For four years the Second Cavalry had served as a fire brigade, responding to emergencies throughout west Texas regardless of distances traveled or weather conditions. Continual service without a break the regiment left "Jeff Davis's Own" a physically and morally depleted force. Disaffected noncommissioned officers were less eager to impose discipline. Troopers who were nearing the end of their enlistment period were less willing to risk their lives. When confronted with criminal temptation, many fell. Although the regiment's nucleus remained solid, its edges were fraying from wear.

Meanwhile, in faraway Washington, a board of officers had convened in January 1859 to make a final selection of a saddle for the mounted service. The board's three senior officers were Colonel Philip St. George Cooke and Lieutenant Colonels Joseph Johnston and Robert Lee. All three were Virginians. Cooke was a veteran Dragoon, and within the tight-knit, pre–Civil War army fraternity was also the father-in-law of a young cavalry lieutenant named Jeb Stuart. Johnston served with the First Cavalry and had seen enough of government-issue saddles that he replaced his own with a Texas adaptation, the Hope saddle. Johnston would be seated on a Hope saddle at the battle of Seven Pines when a federal bullet disabled him, thus opening the way for Lee to ascend to command of the Army of Northern Virginia. Lee was well aware that the Second Cavalry had entered service with the field-tested Grimsley saddle and the new-model Campbell and that neither had been satisfactory. The board examined and tried various saddles. Lieutenant Jenifer of the Second Cavalry did not complete the design of his saddle in time for the board's consideration, although after he patented it the next year, it would prove popular in both the Union and Confederate armies. Instead, the board recommended one designed by Captain George McClellan of the First Cavalry. The cavalry would continue to use the McClellan saddle for the next eighty-four years; it was McClellan's best contribution to the U.S. Army. But history would better remember McClellan as commander of the Army of the Potomac. Completing the circle of fate that bound the members of the cavalry board, McClellan would be in command of the Army of the Potomac when one of its soldiers fired the unfortunate shot—unfortunate at least from the northern perspective—that wounded Johnston. Thereafer he would be the dupe of Lee's counteroffensive that saved the Confederate capital. During one of its battles, Gaines' Mill, Cooke, who commanded McClellan's Cavalry Reserve, hurled a regiment of U.S. regulars that included the Union-loyal members of the old Second Cavalry into a desperate charge against an infantry brigade commanded by John Bell Hood.

BACK WHEN Twiggs had concentrated the Second Cavalry for Van Dorn's campaigns, he had made decisions regarding the economy of force. Outposts on the Rio Grande had always been expensive. The poor, sandy soil produced little for the garrison's gardens. Grain to feed the horses had to be brought from the Mexican interior, and flour and other provisions shipped from New Orleans to Corpus Christi and then brought inland by mule train. Given the War Department's refusal to sanction cross-border pursuits of Indians, Twiggs reckoned that rather than fetter his scarce manpower at near-useless posts, he would abandon garrisons along the Rio Grande. Then as now it proved difficult to close a military base. Adjacent citizens—Twiggs suspected that most of them were merchants, sutlers, barkeeps, and brothel owners—deluged their political representative with petitions demanding that the bases remain open.[2] Those troopers who had been fortunate enough to be assigned to forts along the relatively heavily populated Rio Grande also thought the order a great pity. Unlike their comrades stationed elsewhere, they had been able to attend fandangos and enjoy the company of Mexican girls. Even a married man such as Richard Johnson took note of these sensual, somewhat exotic women: "Every one smokes, and the gracefulness with which a young maiden handles her cigarette is remarkable."[3] Once the army departed, the Indians quickly moved into this region. An officer reported about the dangers of the road linking San Antonio with El Paso: "Scarcely a mile of it but has its story of Indian murder and plunder . . . [it] is but one long battle ground—a surprise here, robbery of animals there."[4]

Captain Albert Brackett commanded Company I, the only cavalry unit that remained behind to operate west and south of San Antonio. In April 1859 he set out with sixty-seven men to scout toward the Rio Grande. The company came to the Great Comanche Trail, the deeply worn and rutted track along which the Indians moved each year to attack the Mexican provinces of Durango and Chihuahua. The cavalry followed the trail south. Like so many before, it was a march most notable for the suffering man and horse endured because there was no potable water. Five allied Indians from the Brazos reserve led Brackett's men. One of them discovered a band of Comanches in camp ten miles away. Upon receipt of this intelligence, Brackett immediately ordered an approach march. Once more poor Indian camp security allowed the cavalry to deliver a surprise charge. The troopers killed two Indians and captured all of their camp equipage. In the running fight, Brackett's reliable first sergeant Henry Gordon again distinguished himself.

Now Brackett found himself in trouble. The patrol had been subsisting on short rations. In this arid territory, game was scarce. All there was to eat was dried horsemeat captured from the Comanches. Although it was against American policy, Brackett led his men into Mexico to obtain food. Persistent Comanche raids had reduced the Mexican side of the Rio Grande to a desolate wasteland. The cavalry had to march a fatiguing fifty miles before coming to a settlement. While they were resting in San Carlos for the return march, a distraught group of Mexicans rode into town to report that Indians were raiding nearby. The alcalde of San Carlos begged Brackett to help. Brackett later claimed that he suspected that the Indians belonged to the same band he had engaged on the American side of the border. This was a convenient, self-serving invention. Like most cavalry officers, Brackett was frustrated with his inability to locate the enemy. The alcalde's request provided a cherished opportunity. Brackett replied that if some Mexicans joined him, he would attack the Indians.

The alcalde raised a motley force of local citizens and then recruited an unlikely ally. A small group of Seminoles had been hounded from place to place ever since being forced to leave Florida, until they finally settled near San Carlos. They too had been victims of Comanche raids and welcomed the chance for revenge. So, one of the strangest punitive forces ever to campaign on either side of the border moved down the Monclova Road to engage the Comanches. Leading the way were the Indian scouts from the Brazos reserve. Company I followed while the Mexicans and Seminoles, riding an assortment of swaybacked horses, elderly mules, and burros—the only animals the Indians had not stolen—and carrying everything from pitchforks to blunderbusses, brought up the rear. The "army" surprised the Comanches and easily scattered them. The cavalry returned to San Carlos to soak up local adulation before beginning the return march.

Brackett's 600-mile-long patrol had violated the prohibition against pursuing Comanches into Mexico. Texans did not care. The *San Antonio Texan* said that the captain was completely justified because "there is no law of nature that will permit outlaws to commit outrages upon citizens of one nation and then flee to another, and thus, be screened from their guilt and punishment that should await them."[5] The War Department found itself able to overlook the awkward details of Brackett's expedition and merely focused on his patrol's endurance and gallantry when it cited Company I in a general order.

Back north, after completing his mission to escort the reserve Indians out of Texas and having won his struggle against General Twiggs regarding the prerogatives of seniority, Major George

Thomas was free at last to conduct field operations. On October 1, 1859, he led five companies on a grand sweep to the headwaters of the Red and Canadian Rivers. As Van Dorn had done, once he entered Comanche territory Thomas established a supply base. Then the command fanned out in search of Indians. When they struck a fresh trail, matters seemed promising. Apparently a large band of Comanches were returning from a raid into Mexico. The cavalry zealously pursued the Indians all the way to the Cimarron River. Here the trail became obliterated in a bewildering maze of buffalo tracks. Probably the Indians had deliberately driven the bison across the trail, to literally cover their tracks. Perhaps if Indian scouts had accompanied the expedition they could have followed the Indian trail. In their absence, a disappointed Thomas returned to his base on October 31.

After five days of rest he set out again. This time the direction was southwest, all the way to the state boundary with New Mexico. Here Thomas divided his command, sending Lieutenant Royall with two companies to the head of Sweetwater Creek while Thomas searched the tributaries of the Red River with the balance of the command. Neither column found anyone. The Cimarron expedition returned to Camp Cooper after a fifty-three-day campaign. Thomas had led half the regiment into the field and failed to encounter one Indian. It was but another demonstration of the futility of the big sweeps, particularly in the absence of allied Indians. As one experienced frontiersman observed, "Then as always before it was a mistake to expect Indians of the wild tribes to give battle to numbers, or to allow themselves to be found and forced to do so."[6]

In contrast to Major Thomas, Corporal Patrick Collins experienced a notable success. Collins served with Company I, which was based at Camp Ives, a temporary post four miles from that oasis of camels, Camp Verde. He set off in early December with a small detachment to intercept a band of raiding Comanches.

After a lengthy pursuit, Collins found the Indians on the north branch of the Guadalupe River on December 14. During a running battle, the cavalry killed four Comanches and captured most of their animals. Collins received an honorable mention in a general order for having "conducted the scout with discretion and energy."[7] Just as the Cimarron expedition had demonstrated the futility of large sweeps, so Collins showed what small patrols could accomplish.

The removal of the Texas Indians had presumably removed most of the state's horse thieves. When depredations continued along the frontier unabated, some people began to ask why. The easy answer was that it was still the Indians, returning with vengeance to raid around their former homes. Near Christmas of 1859, a cavalry patrol from Camp Cooper had discovered the body of a dead white man near the Clear Fork of the Brazos. On his body was a most revealing letter. It conveyed a set of instructions from some white outlaw boss on the Texas border to another outlaw operating near Camp Cooper. It revealed a bandit organization operating on a vast scale from Texas over the border to the north and possibly all the way to Kansas. The organization concealed its crimes by making it seem as if the Indians were the guilty party. In part the letter said: "Tell our friend of the *Whiteman*"—alluding to Baylor's notorious journal—"above all things, to keep up the Indian excitement" through the spate of bad weather since the gang could not steal horses during this period; "also acquaint our friends of Belknap particularly that it will be necessary to keep the matter up; even if we have to kill or shoot at some fellow there." The writer recommended killing emigrants who were passing through since that would create the necessary "Indian scare" but was less likely to produce a thorough investigation. It was important to keep settlers away from the upper part of the state because that area served as the organization's base and corral for the stolen livestock. The writer complained that the quality of stock obtained in the "last drove were very inferior" and had caused some grumbling over the division of the spoils. The next operation would have to raid farther south to get better animals. Thus, it was doubly necessary to simulate Indian raids and play up the "excitement" in the press in order to provide cover for the next drove.[8] The letter made Major Thomas's eyebrows rise. He dutifully sent the letter to the governor, and it disappeared into the state bureaucracy.

The swirl of disorder and lawlessness around the Indian reservations had provided cover for criminals of all sorts. So it was on the Rio Grande, where a lawless population of whites and Mexicans stirred up trouble that threatened to cause a war.

JUAN NEPOMUCENO CORTINA (or Cortinas) was a Mexican army veteran, a rancher, and depending on one's viewpoint, a great hero and friend to the Mexican peons or a fugitive from Texas justice and a dangerous villain. The Brownsville court had indicted him for murder in 1850. His Texas record numbered at least twenty offenses. Cortina evaded arrest until July 13, 1859, when he returned to Brownsville with some of his followers. What exactly transpired next depended upon who told the story. Cortina entered a coffeehouse, where he saw Marshal Robert Shears arresting a ranchero who had been abusing the coffeehouse keeper. Shears, a bully and an ugly brute of a man, was employing characteristic frontier law-enforcement techniques by beating the unarmed man. Cortina intervened. Cortina may have attempted to explain to the marshal that the ranchero was normally mild-mannered but just now was drunk, and this accounted for his difficult behavior. Local tradition has it that Shears replied, "What is it to you, you damned Mexican?" What next occurred is certain. Cortina drew his pistol and fired a shot. Perhaps this was a warning shot, but Shears did not heed it. Cortina's second shot wounded the marshal in the shoulder. With the ranchero in hand, Cortina fled across the Rio Grande.

Mexicans hailed his exploit. Although 90 percent of the two thousand inhabitants of Brownsville were Mexicans who happened to be American citizens only because the victors drew the national boundaries, law enforcement and everything else on the Texas side of the river were firmly in the hands of the Anglo minority. They enjoyed one standard of justice and applied a quite different one to the Mexicans on both sides of the border. In this case, the Americans organized a posse but desisted when they learned that Cortina had a stronger force.

There the matter rested until September 28, 1859, when many of Brownsville's people crossed the Rio Grande to Matamoros to attend a fiesta and ball in celebration of Mexican independence. Those who remained behind awoke around 3 A.M. to the sounds of gunfire and the cries *"Viva Cheno Cortina!" "Viva Mexico!"* Some townspeople believed they heard the cry to kill the gringos, but at all events when they looked outside they saw that Cortina's gang controlled the streets. He wanted to settle scores with old enemies and have another crack at Marshal Shears. His men stormed the jail in a blaze of bullets. Although Shears went unharmed, two lawmen, one citizen, and a Mexican were killed before Cortina withdrew to his mother's ranch, six miles west of Brownsville. At the behest of the terrified citizens, a Mexican army detachment later arrived to provide security.

Two days later Cortina issued a proclamation that in part presented a loud defiance of the law—there were still six or so Anglos Cortina wanted to kill in order to balance the scales of justice—and in part was a revolutionary manifesto on behalf of oppressed Mexicans. Cortina's actions and words inflamed the border.

On the morning of October 24, a militia unit, the Brownsville Tigers, accompanied notably by a Mexican militia whose leaders also judged Cortina an outlaw, marched on the Cortina ranch. This eighty-man army, complete with two artillery pieces, set off bravely enough but broke on first contact with Cortina's men. They abandoned their artillery and fled. Cortina's star was on the ascent. Adventurers, outlaws, and assorted riffraff flocked to the banner of the Robin Hood on the Rio Grande. Raid and counterraid ensued, leaving the Rio Grande border a wasteland of empty ranches and frightened citizens. On November 22 a group of Texas Rangers suffered a rout at Cortina's hands, with three killed. They retreated to Brownsville, where that night they hanged the only prisoner they had manage to capture. Citizens' complaints, matched in wild exaggeration only by Twiggs's telegram to the secretary of war—"Express from Rio Grande City just in. Brownsville burnt. One hundred Americans murdered. Cortinas on the march for the Nueces with eight hundred men"—prompted authorities in Washington to order the U.S. Army to intervene.[9] Major Samuel P. Heintzelman received command of a force whose objective was to hunt Cortina and his band but not to follow them into Mexico unless in "hot pursuit."[10] Twiggs also ordered the majority of nine of the Second Cavalry's ten companies to march to the threatened border.

At Fort Merrill on November 24, 1859, Captain Stoneman's Company E learned that they were to be part of Heintzelman's expedition. Stoneman's instructions required him to march rapidly to Brownsville. In the event, the need to obtain corn to feed the horses and draft animals delayed the mission. The march was full of the hardships typical of the cavalry's operations in Texas. Four days out from Fort Merrill and the column was toiling through deep sand. On November 30, after a 25-mile march, the cavalry went into camp still 13 miles short of the next water hole. There was enough for the troopers to drink, but the horses and mules went without. The following day a work party went ahead to dig wells. Their efforts produced a meager amount of dirty,

In late 1859 and 1860, in response to Cortina, attention shifted to the Rio Grande. (National Archives)

salty water. After a 13-mile march, each horse received a half pail. An overnight 27-mile march led to some deserted ranches where the column found brackish water in old wells. While they were watering, a norther struck. Henceforth, trouble came from too much rather than not enough water. After an all-day rain, the temperature fell below freezing. The men awoke to find grass and trees coated with ice. When it melted, the ground turned slushy. The weakened animals could barely haul the wagons free from the mire. After slow progress, toiling through deep sand, the column encountered a last obstacle at the rain-swollen Arroyo Colorado, some 31 miles from Brownsville. A slow back-and-forth passage on a small ferryboat conquered this final barrier.

The cavalry was now in the disputed lands where lawlessness seemed the norm. Back in 1856, when Frederick Law Olmsted had toured the border, he had listened to a barkeep explain how to profit enormously by luring soldiers with good whiskey and then substituting rotgut when the soldiers got tight. Olmsted inquired if there were not merchants who did a respectable business. "Oh yes," replied the barkeep, "there's two or three smuggles considerable goods over into Mexico."[11] The Mexican side of the border was worse. It had experienced an ongoing war between the clerical and anticlerical factions that caused near anarchy and was soon to elicit French intervention. In 1859 it was a region where raid and counterraid by Cortina and local vigilantes had left a blighted landscape. Stoneman's column entered Brownsville with broken-down animals and tired men. Once again their assignment was akin to military police duty, and again they found themselves interposed between the citizens and their enemies.

Nominally they were supposed to cooperate with state authorities and the chosen armed force, the Texas Rangers. To many citizens, the Texas Rangers were already heroes. Their captains were household names. One Ranger offered a description of the militia: "Imagine two hundred men dressed in every variety of costume, except the ordinary uniform, armed with double-barreled shot-guns, squirrel rifles, and Colt's six shooters, mounted on small, wiry, half wild horses, with Spanish saddles and Mexican spurs; unshaven, unwashed, undisciplined," riding pell-mell in pursuit of the Indians.[12] Whereas the cavalry's blooded horses required high-quality fodder, the "half wild" Ranger horses refused to eat the unfamiliar corn or grain. There was some mutual respect. Captain Stoneman received an invitation to demonstrate his company's drill to a Ranger company and performed with zeal.

Among many differences, the regulars and the Rangers held opposing notions of what constituted military justice. When the cavalry turned over a prisoner presumed to be one of Cortina's men to the designated civilian authority, the Rangers promptly hanged him. Such behavior caused Heintzelman to write of all Rangers, "They are doing no service & only bringing disgrace upon the country."[13] The feeling was reciprocated. Governor Houston, in turn, complained to the secretary of war that the regular army was "useless" in protecting Texas.[14]

Inevitably, having hurried to reach Brownsville, Stoneman's company now sat around and waited at Fort Brown for someone to figure out how to deal with Cortina. Time weighed less heavily on the officers. They made frequent trips into town or across the border to attend routs, balls, and fandangos. A disgruntled Heintzelman complained that they spent more time attending to young Mexican ladies than to their duties. Stoneman tried to display commendable energy by taking his company into the field in response to an alarm that Cortina's men would attack and plunder a border town. It proved to be yet another wild rumor. "I am here with nothing to do or nothing to report," Stoneman wrote to Heintzelman.[15]

When he had assembled an adequate force, Heintzelman resolved to attack Cortina in his position at his mother's ranch. The subsequent encounter proved disappointing. Cortina quickly discovered that he had no answer to Heintzelman's 24-pounder howitzers crewed by regular artillerists. After a short skirmish, he abandoned his position. Over the ensuing days Heintzelman chased Cortina's band. But the outlaw enjoyed excellent local intelligence and managed to stay one step ahead. A series of skirmishes ensued, with the decisive encounter occurring the day after Christmas. The celebrated Ranger Major Rip Ford led his men in a wild charge, reportedly shouting "You d——d sons of b——s, we have got you!"[16] Cortina's men apparently agreed. They broke before contact. Stoneman's cavalry intercepted their retreat. Armed with the latest-model Sharps carbine, the troopers decimated the fleeing Mexicans.

In February 1860, Cortina attempted to recoup his losses with a bold ambush of a Rio Grande steamer rumored to be carrying cargo valued at $300,000. Someone apparently tipped the plan to the gringos. At any event, Heintzelman's infantry and Ford's Rangers killed twenty-nine of Cortina's men and scattered the remainder. It was said that when the Texas Rangers charged, they screamed like Indians, thus giving voice to the rebel yell that was to terrify foes at Shiloh and Gaines' Mill. Thereafter, Cortina lay low—where, no one knew, but excited rumors of his presence, of another pending raid, swept the border.

—— II. The Virginia Back Heel ——

The same month that Cortina performed his best impression of a Comanche raider by disappearing like the mist into the hinterland, Robert Lee returned to Texas. He had been on leave for twenty-eight months, with most of that time spent attending to domestic affairs. An urgent summons from the War Department delivered by Lieutenant Jeb Stuart interrupted Lee's routine. Stuart told Lee that it seemed that something was taking place at Harpers Ferry. Lee had no idea that he was to participate in one of the decade's decisive events. He did not even take time to change from civilian clothes to his cavalry uniform. With his subsequent capture of John Brown, he climbed to the forefront of public attention, a place where he had not trod since his glory days on the road with Scott to the Halls of Montezuma. Communication had improved dramatically during the Second Cavalry's tour of duty in Texas. The troopers of Company I near Camp Verde learned of Lee's exploit only twenty days after it occurred. They joined in the national praise for their colonel.

It was thus natural for the Buchanan administration to turn to this reliable troubleshooter when it learned about the crisis on

273

the Rio Grande. When Secretary of War John Floyd, the future Confederate coward of Fort Donelson, issued Lee his orders, he did so in the belief that Cortina represented a threat almost equal to that of John Brown. The administration had such confidence in Lee that Floyd gave him two signed letters. One authorized him to pursue raiders caught in the act beyond American borders. The second letter contained a potentially inflammatory directive: if the Mexican authorities failed to act to break Cortina's band, then Lee could invade Mexico and do the job with United States regulars. In the hands of a Mexican-loathing aggressive hothead, the typical army officer of the 1850s, such command latitude would have provoked an international incident in short order. The Buchanan administration believed it had chosen a soldier who could perform as a skilled diplomat.

Lee arrived in San Antonio on February 19, 1860. He found a booming city that had tripled in size over the past three years. It was no longer a raw frontier outpost but rather a somewhat more sophisticated place. No longer did gentlemen traverse the streets armed to the teeth, their wives on one arm, a shotgun cradled in the other. But when Lee replaced Twiggs, who was going home on leave, as acting district commander he learned that on the frontier little had changed. Although events on the Rio Grande seemed critical, Indian troubles on the northern and western frontiers were worse. The redeployment of soldiers to the Rio Grande left the settlements vulnerable. Indicative of the ongoing guerrilla war was a recent Indian raid into the very heart of supposedly secure territory around Camp Colorado. On February 17, raiders stole mules from Camp Cooper itself. The cavalry pursuit recaptured twenty-three mules, but the Indians made off with forty mules and three horses. It was too dangerous for single riders to depart Camp Verde, another heretofore reasonably secure outpost. Like his predecessor, Lee found himself confronting too many threats with too few troops. When he examined the status of his own regiment, Lee learned that the unit's horses were "so worn down by constant service, exposure, and the scarcity of grass" that several perished every time a patrol went out.[17]

Turning his attention south, Lee suspected that the threat posed by Cortina was exaggerated. He referred to the outlaw as "that myth Cortinas." Still, like mushrooms sprouting from wet earth, outlaws flourished over a region from Brownsville to Rio Grande City. Raid and retaliation across the border drove the law-abiding from their ranches. In the face of so many contradictory reports, Lee decided it best to see the Rio Grande frontier in person. "If I can hear of the whereabouts of Mr. Cortina," Lee wrote, "I will endeavor to pick him up."[18] For his journey his nephew Fitz gave him Minnehaha, the beautiful mare that once had belonged to Lieutenant Van Camp. Lee mounted Minnehaha on March 15 and set off with a cavalry escort toward the troubled border. Along the way, Lieutenant Eagle's Company H and Captain Brackett's Company I joined him. Lee maintained a strict march schedule: 4 A.M., reveille; 5:30 A.M., to horse; 2 P.M., final halt to allow horses ample time to graze on the sparse desert vegetation. While they were passing near Laredo a fierce norther descended on the cavalry. Lee ordered the column to break camp and continue until they could find a sheltered campsite with firewood. Forsaking the comforts of town, Lee personally finished supervising the loading of the wagons and set off to rejoin his men. The rain switched to sleet and snow. He failed to find his men until the next morning. In his absence two troopers perished from exposure. Apparently, illicit town whiskey had contributed to their deaths.

When the cavalry finally reached Ringgold Barracks near Rio Grande City, Lee learned that the active Captain Stoneman had been at it again. A Mexican general had informed Heintzelman that Cortina's band was at a ranch named La Mesa, about four

275

miles inside of Mexico. The major passed on the intelligence to Rip Ford. Ford was skeptical but when Stoneman appeared with his cavalry company the next day and said he was heading over the river to bag the outlaw, Ford and his Rangers went along. It was a bungle from the beginning. High water compelled the troopers to cut a ramp one horse wide down to the river and then swim the animals across the Rio Grande. It was slow, noisy work. A wiser man than Stoneman might have realized that the laborious river crossing could not go unnoticed. By 3 A.M. the cavalry and Rangers were in position on the direct road to La Mesa. Ford scouted ahead and found an enemy outpost guarding the road. He led Stoneman along a back route to within a half mile of the ranch. Here an alert group of pickets opened fire. Stoneman heard drums beating the long roll and knew that his foe was alerted.

Stoneman ordered the deployment and charge. The howling troopers overran the ranch after a brief skirmish. As they disarmed their foes the troopers realized the error. These Mexicans belonged to the militia, the Guardia Nacional, and were apparently defending the ranch against Cortina's band!

Naturally the affair infuriated the Mexicans. It did nothing to daunt Stoneman. Within a few days he and his cavalry were back in Mexico. This time, a 60-mile approach march to Cortina's rumored hideout brought the cavalry to the town of Maguey. As Stoneman's command approached, troopers saw a rider break from cover and gallop into town. The cavalry spurred their weary horses in pursuit. Ahead they heard a noisy fusillade, undoubtedly the enemy preparing for battle. Pulses racing, Stoneman led the cavalry into the plaza, where they found the townspeople firing weapons into the air. It was St. Joseph's Day and the Mexicans were celebrating in style. Would the cavalry like to join the fiesta?

* * *

FOR THE DIGNITY of the Second Cavalry and for the nation, saner heads prevailed once Lee arrived on the border. As the command, now reinforced by two more cavalry companies, neared the Rio Grande, it was as if they had marched into a war zone, a region of smoke-blackened chimneys looming above gutted homes, broken-down fences, untilled fields, abandoned homesteads. (Lee could little imagine how soon he would see his beloved Virginia reduced to such scenes.) On Sunday, April 8, Lee rode into the border town of Edinburg. He learned that during the morning Texas Rangers and Mexican soldiers had been exchanging shots across the river. The Rangers claimed that the Mexicans had fired first. In contrast to Stoneman's conduct, and even though he, unlike Stoneman, possessed orders permitting a cross-border attack, Lee acted cautiously. Reynosa, the Mexican town across the river, appeared curiously deserted. Lee sent a trooper to the river waving a white flag of truce. There was no response. A fierce wind began blowing dust everywhere. It was an eerie situation that had the possibility of becoming something much worse. Lee sent Captain Brackett across the river under a flag of truce to demand that the Mexicans cease firing across the border and to inquire about Cortina.

Brackett found the town in a state of high excitement, the streets barricaded, artillery in place, four infantry companies assembled in the plaza. The Mexican commander expected reinforcements momentarily. Five anxious hours later a courier delivered a message to Lee. It was a chronicle of Mexican complaints beginning with the time that Ford's Rangers had crossed into Reynosa and occupied the town. Since then, the citizens of Reynosa had been afraid even to go to the river to draw water because they had been repeatedly fired upon. Lee queried Rip Ford, and the Ranger confirmed that he had scouted the town while searching for Cortina. Here was the tinder to ignite a cross-border conflagration: aggressive, heedless Texas Rangers; prideful

Mexican authorities whom Lee suspected were harboring Cortina's gang. However, Mexican authorities acknowledged that someone on their side of the river had fired first this day. For this they apologized. Regarding Cortina, the alcalde as well as military officers insisted that he had fled to the interior and pledged their help to arrest him if he returned.

The day had been tense. A misstep by Lee, Brackett, or the Mexicans might have led to war. Instead, Lee handled matters delicately and by so doing defused a dangerous moment. Rip Ford described his impressions of Colonel Lee's commanding presence: "His appearance was dignified, without hauteur, grand without pride, and in keeping with the noble simplicity characterizing a true republican. He evinced an imperturbable self-possession, and a complete control of his passions. To approach him was to feel yourself in the presence of a man of superior intellect, possessing the capacity to accomplish great ends, and the gift of controlling and leading men."[19]

Rather than set off in pursuit and risk exacerbating border tensions, Lee proceeded to Fort Brown. He began a series of written exchanges with Mexican authorities that were a well-calculated mix of threat and cordiality. To Governor Andres Treviño of Tamaulipas he showed his assertive hand: "In consequence of the recent outrages of Cortinas and his followers upon the persons and property of American citizens, I have been instructed by the Sec'y of War of the U.S. to notify the authorities of Mexico on the Rio Grande frontier, that they must break up and disperse the bands of banditti which have been concerned in these depredations and have sought protection in Mexican territory."[20]

When he contacted other Mexican authorities he emphasized the mutual benefits of preserving peace. After some back-and-forth negotiation—Lee described them as a "sharp correspondence"—Lee concluded that he had received the desired promises from Mexican leaders.[21] In fact, Mexico had descended into near anarchy, so there was little likelihood that the government, regardless of its true intent, could control Cortina and his ilk.

Having assessed the border environment, Lee concluded that Indians, Mexicans, and Americans would commit crimes when it could be done with impunity. He judged that it would require twenty thousand troops to defend adequately the region's isolated ranches and small towns. As for Cortina, his most reliable intelligence placed the outlaw some 135 miles inside Mexico. Although Mexican authorities pledged that they would capture him, Lee doubted it. On the other hand, he did not want to conduct a blind pursuit so far into the interior. His troopers' horses were already broken down and the region's thin chaparral and mountains would not provide adequate forage to sustain a chase.

Lee assigned 40 percent of the Second Cavalry to patrol the border and returned to headquarters in San Antonio. The four cavalry companies were inadequate, yet in the absence of the Second Cavalry the Comanches had intensified their attacks along Texas's western border. Lee's mission had been successful only as a show of force. The sight of uniformed troopers riding patrol heartened the citizens. A delicate border situation had been stabilized. But the underlying problems had not been dealt with. "That myth Cortinas" would return to raid the border, rise to become a general in the Mexican army, and eventually serve as governor of Tamaulipas. Overall, the entire affair foreshadowed events in 1916, when Pancho Villa and General John Pershing confronted each other along this same border.

For the Second Cavalry, the Cortina affair was simply more of the same sort of arduous and fruitless patrolling that they had experienced against the Comanches. Cortina's raid affected many Texans differently. They had barely digested the shocking news of John Brown's raid when, to their minds, something very similar happened in their own state. Comanches to the north, Cortina to the south—to them it seemed that in spite of the Second Cavalry's best efforts, the federal government was unable to provide security for Texas.

IN THE FALL of 1859, the cavalry abandoned Camp Radziminski. It was simply too difficult and too expensive to supply this isolated camp. Before the cavalry departed, the camp witnessed another memorable horserace. The irrepressible Fitzhugh Lee had recovered so completely as to accept Lieutenant Royall's challenge. Each rider could name any horse to serve as his mount, and each would ride the race himself. Royall believed that he had a secret advantage. He had recently purchased a splendid animal at Fort Smith that had won every contest run. But Fitz Lee rode Bumble-Bee, the still-undefeated victor of the Fort Mason Derby. Moreover, until recently Bumble-Bee had been receiving tender stable care as the regiment's equine champion, while Royall's horse had been depleted by field service. In the presence of the entire garrison the race was run. Fitzhugh Lee, riding the invincible Bumble-Bee, triumphed.

Fitz Lee was once again enjoying life. He was not a deep thinker, preferring to view life as a series of grand adventures to be met as they came. In a letter home he reflected about how he survived "a severe ordeal." He described the rigors of patrolling in Texas, the hostile climate, the poor food, and thirst. There was little chance for glory, yet he concluded that he enjoyed the life because, "apart from the excitement of catching Comanches, there is always fine hunting and fishing."[22]

The troopers rode south to Camp Cooper. Their "little major," Van Dorn, was no longer with them. In recognition of his two successful campaigns, he received a posting to Fort Mason, where he served as assistant regimental commander. This left the senior captain, Kirby Smith, to grapple with his first important exercise in independent command. Recent expeditions had again depleted the regiment. In camp were 150 broken-down horses and some fifty to sixty sick men. Smith had only one officer to assist him. Somewhat to his surprise, Smith learned that his shoulders were broad enough to carry "all the trouble of six companies."[23] By Christmas, Smith moved from the dreary Camp Cooper to Camp Colorado. Although this post was forty miles from the settlements, it was altogether an improvement. It had comfortable quarters built from pickets and enjoyed good water. Like most of the regiment's officers, Smith was an avid hunter. Game around Camp Colorado was amazingly abundant. For Christmas dinner, Smith shot six large turkeys within fifteen minutes. Still, at this poignant time of year he longed for home. "I would relish," wrote Smith to his mother, "a dish of ripe tomatoes, some old-fashioned boiled potatoes, or a generous pile of smoking roasting ears."[24] Worse, it would be a dry Christmas without a celebratory glass of eggnog. Fortunately, the camp was on the route linking San Antonio with Fort Belknap. Thus Smith gratefully received a Christmas gift from his mother, a book in which to immerse himself and thereby live, at least for a while, in another, more comfortable place.

The persistent attacks by small parties of Indians drew the cavalry out in all sorts of weather. Occasionally, those "dangerous visitors," the ferocious Texas northers, struck without warning. One sleet storm caught Smith's patrol thirty miles from Camp Colorado. The troopers took shelter in a ravine and waited as one storm came hard on the heels of another. But for the presence of a demijohn of whiskey, Smith believed, they might have perished. Although his patrol safely returned to camp over snow-covered ground, the storm's lethal potential was manifest when he learned that a teamster had been caught overnight and frozen to death. To endure in such conditions required great hardihood. With considerable pride, Smith described his troopers as "perfect Cossacks, they ride day and night, carry 7 to 10 days provisions on their backs, sleep out on their saddle blankets in cold and rain without murmur and take their rifles, and ambush" the Indians.[25] Around the time that he penned these words, Smith was reminded that sometimes the Indians ambushed the cavalry.

Near midnight on January 14, 1860, a settler rode into Camp Colorado to report the Comanches were raiding about sixteen miles away. So far they had stolen twenty-four mules and horses. Lieutenant Fitzhugh Lee had just returned that same evening after attending the galas surrounding the inauguration of Governor Sam Houston in Austin. Perhaps the alcoholic cheer of that event had yet to wear off. At any rate, Lee volunteered to lead a detachment against the raiders. Twenty troopers, a noncommissioned officer, and a bugler from Kirby Smith's own Company B followed Lee's Minnehaha out into a cold Texas night. A howling norther was blowing. Progress reduced to a walk through ever-thickening drifts. Finally, at daybreak the patrol reached the area where the Indians had been active.

Surprisingly, in spite of the wind, the troopers could plainly follow the Indian tracks through the newly fallen snow. For eighteen hours the detachment trailed the raiders without a halt. On the night of January 15, Lee ordered the first rest for his iron troopers. He forbade fires, so they ate hardtack and frozen pork before bedding down. At dawn the patrol continued. Some troopers were so stiff from the cold that their comrades had to help them into the saddle. As the day progressed, a bright, warming sun appeared. The melting snow still revealed the Comanches' path. By midafternoon the detachment overtook the raiders, who were driving their herd up Pecan Bayou. The overconfident Indians were oblivious to the pursuit. Lee ordered his troopers to draw their revolvers and charge.

The Indians scattered into the trees in shocked surprise. The charging cavalry trapped two warriors who were at the rear of the herd. A trooper shot one. The other aimed his bow and shot two arrows at Lee and his faithful bugler, Jack Hayes, before running into the tree line. This was entirely too personal for Lee, and he set off in pursuit. It was easy to follow the Indian's tracks through the snow, although Lee only caught glimpses of the man himself when his foe entered the open glades among the trees. The terrain became rugged, hills separated by deep and crooked ravines, the ground covered with a close growth of cedar. The Comanche realized that his mount could not outrun Lee's fleet Minnehaha. While out of sight, he dismounted, concealed his pony in a ravine, and attempted to escape on foot. Lee recognized the ploy. He, Hayes, and four troopers also dismounted and followed the moccasin prints through the snow. They tracked the Indian for three hours but became scattered. This gave the brave warrior his chance. He baited his trap with his blanket and then crouched in ambush. In Lee's words,

> [I] finally came to a little precipice, down which I saw his red blanket, which he had dropped. Clambering down that, I picked up and examined his blanket. I was then within six feet of him and did not know it. Seeing where he had jumped down another little descent by a ledge of rocks, I jumped down also and in an instant he sprang upon me, leaping in the air and alighting with his breast upon my head. He had an arrow in his bow, the sharp point of which he placed against my breast, but, just as he shot, I sprang to one side and the arrow passed through the sleeve of my coat.

Lee carried an older-model muzzle-loading carbine and had a navy Colt attached to his waist. The arrow shattered the carbine's stock. Dropping his useless carbine, Lee began grappling with his assailant. His heavy overcoat and cape restricted his movements. Perhaps memories of the martial arts training he had received from George Cosby back at West Point came to the fore. He wrenched the bow away, drew his revolver, and began hitting the Indian across the head and eyes. The warrior replied with slashing knife strokes. "Finding however, that he pressed me so tight that I could not get a chance to cock my revolver, I dropped it, and seizing him with both hands near the waist, raised him high above the ground, tripped him, and fell with my whole weight upon him; but then I was in a quandry. Here was I on top, holding down, breast to breast, a live Camanche, and a very slippery one, with nothing to kill him!"

At that point Hayes arrived. Together they restrained the warrior until Lee recovered his revolver and shot him through both cheeks. A second, better-aimed shot killed. Lee searched himself for wounds. Although the knife strokes had slashed his outer garments to ribbons, his skin remained untouched. When Hayes asked him how he had brought down the Indian, Lee explained that his opponent, although very strong, "knew nothing of the science of wrestling." Lee employed a wrestling trick he had learned during his school days in Virginia: the Virginia back heel. "I tried it on him and fotched him down." Lee gathered the fallen warrior's weapons and led the triumphal return to Camp Colorado. In addition to having killed two Indians, the patrol recaptured twenty-five horses. But the lieutenant was proudest of the spoils of war captured in single combat. According to Captain Smith, Lee displayed the Indian's "shield, head dress and arms with great pride."[26]

10

Twiggs's Treachery

I have a great deal of charity for many men who drifted away into the rebellion, but for General Twiggs none whatever. He knew his duty and did it not.

—Richard Johnson, 1886 (in *A Soldier's Reminiscences in Peace and War*)

___ I. Full Circle ___

Along the thousand miles of Texas frontier defended by the Second Cavalry, one word dominated soldier talk: secession! For most troopers it was an abstract concept. They had turned their backs on home when they enlisted in the Second Cavalry. Thereafter, the regiment served as their family and government. Their interests and loyalty focused on the Second Cavalry. The officers, on the other hand, had retained close ties to their homes, in part because local politics influenced their future chances at promotion. For them the news from home was unsettling. Captain Kirby Smith learned from his mother back in Florida how secession talk was becoming ever more popular. The South's belligerency was incomprehensible to him. Few outdid his own mother: "Southern men and Southern women will not sit down with folded hands if the masses elect a Black Republican President." Smith sadly replied, "A fratricidal war looms on the horizon."[1]

John Brown's bid to foment a slave insurrection inspired fear throughout the South. Texas was no different. All during 1860, conspiracy rumors swept the state: reports of northern agents-provocateurs, abolitionists, and rebellious slaves setting fires and poisoning wells. Committees of public safety formed. Texas teetered on the edge of lynch-mob rule. Yet the Second Cavalry's duty remained unchanged. The excitement over Cortina subsided. By the late summer the Rio Grande presented a quiet border, interrupted only by outbursts of horse stealing. Captain Stoneman reported that Mexicans, presumably members of Cortina's gang, crossed the border to steal Texas horses and that Rangers and Knights of the Golden Circle bought them for profitable resale. As for Cortina himself, no one seemed to know where he was or what he was doing.

A hot, drought-stricken summer arrived to parch the land and to dry up the watercourses. In spite of, and perhaps because of, the eviction of the Texas Indians from their reserves, 1860 seemed to bring increased raiding. Dispersed groups of two or three Comanches and Kiowas, separated by ten to twelve miles and operating on foot so as to leave no trace on the dry rocky soil, entered the settlements. They waited for a moonlit night, the Comanche moon, and rounded up scores of horses. Then they took off on a hard ride for the Staked Plain. Their goal was to reach buffalo country along the upper Canadian River, where the still-great herds would obscure their tracks. Switching horses frequently, leaving the lame and hobbled behind, these raiders covered eighty miles a day. They hit particularly hard at the area west and northwest of San Antonio. In a typical incident, Buck Barry led a cavalry patrol from Camp Cooper in the hopes of avenging the murder of Mrs. Woods and Mrs. Lemley and the capture of two Lemley girls. Barry discovered where the raiders had crossed the stage route and led the cavalry toward Fort Phantom Hill. Here they lost the trail. The patrol counter-marched six miles to find a fresh Indian trail made by a different set of raiders. That night Indians stole horses from the cavalry's picket line. If the troopers could not even secure their own horses, it was unlikely they could do much to protect the live-stock of the settlers. Even Buck Barry had a similar experience later in the year, when he returned from chasing Indians to learn that during his absence raiders had taken his own horses, includ-ing his nine-year-old son's favorite mount.

Another Ranger captain described how he sent out far-ranging patrols to crisscross the land between Fort Mason and Camp Colorado. Because he was an experienced frontiersman, he doubted the effort would prove worthwhile: "I hope and trust I may be able to come up with Indians in a conciderable body for that is my only hope of any success as they come down on foot and in small parties and its impossible to know any thing of there whar bouts until they deprecate and then its next to imposible to catch them."[2]

The Second Cavalry was evolving along a path followed by all combat units. Many skilled veterans had become somewhat war weary, others grew cautious as their term of enlistment neared its end. Regimental strength declined. The reality of ser-vice in Texas had triggered heavy desertion back in 1857. A sec-ond large group of enlistments had replenished the ranks, but now their enlistments ran out and many returned to civilian life. Another 102 troopers deserted during 1860. Then there were battle losses. In July 1860 a trooper named Flinn left Camp Verde for San Antonio. On his return he rode to within five miles of camp before the Comanches killed him. In August, Corporal John Rutter led a patrol from Company B out of Camp Colorado to chase Indian raiders. Because a succession of thunderstorms persisted for the next two days, he was able to track the Indians until he came to swollen Sabano Creek. The water was so high that several troopers and their mounts disappeared briefly beneath the waves when the patrol forded the creek. Rutter's men reached the opposite shore to find themselves directly below the Indian camp. The corporal ordered an immediate charge. Powder had been soaked during the crossing. Only a few weapons could fire. A brief melee ensued but the Comanches perceived that the troopers' firearms were disabled. They managed to kill Private James Cunningham and escape. Captain Smith wrote, "One of my men was unfortunately killed the other day in action with the Comanches, his was a soldier's fate—the shouts of his victorious comrades was his funeral requiem."[3] Fourteen other troopers shared Cunningham's "soldier's fate" during the year.

On July 23, Major Thomas led one of the last major cavalry expeditions. He departed Camp Cooper to scout the headwaters of the Colorado and the Concho. Because four companies were still stationed on the Rio Grande, Thomas compensated by ordering every able-bodied trooper into the field. Thirteen soldiers of the regimental band left their instruments behind and accompanied Thomas, along with a handful of recruits awaiting assignment. While on the march, companies commanded by Captain Richard Johnson, Lieutenant Fitzhugh Lee, and Lieutenant A. Parker Porter joined Thomas. With a combined strength of more than a hundred men, the cavalry carried out a thorough reconnaissance. Typically, they failed to find any Indians. Thomas divided his command so they could cover more ground and led his own detachment back toward Camp Cooper. On the return journey a Delaware scout reported that he had cut an Indian trail 25 miles away. Thomas immediately set out on a hard, fast pursuit. Belying his Civil War name of Old Slow Trot, his detachment covered 40 miles before resting. At daybreak the following day, they rode another 20 miles until the Delaware scout surmounted a small butte. He motioned to the troopers. A mile

A Mexican War–era feud with General Twiggs relegated Major George H. Thomas to rear-area duty when Van Dorn marched north. Thereafter he served as regimental commander during the summer of 1860 and received a serious arrow wound. (National Archives)

away was a small Comanche encampment. There appeared to be about a dozen warriors. Their horses were grazing nearby. A deep ravine separated the cavalry from their prey. The troopers negotiated a buffalo track single-file aross the ravine. By that time the Comanches had fled. However, their horse herd slowed their flight. After a 4-mile chase, they abandoned their twenty-eight stolen animals. Still the cavalry pressed the Comanches.

A solitary warrior detached himself to fight a sacrificial rearguard. The tactically adroit response was to detail some men to deal with this man while the balance continued the pursuit. But most of Thomas's men were new to combat and he apparently lost control of them. All the cavalry attacked the solitary warrior. Armed with lance and bow, he defied the swarming troopers, who in their eagerness to participate in the kill seemed to get in one another's way. The Indian was an old man, but his age did not impair his fighting ability. His accurate archery mortally wounded Private William Murphy in the left shoulder. His arrows inflicted serious wounds on bandsmen John Zito and Casper Siddel. Another shot pinned Thomas's chin to his chest, the only combat wound Thomas ever endured. The troopers' revolver fire hit the warrior repeatedly. Still he struggled, jabbing weakly with his lance at the encircling crowd. Private Hugh Clark dismounted to fire his carbine more accurately. Clark's excited horse lashed out with a stunning kick. The Comanche advanced to try to finish off the dazed trooper, but his weak thrust only managed to inflict a slight wound. His lance caught Chief Bugler August Hausser in the left breast before the warrior fell with some twenty wounds.

Thomas instructed the Delaware to ask the Comanche to surrender. The resolute warrior replied, "Surrender? Never! No never! Come on, Longknives!"[4] This brave man's sacrifice covered the escape of his comrades. By the time Thomas had his men in order the Indians were two miles away, riding hard. Many if not most of the officers in the Second Cavalry, certainly Van Dorn or Hood, would have continued the chase. Perhaps his wound disordered his thinking, but Thomas decided that his patrol had done enough.

THE RAIDING SEASON in the autumn of 1860 began with a vengeance. By the time of the dreaded Comanche moon the raiders had again brought terror to the settlers of Parker, Young, Palo

Pinto, and Jack Counties. In the fall of 1860, the scene around Camp Cooper was a frontier in turmoil. Rumor fed on rumor as frightened settlers abandoned their homes, moving their families in "trains of wagons, miles in length," to Camp Cooper or anywhere east to escape.[5] It seemed that Governor Houston's preferred frontier defensive forces, the Texas Rangers and the emergency militia, were no more effective at providing security than the regulars. The *Austin State Gazette* complained that the protection the state troops provided "is a humbug."[6]

In December 1860, the new graduate of Alabama's Florence Wesleyan University, Lawrence Sullivan "Sul" Ross, returned home to receive a commission as captain in the Texas Rangers. The much-feared Comanche chief Peta Nocona was raiding through Parker County. The county was named after the Parker clan, the family who had suffered the appalling raid at Parker's Fort back in 1836. Ross prepared to intercept Peta Nocona but could muster only forty men. He asked Captain Nathan Evans, who was back on duty at Fort Cooper, for reinforcements. Based upon their association during the Wichita campaign, Evans had grown to like Ross. Accordingly, Evans sent Sergeant John Spangler and twenty troopers to assist him.

For six days, Spangler's troopers experienced the familiar cold weather, bad water, and poor grass as Ross's guide led them northwest toward the Pease River. On December 18, a herd of buffalo came thundering toward the column. Ross figured that Indians must have spooked the animals. While the column proceeded down the valley, he personally scouted all the nearby rises until he found what he was looking for: four fresh pony tracks on a sandy hill, marking an enemy scout's outpost. Ross pressed on and saw a Comanche village located on a small winding stream. Because a piercing norther was blowing sand, the Comanches did not see Ross. Alerted by their scout, the Indians were busily breaking camp. Ross sent Spangler's men to circle to the opposite side of a low range of hills where they could intercept the Indians' retreat. Then he led his Rangers in a frontal charge.

It was the usual story. Surprised, the dismounted Comanches fell to the Rangers' shotguns and pistols without offering effective resistance. An Indian leader, easily distinguished by his magnificent gold accoutrements and bison horn headdress, organized a rearguard action. He directed his warriors to form a defensive circle by using their horses as breastworks. The Rangers methodically shot apart the rearguard, but the Comanches' sacrifice allowed their women and children to flee. Unfortunately for them, they ran into an ambush set by Spangler's troopers. Most of the women rode horses heavily laden with buffalo meat, tent poles, and camp equipage. Consequently they moved slowly, and by so doing presented splendid targets. Spangler's detachment gunned them down, killing "every one of them, almost in a pile."[7] A Texas Ranger later wrote that Spangler probably could not recognize the men from the women and probably did not care.

Meanwhile, the survivors of the rearguard scattered. Ross and one of his lieutenants chased a party composed of a pony carrying two mounted warriors and a second horse with a single rider. Ross could see that one of the two riders sharing a horse was the warrior who had organized the rearguard. After a mile-long pursuit, Ross drew near the single rider and was about to shoot when his target held up a bundle and reined in. The rider was a woman and the bundle shrouded an infant child. Ross motioned to one of his Rangers to seize the women and spurred onward. He chased for another half mile. At twenty-yard range he fired his pistol, striking the rearmost rider. This person turned out to be a young girl, about fifteen years of age, but because she rode like a man and was wrapped in a buffalo robe, Ross had mistaken her. Mortally wounded, the girl fell from the horse, dragging the leader with her. Ross galloped forward to administer a killing shot, but the surviving Indian skillfully managed to unleash a volley of arrows. One struck Ross's horse, causing him to buck and almost unseat Ross. While clinging to his pommel, Ross fired again. His lucky shot broke the Indian's right arm at the elbow, rendering him defenseless.

Ross related, "My horse then became quiet, and I shot the chief twice through the body, whereupon he deliberately walked to a small tree, the only one in sight, and leaning against it, began to sing a wild, weird song." In his left hand he held his lance. Ross's Mexican servant rode up. He had once been a Comanche captive and spoke the language. At Ross's request he summoned the wounded man to surrender. The Indian replied with a thrust from his lance. Ross "could only look upon him with pity and admiration." His sentiment did not last long. Ross ordered the Mexican to finish him with his shotgun.

Ross did not immediately realize it, but he had just executed Peta Nocona. Examining the captive squaw, Ross looked at her face: "This is a white woman, Indians do not have blue eyes."[8] He did not know it but the woman was Cynthia Ann Parker, Peta Nocona's wife, a captive of the Comanches since age nine.

Ross's patrol returned to Camp Cooper with the prisoner, for prisoner she was, having wholly absorbed Indian culture. She spoke no English but through an interpreter revealed an anxious concern about the fate of her two sons, Pecos and Quanah. The whites assured her that no boys had been killed. The knowledge that the sons of Peta Nocona lived seemed to calm the woman. Captain Evans's wife cared for the captive and her infant daughter until relatives came to claim her. Isaac Parker was uncertain of the woman's identity. He happened to mention that his niece's name had been Cynthia Ann. The woman's blue eyes blazed. She slapped her chest and said, "Me Cincee Ann."[9] A short, restless life of deep unhappiness lay ahead for the woman once known as Cynthia Ann Parker.

Although her relatives cut her hair and dressed her in
Anglo clothes, Cynthia Ann Parker's deep unhappiness over her forced separation from her Comanche
family was apparent. (The Texas Collection, Baylor
University)

For Sul Ross it was an episode that enhanced his burgeoning
fame. His triumph had been one-sided. Without any casualties
his command killed fourteen people, captured three warriors
and several women, and seized forty-five horses. Ross sent Governor Houston Peta Nocona's lance and shield for deposition in
the state archives as mementos of this encounter. Houston re-

sponded with praise: "Your success in protecting the frontier gives me great satisfaction. . . . Continue to repel, pursue, and punish every body of Indians coming to the State."[10] For John Spangler and his men, the fight on the Pease River was just one more skirmish. Yet it is fitting that Sergeant Spangler, the regiment's most prominent fighter, received another honorable mention in general orders, because it turned out to be the last combat the Second Cavalry fought in Texas.

—— II. "The Fortunes of War" ——

Prior to statehood, Texas attracted bold frontiersmen, quick-buck artists, drifters, criminals. They had either voluntarily distanced themselves from the eastern union or been involuntarily expatriated by the need to avoid financial or criminal writs of law. If anything united them, it was a proud sense of being a Texan and a dislike of outside authority. Texas had been born in rebellion against Mexican rule less than twenty-five years ago and had been a state for only the past fifteen; hardly enough time had passed for its inhabitants to feel much connection or loyalty to a federal government in distant Washington. One of the promises of the Union was the provision of security. Back in 1858, Rip Ford had declared: "There is no better principle established than, that when a government fails or refuses to protect its citizens the ties of allegiance are dissolved."[11] States' righters pointed at the inability of the federal government to defend the border against the Indians and against Cortina. Militants hinted that abolitionists may have inspired Cortina. In the past thirty years Texans had pledged their loyalty to three different governments: Mexico, the Republic of Texas, and the United States. Comanche raids and Cortina were two reasons that made them ready to pledge loyalty to a fourth government.

Pro-Union sentiment was strongest among the state's large number of German immigrants. In addition, the frontier counties possessed some regard for federal government, partially because they appreciated the army's efforts to defend them, but more important, because the army bases were almost the only market for their goods and services. But the eastern third of Texas politically dominated the state. It had been settled by immigrants from the deep South and had a cotton culture based upon slavery. The bonds of kinship, friendship, and commerce made their regional association with the South stronger than any connection to the Union. A Union-loyal Texan recalls that in 1860, "the ties of legal obligation to the Union and the love for the Union were very feeble forces upon many, if not the most, of the leading men of Texas."[12]

The state also had a large, active organization known as the Knights of the Golden Circle. The state held more than thirty castles, the Knights' name for their lodges, and each had its paramilitary division. The Second Cavalry first encountered them in force during the conflict against Cortina. The Knights were a shadowy, secret organization that combined ardent states' rights with a fear of the spread of Roman Catholicism and the influx of immigrants. Among their inchoate objectives was the expansion of slavery into a great slaveholding empire. Mexican territory just over the border from Texas seemed a fine opportunity, so the Knights had begun massing in Brownsville, where they joined forces with adventurers, soldiers of fortune, drifters, and assorted riffraff.

Likewise, Texas governor Sam Houston still dreamed of military and political glory south of the Rio Grande. He sent an emissary to Robert Lee to inquire if that officer would participate in an expedition into Mexico. The emissary apparently was a Knight of the Golden Circle. Lee stiffly declined, stating that he trusted that peace could be maintained inside of Texas in conformity to federal law and the Constitution. Regretfully, the Knight reported, Lee "would not touch anything that he would consider vulgar filibustering; but he is not without ambition."[13]

The day after news arrived in San Antonio that Lincoln had won election, a published notice circulated to announce a political meeting for proponents of secession. The Knights of the Golden Circle controlled the meeting. Among the speakers was a local lawyer who had emigrated from New York. He uttered proslavery gushes, "out-heroding Herod" in the strident manner of northerners determined to display their southern sympathies. He helped demonstrate that in Texas, as was true throughout the South, the fire-eaters controlled the agenda.

On December 13, Brevet Major General David E. Twiggs returned to district headquarters. He had been enjoying an extended leave in his native Georgia and in New Orleans when he learned of Lincoln's election. The next day he applied to the War Department to resume command. Twiggs was one of the army's most senior officers. He had served as a captain during the nation's second war for independence in 1812 and thereafter steadily rose in rank. Never before—not in the Florida swamps while fighting Seminoles, or in the arroyos of Mexico while serving in Scott's campaign, or as commander of the Department of Texas—had he confronted such a momentous decision. One-fifth of the entire army of the United States was in Texas, and now that state threatened to secede. Twiggs never doubted where his loyalty lay. The day before South Carolina voted for the ordinance of secession, Twiggs confidently told Samuel Heintzelman that the Union was doomed.[14]

On the day he returned, Twiggs sent his first of three formal requests to Washington asking for instructions in the event Texas left the Union. He specifically wanted to know how to dispose of troops and property. Communications between Texas and the War Department slowed to a miserable crawl at this vital

Brigadier General David E. Twiggs was the only regular army officer who performed a dishonorable deed before resigning to go south. (National Archives)

juncture. Part of the problem was that the bureaucrats at the War Department confronted an overwhelming barrage of messages. Worse, General Scott fell sick. Because of the resulting chaos, the War Department did not send a reply for more than two weeks, and Twiggs did not receive it until mid-January, more than a month after he sent his query. Because Scott was too ill to contribute, the War Department's communication was a mere survey of the political horizon and lacked any concrete advice.

298

To his discredit, however, Twiggs did not wait for this reply. Instead, he discreetly let it be known to Texas secessionists that he would surrender federal posts and property to the first armed body who demanded capitulation. Having set the wheels in motion, on January 13, 1861, Twiggs asked to be relieved of command of the Department of Texas.

Just as Twiggs had expected, on February 1 a Texas convention overwhelmingly passed an ordinance of secession. The state legislature affirmed the ordinance and said it was to go to the voters on February 23. Anticipating events, on the day after the approval of the ordinance, the legislature formed a Committee of Public Safety. Its particular mandate was to take over federal property. Thus, a potential collision between Texas citizens and the Second Cavalry loomed. In the words of one irate Union-loyal Texan, the troops had come "only to save our Texas scalps from the Comanches and Mexicans" and now they were the unwitting pawns in a great power struggle.[15]

At this time, federal troops garrisoned some twenty posts ranging from 56 to 675 miles away from headquarters in San Antonio. The typical garrison numbered 50 to 150 soldiers. These weak, isolated outposts were ignorant of developments inside Texas, let alone the gathering wave of insurrection back east. On February 3, 1861, Kirby Smith returned from a scout to write his mother. Although he lacked current news, he observed that by now Florida had probably seceded. Like Twiggs, Smith had decided where his loyalty lay: "I am a southern man in all my feeling and will stand by the fireside whilst the roof tumbles about my ears—and such I fear will be the result in the event of a violent secession."[16] Events would prove that, unlike Twiggs, Smith preserved a sense of duty.

In contrast to the garrison commanders, the key actors in the developing plot to seize federal property in Texas were very aware of every change in local and national affairs. Moreover, both the Knights of the Golden Circle and the Committee of Public Safety knew that they had an ally in Twiggs. However, they doubted that his replacement would be so compliant. Consequently they accelerated their preparations. Five days before voters had their say, representatives of the secession convention brought Twiggs his long-invited request regarding the transfer of United States property. Twiggs cited the convenient absence of orders from the War Department and took it upon himself to appoint commissioners to negotiate surrender terms. On February 18 Twiggs made it official. Claiming that Texas had demanded surrender and that he wanted to avoid any collision between state and federal troops, Twiggs ordered all United States soldiers in Texas to hand over their posts and march to the coast. By this act David Twiggs became the only regular army officer who performed a dishonorable deed before resigning to go south. On March 1, President Lincoln dismissed him from the army "for his treachery to the flag of his country."[17]

AFTER YIELDING district command to Twiggs, Robert Lee rode north to regimental headquarters at Fort Mason. Lee had often experienced some of the worst weather Texas had to offer, and this journey was no different. A blue norther struck, soaking Lee with freezing rain. A biting, cold wind made his roadside campsite miserable. While he was en route, in South Carolina a convention voted unanimously for secession. Lee reached Fort Mason in time to partake in the holiday festivities. He assumed command on Christmas Eve, not knowing that Fort Mason would be his last duty station in the service of the federal government. He expected that Texas would soon secede and pondered a plan to lead the regiment north to safety. In the meantime, the presence of suspicious-looking strangers lurking around the fort worried him. He had personally resolved to defend his post but he did not know how much support he could expect. He summoned Captain Johnson to inquire if he could rely upon him. Johnson replied that as long as he held a commission in the Union Army, he would remain loyal to its flag.

Events were moving fast. During January, Lee was again embroiled in the details of regimental command. On January 30, 1861, word came of an Indian raid. Lee organized a pursuit party. Two weeks later he received a summons to report to General Scott in Washington. As he prepared to depart, there occurred a celebrated exchange. Johnson asked him: "Colonel, do you intend to go South or remain North?"

Lee replied, "I shall never bear arms against the United States,—but it may be necessary for me to carry a musket in defence of my native State, Virginia, in which case I shall not prove recreant to my duty."[18]

On his return ride to San Antonio, Lee encountered Lieutenant George Cosby. Cosby suspected that Lee's recall indicated that Scott wanted to consult with the Virginian about a campaign to suppress the southern insurrection. Lee feared that this was indeed the case. Again he affirmed his intention to resign his commission and offer his services to his native state.

Lee found San Antonio a confused swirl of conflicting loyalties. Already grim-faced men wearing red insignia sewn on their shoulders controlled the streets. Lee asked, "Who are these men?" A woman replied, "They are McCulloch's. General Twiggs surrendered everything to the state this morning." With trembling lip, Lee replied, "Has it come so soon as this?"[19] Next Lee experienced an ugly scene when he found that three ardent secessionists representing the Committee of Public Safety had commandeered district headquarters. They told him that Texas was out of the Union and demanded that Lee join the state in declaring for the new Confederacy. Even among friends Lee possessed a "grave, cold dignity of bearing" with a reserved manner

The Texas flag flies over Twiggs's headquarters as armed secessionists parade in front of the Alamo. (*Harper's Weekly*, March 23, 1861)

that "rather chilled over-early, or over-much intimacy."[20] Faced with this rude test of his loyalty, Lee icily replied that he was still a federal officer, and a Virginian, not a Texan, and he reserved the right to make up his own mind without pressure. He turned on his heel and angrily strode from the room.

The episode reinforced Lee's disdain for the secessionist movement in Texas. Had he not been recalled to Washington, there is every likelihood that the opening engagement of the Civil War would have taken place at Fort Mason instead of Fort Sumter. Instead, Lee's departure from Texas left the Second Cavalry without senior leaders: Johnston and Lee on special duty; Hardee reassigned to the First Cavalry; Thomas on leave; Van Dorn already in Confederate service. At this time the regiment numbered 739 officers and men.[21] They were well-armed, veteran soldiers and by far the most formidable force in Texas.

But they were scattered across Texas and led by junior officers unused to the exercise of higher command. If there was to be a confrontation between the Second Cavalry and the Texas State troops, each company officer would have to decide for himself what to do. To them it seemed that after the Second Cavalry had shed some of their best blood in the state's defense, the very people they had struggled to defend were now turning against them.

When the U.S. Army and the state of Texas had first begun surrender negotiations, the attitude of Texas authorities was different. The Committee of Public Safety solemnly stated its desire to afford the regulars every facility on their journey from the state. "They are our friends," the committee reported. "They have heretofore afforded to our people all the protection in their power, and we owe them every consideration."[22] Once the regulars surrendered, militant secessionists had second thoughts about the terms granted to the United States troops. Ben McCulloch, a onetime leading candidate to command the Second Cavalry, complained that the regulars represented both a powerful enemy if they escaped and an invaluable resource if they could be persuaded to remain. He wanted recruiters sent immediately to intercept the regulars before they departed. Other ardent secessionists wanted something more powerful than persuasion employed. They cared nothing about means: somehow the regulars should not be allowed to slip through Confederate fingers.

While the newly forming Confederate state government pondered all of this, in north Texas Ben McCulloch's brother Henry began executing his assignment to seize federal property. In south Texas, the Second Cavalry's former comrade in arms Rip Ford had the same mission.

* * *

ALTHOUGH TEXAS departed the Union on February 1, 1861, and the district commander was in the process of betraying it to the enemy, the Second Cavalry continued to do what it had done for five years. In midmonth, Captain James Oakes, who had returned from duty after partially recovering from his lung ailment, learned that Comanches were raiding nearby settlements; he ordered a detachment led by Lieutenant Abraham K. Arnold to depart Fort Inge in pursuit. Arnold almost caught the raiders. His close pursuit compelled them to abandon their stolen property. The troopers might have engaged the Comanches themselves except that just ahead lay the Rio Grande. The Indians well appreciated the cavalry's reluctance to enter Mexico. They splashed across the river to safety and left behind the panting troopers to grind their teeth in frustration. Oakes received a vote of thanks from the secession convention. This patrol proved to be the regiment's last mission in Texas.

The Second Cavalry began abandoning its duty posts on February 21, when Captain Innis Palmer led Companies D and H out of Camp Cooper. The same day the cavalry left Camp Verde. A careful accounting of federal property here noted that by far the most valuable asset was the fifty-three camels.

The next day Henry McCulloch and several companies of state troops arrived at Camp Colorado to demand the surrender of the camp, the troopers' arms, equipment, and horses. By so doing McCulloch was exceeding the terms negotiated with Twiggs. Captain Smith did not yet know about Twiggs's perfidy. Exhibiting considerably more strength of character than had that officer, Smith pointedly explained the situation to McCulloch, telling him he could never "negotiate upon terms that would dishonor the troops under my command." If McCulloch forced the issue, Smith would mount his troopers and "endeavor to cut my way through any force opposed to me."[23] It was a delicate moment—on one side, rowdy, loosely disciplined Texas militia;

on the other, angry, irritated veteran cavalrymen. To avoid violence, Smith negotiated to surrender the camp if his men retained their horses, arms, and ten days' rations. Before signing an agreement, Smith received Twiggs's surrender order and saw that it required no substantive changes to the agreement already in place. So Company B evacuated Camp Colorado. It was so hastily done that the officers and men left behind their private property. In Smith's case, this included his cherished bird dogs, Nell and Ugly. For almost four years the Second Cavalry had guarded the nearby crossing of the Colorado River to permit freight, mail, and private travel in safety from San Antonio to the northern frontier. During the Civil War, Camp Colorado became a base for outlaws and deserters to launch raids against the settlements.

At Fort Mason a few days later, Smith learned that he had been promoted to major. Promotion had been painfully slow in the old army. The honor filled him with pride since, at age thirty-six, he was the army's youngest major. He calculated that in the great race to higher rank, he was twenty years ahead of his contemporaries. It was a cherished position, but on March 3 he voluntarily gave it up: "What my future may be I cannot tell. . . . I only know that I sacrifice to my principles more than any other officer in the army." He sadly reflected how his resignation severed "all the associations of my life."[24]

SOME NORTHERN-BORN cavalry officers briefly considered resistance. Captains Oakes, Stoneman, and Whiting met at Fort Inge to discuss uniting their companies and cutting their way north to freedom. They well knew that such an operation required a certain irreducible minimum of logistical support. An inventory of resources revealed that there were simply too few wagons and draft and pack animals, and not enough grain and forage to feed what animals there were. Reluctantly they agreed to adhere to Twiggs's order. Later, some soldiers as well as Union-loyal citizens hinted darkly that the absence of transport and supplies had been carefully orchestrated by Twiggs and his cronies in the Knights of the Golden Circle. Richard Johnson avowed that the movement schedule of troops out of Texas was planned in such a way as to prevent a massing of men sufficient to challenge the armed secessionists. At this remove it is impossible to verify these charges. Probably the same logistical constraints that had plagued cavalry operations throughout its tour of duty accounted for the situation in 1861.

The last post the cavalry held on to was its headquarters at Fort Mason, and it was here that tension almost snapped into violence. In garrison at Fort Mason was Johnson, with headquarters and Companies A and F. Patrolling the nearby countryside was a disagreeable Texas Ranger officer named A. B. Burleson and a group of state troops. Burleson tried to isolate Fort Mason and went so far as to intercept four troopers who were carrying dispatches. His Rangers opened and read the dispatches, something that honorable men simply did not do, and then made the troopers walk sixty miles as virtual prisoners while their captors gleefully rode their horses. Of course, Johnson protested. He received a revealing, candid reply from Burleson: "In doing what I have done I think I have acted right, and I think the commissioners on the part of the State of Texas are a set of jackasses in allowing the regular troops in leaving Texas with their arms; and, to be plain with you, if I had a sufficient force I would make all of you lay down your arms in short order, and if I can get men I will yet do it."[25] Burleson politely concluded by thanking Johnson for the kind treatment he had received while at Fort Mason.

Burleson's superior, Henry McCulloch, disapproved of the Ranger's conduct and handsomely apologized for the incident. So affairs remained calm until March 29, when Johnson ordered the flag hauled down from the parade ground at Fort Mason for the last time. As the disgruntled cavalry withdrew, Johnson turned a blind eye when troopers set the post ablaze.

ANY ARMY OFFICER could resign his commission at any time without a stain on his character. Still, Earl Van Dorn set a rather unseemly example. He had always been an avowed secesionist, which was one reason he got on so well with Twiggs. Like his idol, Napoleon, he possessed boundless ambition. During his time in Texas he believed that he was on a fast track toward promotion. After the fight on Crooked Creek he heard rumors that he was a leading candidate for elevation to major. He happily boasted to his wife that this gave him hope of someday becoming "general of the army." After Lincoln's election, Van Dorn sensed a more immediate opportunity. He sought Twiggs's advice. The old veteran told him to go home and settle his affairs because war loomed. Thus, the breakup of the Union found Van Dorn conveniently back east with his finger on the pulse of rapidly changing events. Whereas almost all southern officers followed their state's lead, Van Dorn anticipated Mississippi's decision. Six days before his state seceded, Van Dorn resigned his commission. He was the first officer in his regiment to do so.

Van Dorn had his eye firmly fixed on the main chance. When Mississippi named Jeff Davis as its major general, it nominated Van Dorn as his senior brigadier. After a short stint helping organize state forces, Van Dorn ascended to Davis's spot when Davis became president. The fame he had achieved in Texas accounted for this rapid rise. But the former captain was a man of action, and this posting was a tedious administrative job. In March he resigned, reported as a volunteer to nearby Fort Jackson, and immediately became an infantry colonel! Then Van Dorn received orders to return to the scene of his exploits: his mission was to travel to Texas to recruit for the Confederacy. The Confederate government had digested reports from Texas claiming that many regulars were merely awaiting direction before joining the Confederate service. One letter to Jefferson Davis specifically mentioned that "a large majority of the Second Cavalry" stood ready to enlist if the proper officer was present to encourage them.[26] Ben McCulloch said that one potentially excellent recruiter had already said that he did not want to leave Texas, namely the renowned Sergeant John Spangler.

As the colonel walked across the gangway to board the steamer *Southern Republic*, he knew he had entered a larger stage, and it pleased him. The public was aware that Van Dorn was bound for Galveston on what they believed to be a momentous, dangerous assignment. Young ladies came to the dock to see the handsome hero of the hour. Men doffed their hats. The dapper Van Dorn stood on the upper deck basking in the glory. Dramatically he lifted his Mexican sombrero adorned with the Texas star to return their salute. When the steamer pulled away from the dock, its calliope played martial music in honor of its famous passenger.

His mission proved anticlimactic. Van Dorn tried to persuade the regular army soldiers, including men of the Second Cavalry, to join the Confederacy. Most officers did not need Van Dorn's velvet tongue to tell them their duty. Kirby Smith, Nathan Evans, John Hood, and many others had already resigned. By the end of March only fourteen officers remained with the regiment. Resignation was not a privilege accorded enlisted men. They knew that failure to complete their terms of service would brand them as deserters. Furthermore, while Van Dorn tugged in one direction, officers such as Hood encouraged them to honor faithfully their obligation. During the regiment's march to the Texas coast, about a hundred men, one-seventh of the regiment's strength, deserted. Almost all were privates. Only one senior noncommissioned officer, a first sergeant in Company B, was among them. Ben McCulloch had seriously misestimated Sergeant Spangler. More days of glory lay before him, but all of them would be in federal uniform.

Having failed to encourage widespread desertion, Van Dorn received a new assignment. Jefferson Davis personally instructed him to use force to block the army's departure from Texas.[27] He was to capture all the regulars he could and to regard them as prisoners of war unless they joined the rebel army. This was a shabby business. The Confederate president took the narrow view that Twiggs's agreement had lost its force when South Carolina opened fire on Fort Sumter. Van Dorn accepted the mission without hesitation: "It may be that in this sad war I shall have to fight some of my old comrades—that would be hard; but it cannot be helped."[28]

Van Dorn threw himself into the effort to round up his former comrades with unseemly zeal. His crowning moment came when he employed a ruse to capture a federal vessel carrying troops out of Texas. The vessel was the *Star of the West*, the famous steamer that had tried to deliver supplies to the beleaguered garrison at Fort Sumter. Van Dorn approached the *Star* on a dark night. He responded to a challenge with the claim that he was a friend bringing more federal troops for transport. The rest was simplicity itself. A sailor passed a line, Van Dorn's volunteers boarded. They easily subdued the surprised crew and the infantrymen belowdecks. Reputedly, the *Star*'s captain accused Van Dorn of "a damned scurvy trick." Van Dorn replied, "You can consider it the fortunes of war. All things are fair when you play that game."[29]

FORTUNATELY FOR the Second Cavalry, the regiment had already departed Texas before Van Dorn began his campaign. Captain

Whiting led a battalion toward the coast during the turbulent days of late March. The unit paraded through San Antonio in style, company guidons and regiment standard displayed proudly, the band playing "Yankee Doodle" and "Hail Columbia." A large group of Union-loyal civilians marched alongside. At a time when emotions ran high, and in an environment where men with guns ruled, theirs was a bold gesture. A citizen who eventually fled Texas recalled, "I could count on the fingers of my hands every Union man, not a German, I knew of whom I could trust."[30] As the troopers departed they courageously presented Whiting with a large United States flag. The next afternoon the battalion entered Goliad. Flying above the square was a secession flag. Some of its enlisted men cut the flag down and used it to make head streamers for the train mules.

Twiggs's orders required the regiment to converge on Indianola, where steamers would be waiting to embark the troopers. The steamboat *Mustang* conveyed Company E to the transports. During the early-morning hours of May 21, First Lieutenant James B. Witherell apparently arose to relieve himself. Witherell had been with the regiment since its birth and, in spite of his nearsightedness, distinguished himself often in combat, beginning with an honorable mention in general orders back in September 1856. The night was dark. The *Mustang* floated low in the water and was without guardrails. Witherell misjudged his step and disappeared overboard. His inglorious end marked the regiment's last fatality during its tour of duty.

One officer remained behind to be caught up in the net cast by Van Dorn and his ilk. Because of illness, Captain Kenner Garrard had stayed behind when the Second Cavalry evacuated Camp Cooper. Garrard had spent most of his service time with the Second Cavalry in staff positions, so it was unsurprising that a rebel roundup of Union troops caught him at departmental headquarters in San Antonio. Fortunately for Garrard, his captors failed to discover the reason he was there. Garrard knew the whereabouts of a large sum of money earmarked as soldiers' pay. He managed to hide about $20,000 on his person before being caught. He accepted a parole and with difficulty made his way to Washington, where he handed the money over to the Treasury. His financial feat was the Second Cavalry's most effective retaliation against the forces of Texas secession.

WITH A NEWLY CONFERRED Confederate lieutenant colonel's insignia on his shoulder, George Baylor—former Comanche Indian agent and leader of the mob who drove the Indians from their Texas reserve—scoured the countryside for enemies. At the same time he eagerly looked out for the return of Albert Sidney Johnston, who was rumored to be en route east from California. Baylor's pickets caught a man trying to steal some of his troopers' horses. After close questioning, an officer said, "You do not bear the appearance of a horse thief."

With no apparent irony, the man replied, "No Sir. I am no thief. I was trying to get them because I need them."[31]

In fact, he was trying to obtain fresh horses for Johnston's weary band. When everyone's pro-Confederate loyalties had been established, the man led Baylor to Johnston. They had known each other back in the days of the Texas Republic. The men embraced. Baylor impetuously offered Johnston command of the local forces, but Johnston replied he was in a hurry to reach the Confederate capital. After a brief rest, Johnston continued east. Before leaving the Texas Cavalry, he said to Lieutenant John Baylor that he did not know if he was to receive a command, but if he did, he wanted the lieutenant to serve on his staff. Johnston proved good to his word. John Baylor was with Johnston at Shiloh and claimed that Johnston died in his arms.

*　*　*

THE SHOCK WAVES of secession had yet to be fully felt while Major George Thomas, on leave from his regiment, contemplated his future. Because of his recent wound and a subsequent accidental fall, he doubted his physical capacity to continue the life of a soldier. Thomas contacted the superintendent of the Virginia Military Institute. Thomas had seen an advertisement in the *National Intelligencer* for a commandant of cadets and an instructor in tactics. It was natural for a West Point graduate, a Mexican War veteran, and a Virginia native to apply for this job. Had Thomas joined VMI's staff, he would have become an instructor alongside a then-obscure professor named Thomas Jackson. Instead, Thomas decided that his oath of allegiance to the United States superseded all else. Among the many personal problems this posed was the fact that he owned a slave. He knew that if he sold her, her fate passed from his hands. Accordingly he arranged for her to return to the family lands in southern Virginia. On April 10, 1861, Thomas's leave was canceled and he was ordered to New York City to take charge of the first echelon of returning Second Cavalry troopers.

Captain Richard Johnson's company was in the second contingent to depart Texas. Their last duty was to turn over their horses to state authorities. Forty-four of their original Kentucky horses remained alive and fit. Johnson's steamer, the *Empire City*, crossed the storm-tossed Gulf of Mexico to Havana, where it stopped to load coal. There the men learned the appalling news that Fort Sumter had been fired upon. The troopers entered New York harbor to see the city bedecked with the Stars and Stripes flying from every housetop, dome, and steeple. A tremendous excitement pervaded. The streets were abuzz with news of the recent riot in Baltimore, where citizens tried to block the passage of a Massachusetts volunteer regiment on its way to Washington. It appeared that the nation's capital was in peril. Yet "everything wore the aspect of a gala day, and the people

The Second Cavalry at dress parade at Carlisle Barracks. The troopers wear the Hardee hat with the crossed saber brass insignia on the front. (U.S. Army Military History Institute, Carlisle Barracks, Pennsylvania)

seemed to be on one grand picnic."[32] To the weathered veterans of the Second Cavalry this seemed incongruous. Unlike the New York civilians, they well knew what war meant.

A sad severing of ties followed as those officers whose loyalties drew them south departed while the remainder joined the enlisted men for the train ride to Carlisle Barracks. An episode on the train partially relieved their gloom. A committee of patriotic Dunkers was distributing sandwiches and lemonade to soldiers passing through. One asked what state the men were from. Johnson's emphatic reply caused the good Samaritans to seize their trays and flee: "This is the Second Cavalry from Texas."[33]

11

Cradle of Leadership

*It is a historical fact that the officers thus selected were superb soldiers,
and that they were from the best to be found in the army and in civil life.*

—George F. Price, *Across the Continent
with the Fifth Cavalry*

SERVICE IN TEXAS provided the officers in "Jeff Davis's Own"
little opportunity for advancement. No one distinguished himself
more than Earl Van Dorn, yet he rose only one step, from senior
captain to major. The plight of Robert Lee was entirely typical.
He had performed with unsurpassed brilliance during the Mexican War, yet by 1860 the fifty-three-year-old officer had spent
twenty-two years advancing from captain to lieutenant colonel.
Prospects for further promotion were negligible. Jefferson Davis
had been able to ignore the claims of seniority when he selected
officers for the Second Cavalry. It had been a unique opportunity.
In 1860 Lee well knew that the rules of seniority appertained.
Between him and the rank of general were twenty-two senior officers. He had been away from his family for most of his military
service, but his personal sacrifice had netted his family little, since

his salary was hardly sufficient to meet his own modest needs. After holding a commission for thirty-one years, his pay was $1,205 per year. On this he had to support a sickly wife and four unmarried daughters.

Even if there had been an opportunity to leap over one's seniors, it is doubtful that anyone would have chosen Lee. His Texas service had been without solid accomplishment. He had tried to "chastise" the Comanche raiders and seldom encountered them. He had tried to keep the reserve Indians on the "white man's road," and they had left the reserve whenever able. He had begun to build Camp Cooper into a permanent, modern post but was reassigned before he had finished. He had tried to capture Cortina and failed. Given this record, it is unsurprising that early in the war, when the Confederate government organized command responsibilities, it placed Lee in decidedly secondary assignments.

Closer inspection of Lee's time in Texas shows that his tour of duty had not been profitless. His long months in a lonely garrison had taught him a commanding stoicism. Nearly everyone who met him commented about it. Through tribulations small and large, Lee also perfected a compelling courtesy. It was a major reason that the junior officers in the Second Cavalry so admired him. It was an attractive part of his character that would serve him well when he took command of the Army of Northern Virginia. Having devoted "the best years of his life" to the army, Lee tendered his resignation to General Scott. The words he chose reveal the inner man: "I have experienced nothing but kindness from my superiors and a most cordial friendship from my comrades."[1]

Because the pace of promotion was so slow in the prewar army, no one anticipated how quickly this would change when North and South mobilized for war. Lee's resignation created a vacancy within the Second Cavalry. On April 25, 1861, Major

Thomas received a promotion to lieutenant colonel to fill it. Eight days later he ascended to colonel to fill the vacancy left by Sidney Johnston's resignation. This was a steep ascent indeed, but it came with a challenge to Thomas's sense of honor. When hostilities began, the United States government required all officers to take the oath of allegiance. Officers viewed this as an uncalled-for insult since they had given this oath when first entering service. Because there were so many real and pressing challenges, Thomas did not think that officers should stand on pride over this issue: "I do not care a snap of my finger about it. If they want me to take the oath before each meal I am ready to comply."[2] It was one of many ways that this extraordinary officer set himself apart.

The Virginia-born Thomas lost much by staying in the U.S. Army. He was an amiable man and had many friends. Henceforth his southern friends and even his family shunned him. Compared to the wounding nature of this behavior, it probably did not bother Thomas that during the war's first summer, when he led his troopers of the Second Cavalry toward Harpers Ferry, awaiting him was his former subordinate Kirby Smith, who now referred to him as "a Virginia renegade."[3]

THE OUTBREAK of Civil War found the Texas secession convention compelled to compensate for the void caused by the departure of the Second Cavalry. It assigned responsibility for defending the frontier against the Indians to the state militia, the Texas Rangers. These men occupied the posts abandoned by the cavalry. They put to the test Sam Houston's claim that Rangers could provide better security than had the regulars. In the event, the militia's experience was little different from that of its predecessors: a great deal of futile patrolling amid enormous physical hardship, with occasional sudden, violent encounters. In April

1861, Earl Van Dorn assumed command in Texas on behalf of the Confederacy. He could come up with nothing more original to defend against Comanche raids than to draw two lines of defense on the map. They proved far too extensive for the available forces.

The same month that Van Dorn assumed command, Confederate agents arranged a council with the Comanches. Their hope was to conclude a peace that would keep the Indians from raiding Texas. According to a member of the diplomatic party, one day and one night spent with the Indians demonstrated the futility of negotiation: "The Comanches flatly refused to join the Confederacy, saying we Tesas were heap rich in cattle and horses, and that they preferred to fight us and steal from us and trade to Mexico—which they did."[4]

As the Civil War progressed, Confederate manpower demands drained the frontier of most able-bodied men. For example, among the 1,160 Texas Rangers who marched east to participate in the early-war struggle for Tennessee were many of the state's most experienced Indian fighters. At their own request, they were allowed to report to Sidney Johnston. They were on the field of Shiloh when Johnston received his mortal wound.

In their absence Texas raised a regiment specifically for frontier defense. The regiment established company-sized outposts a day's ride apart and patrolled the intervening ground frequently. As a veteran frontiersman remarked, "This plan had proved a failure in the first Indian war during the revolution, and it did not answer now."[5] The settlers' plight worsened as the war ground on. By 1863 increasing numbers of lawless white men, their ranks filled with deserters and conscription evaders, began also preying on the frontier settlers.

The Second Cavalry's effectiveness in defending the Texas frontier can be partially measured by what transpired after the regiment departed. So ferocious were the subsequent Indian raids that an entire tier of frontier counties became depopulated as the settlers abandoned their homesteads. The handful of remaining families took shelter at a now vacant Fort Belknap. The wild, natural frontier returned to fill the void. It is said that during snowstorms, buffalo sought shelter in forts' abandoned buildings.[6]

BACK EAST, four companies of the Second Cavalry marched with the Union Army to the battlefield of Bull Run. During the battle proper they did not fight, but they stood firm amid the dreadful panic in the battle's aftermath and by so doing helped cover the retreat. A month later, in August 1861, Congress passed a bill that organized all of the mounted troops into one branch. Henceforth they would all be called cavalry. The regiments received new numbers by seniority, with the Second becoming the Fifth Cavalry.[7] The regiment was unhappy. They were extremely proud of the reputation they had established in Texas and felt that unjustly they now had to begin over again under a new name.

Virginia-born William Royall, a onetime lieutenant in the Second Cavalry, was like George Thomas and stood by his oath of allegiance. Junior officers in the old Second Cavalry had led from the front, often exhibiting reckless disregard for their personal safety. As if determined to prove that nothing had changed just because the regiment had a new name, Royall led two squadrons of the Fifth Cavalry in a dashing charge outside of Richmond in June 1862. His men encountered an overwhelming counterattack. Royall met the Confederates as he had faced the Comanches. He stood at the front of his unit fighting desperately. Surrounded by numerous opponents, he received six saber wounds. Although grievously hurt with a slash on his right wrist that severed a tendon, two cuts on the right side of his head, a two-inch cut on his forehead, a long cut on his cheek, and a skull fracture, Royall managed to fight his way clear. Few doubted that this gallant officer was bound for higher rank, but his injuries cut short a promising career and prevented him from returning to active duty.

In a war that saw former comrades oppose one another in lethal conflict, the old Second Cavalry saw more than its share of fratricidal combat. During Stuart's cavalry ride around McClellan in June 1862, Fitzhugh Lee's First Virginia Cavalry encountered a federal patrol of 150 troopers belonging to the Fifth Cavalry. Whether chasing Comanches or chasing Yankees, for Lee it was all one fine hunt. Among the prisoners his Virginia cavalry captured was a well-remembered sergeant. Amid laughter and jokes, Lee solicitously inquired about the men from his former company. Who had been promoted? Where were they serving? He never stopped "until he found out everything."[8] Since the prisoners could expect to be exchanged soon, the affair was a not entirely unpleasant meeting of old friends. The Fifth Cavalry encountered another former lieutenant in a much more deadly action two weeks later.

On the slopes of Gaines' Mill, the battle's outcome hung in the balance. General Robert Lee's offensive to save Richmond had bogged down against tenacious Union resistance. Lee determined to risk all in one last charge. He summoned John Hood, now an infantry brigadier in command of the army's only Texas soldiers, and explained that the enemy's position had to be stormed or the battle was lost. Lee asked, "Can you break his line?" Hood replied, "I will try."[9] Upon his promotion to brigadier, Hood had promised that he would personally lead the Texas Brigade in its first battle. Now came the time to redeem his promise. In an epic charge Hood's brigade did break the federal line. The impetuous gallantry, and the cost, were like Hood's fight against the Comanches on Devil's River. The brigade lost 570 casualties, one in four men. Hood's old regiment, the Fourth

Texas, suffered a loss rate of about 50 percent. Having pierced the Union defense, the victorious infantry climbed toward the Union batteries on the crest.

Out of their view on the hill's reverse slope were five companies of the Fifth Cavalry. The sun had sunk below the horizon. Battle smoke shrouded the slope. General Philip St. George Cooke rode up to the regiment's commander, Captain Whiting, and ordered Hood's former company commander to charge when he saw the Confederates ascend the crest. Whiting shouted out the order, "Cavalry! Attention! Draw sabre!"[10] Some of these troopers had charged the Comanches at the Wichita village and also rooted them out of their firing positions in the Crooked Creek ravine. Nothing in their experience compared to the volume of fire that met this charge. The Texans in Hood's brigade shot the attack apart. Six of seven officers were hit. Enemy fire dropped Whiting's horse out from under him. He fell dazed to the ground. Two other Second Cavalry veterans, Captain Chambliss and Lieutenant Arnold, were among the casualties. Only Captain Joseph McArthur escaped unharmed.

That night Hood rode over the field looking for his wounded. Around 2 A.M. he heard a voice calling his name over and over again. It was Chambliss, formerly a lieutenant in the Second Cavalry, another Union-loyal Virginian and one of Hood's good friends. He lay on the ground, gravely injured with six wounds. Hood sent a soldier to provide assistance. At dawn Hood's men carried Chambliss to the rear. Miraculously he later recovered in a Richmond hospital, although his crippling wounds prevented his return to active duty. So ended another promising career.

The impact of the Fifth's charge would be debated by the participants during postwar decades. Cooke's aide Wesley Merritt wrote that "the daring charge of the cavalry . . . prevented . . . the capture or dispersion of Fitz John Porter's command." Porter asserted that the charge was unauthorized and after its repulse

The Fifth Cavalry's charge at Gaines' Mill. The Second Cavalry's modern successor bears a coat of arms that includes a cross moline, symbolizing the charge at Gaines' Mill, and five arrows tied with a rattlesnake skin having five rattles, to correspond to the unit's numerical designation and to honor its Indian campaigns. (National Archives)

the regiment's fear-stricken, riderless horses stampeded back through his lines and caused the collapse of the position.[11] What was certain was that one officer and three enlisted men died; three officers and twenty-seven enlisted men received wounds; and two officers and nineteen men—some of whom were also wounded—became prisoners. In a combat that lasted less than five minutes, the regiment suffered more casualties than the combined total of its two biggest battles in Texas. Their sacrifice demonstrated that an impetuous cavalry charge, a tactic appropriate against the Comanches, would fail against rifle-armed infantrymen.

* * *

A SUMMARY OF the Second Cavalry's achievements in Texas must begin by recalling the context of its tour of duty. The United States Army had achieved brilliant victories during the Mexican War. When Texans learned that the army would come to their state to defend them from the Indians, they fully expected a new era of security. Instead, murder and rapine devastated the frontier from 1849 until 1861. When the Second Cavalry departed Texas, little had changed since the time of the unit's arrival. As the people of Texas reflected upon the cavalry's battles with the Comanches, some carefully separated their esteem for the men themselves from their criticism of its accomplishments. A Texas Ranger observed, "The federal government had quartered gallant officers and men in this country but . . . the defense had been inadequate."[12] A rancher who had watched Indians drive off his horses and rape and kill his neighbors was less restrained with his comments. He complained to Governor Houston: "We have been battling here nearly 7 years, and a few sleepy regulars at posts so far from the neighborhoods infested by Indians that they knew and could know nothing of their being in the settlements till they had consummated their mischief and fled have been almost our only protectors."[13]

In retrospect, the Second Cavalry had been given an impossible task. Texas's vast territory included too many invasion corridors, too many regions of alternating valleys and hills covered with scrub cedar and oak for the troopers to patrol effectively. There were simply too few men with too big a mission. Neither the cavalry nor their Confederate successors could prevent Indian raiders from reaching the settlements. The veteran Indian fighter Buck Barry addressed the futility of most defensive measures. Referring to the ease with which the Comanches exacted such a heavy toll of stock from the settlers, he wrote, "In later years, even the trained and especially mounted soldiers could not match the skill of the invaders at this game."[14] Although the cavalry could not defend the frontier, it could have accomplished another part of its mission, namely protecting the Indian reserves. Texas historian Rupert Richardson criticized the job the cavalry performed in these words: "It must be said that during much of the four years of the reservation's history the United States Army did not give the protection which even its limited means might have permitted."[15] It seems clear that the regiment's failure in this regard was more a matter of will than of means.

The enormity of the regiment's challenge is underscored by the fact that the end of the Civil War and the return of hundreds of Confederate veterans to Texas had little effect on reducing Indian attacks against the frontier. The line of settlements continued to recede southward before the savage raids. Indian fighting continued into the 1870s. General William Tecumseh Sherman narrowly escaped from an ambush east of Fort Belknap in 1871. Later, Ranald Mackenzie and Nelson Miles led Indian-hunting expeditions through some of the same bleak territory that the Second Cavalry had formerly patrolled. The physical dangers presented by the Texas environment remained constant. In 1877 a cavalry scout of the Staked Plain picked up an Indian trail. The troopers drank all their water during a vigorous, unsuccessful pursuit. Then their guide became disoriented. The patrol searched fruitlessly for water. Troopers drank horse blood and urine in order to stay alive. For eighty-six hours they went without water. By the time the thirst-maddened patrol stumbled to safety, four men, twenty-three horses, and four mules had died.

Although small parties of Indians would occasionally continue to plague the Texas frontier, when this debacle occurred attacks by organized Comanche bands were a thing of the past. In 1875, Quanah Parker, the son of Cynthia Ann, surrendered the last band of raiding Comanches. The fear of the Comanche moon receded into frontier folklore.

* * *

Fifteen years after the Second Cavalry departed
Texas, Cynthia Ann's son Quanah Parker surren-
dered the last Comanche raiding band. (National
Archives)

IF THE SECOND CAVALRY had been unable to solve the near-
impossible challenge of defending the frontier, it achieves much
higher marks for its ability to nurture officers who would play
decisive roles in the Civil War. The bloodshed of the Civil War
persuaded some veterans that their prewar military preparation
had been inadequate. Jacob Cox caustically asked, "What could
you expect of men who have had to spend their lives at a two-
company post, when there was nothing to do when off duty but

324

play draw-poker and drink whiskey at the sutler's shop?"[16] Richard Ewell reflected that he had learned everything there was to know about commanding fifty Dragoons and not a thing more. In contrast to these postwar comments are words Kirby Smith wrote in 1860: "Our cavalry service on this frontier makes us good partisans . . . and is a school that may be invaluable when the irreversible conflict comes."[17]

Part of the schooling officers received while in garrison in Texas arose out of necessity. The frequent departure of senior officers for court-martial duty left junior officers in charge. Thus, Kirby Smith found himself commanding a large garrison for several months in 1856. Robert Lee left Camp Cooper for court-martial duty at Ringgold Barracks and did not return for more than eight months. During such times the Second Cavalry's lieutenants and captains confronted many of the same challenges that they later faced in the Civil War: administration (including selecting privates worthy of promotion to corporal and sergeants capable of conducting patrols independently), logistics (maintaining the stamina of man and horse in a harsh operational environment), and morale (disciplining the refractory, encouraging the dutiful).

One of the extraordinary aspects of service in the antebellum army was that it put men in intimate contact with officers against whom they would fight in the Civil War. In the Second Cavalry, not everyone profited from the experience. While serving as Major George Thomas's adjutant, Lieutenant Hood learned to respect "his manliness and dignity."[18] But judging from his campaign against Thomas in 1864, he apparently did not absorb anything of military utility. In contrast is an experience related by Richard Johnson. In 1864, Johnson, who commanded a division in Sherman's army, encountered an old colleague from Texas. This officer had known Lieutenant Hood well. He predicted that today there would be a hard fight. Johnson asked him to explain. He replied that he had learned that Hood had just assumed command of the Confederate force defending Atlanta. He had seen Lieutenant Hood play poker, and "a man who will bet a thousand dollars without having a pair in his hand will fight when he has the troops with which to do it."[19] The prediction proved accurate.

The anatomy of leadership is complex. Captain George Stoneman impressed both his fellow officers and important inspectors with his zeal to improve his company. Almost fifty years later, Richard Johnson still remembered him as "strict in discipline and exemplary in habits."[20] Although he assumed command of divisional and corps-sized cavalry units during the Civil War, Stoneman's leadership never rose above mediocrity. However, often there was an essential relationship between a leader's ability to manage his unit's internal economy and the skill he would display in war. As an inspector at Camp Cooper reported, "The post is very well commanded by Col. Lee & in good discipline."[21]

Turning from administration to field operations, with the exception of Van Dorn's two campaigns, the fighting experienced by the Second Cavalry consisted of small-scale skirmishes. At this level, leadership was of the sort unchanged since the dawn of warfare: compel a man to overcome his instinct for self-preservation and close to engage the enemy. This the troopers of the Second Cavalry did repeatedly. Because they typically fought while mounted, troopers had every opportunity to use their mobility to flee. Instead they spurred their horses closer to danger. Their confidence that they held a dominant weapon, their Colt's revolvers, contributed to their aggression, but their trust in their leaders played a larger role.

Success in the field against the Comanches had depended upon bold aggression. The typical engagement required instant decision because any delay would permit the enemy to disperse. This was decidedly not the case in the Civil War, but it was a distinction that some of the Second Cavalry officers failed to discern. In the two battles he conducted as field commander—Elkhorn Tavern and Corinth—Van Dorn behaved as he had in Texas. He conducted a rapid approach march toward the enemy, weather and logistical support be damned. At Elkhorn Tavern his army was weakened by exposure and lack of food, yet still he insisted upon a long flank march in an effort to gain his enemy's rear. At Corinth he relied upon surprise to defeat his foe. This time his men marched beneath a blistering sun through a countryside where many wells were low or empty. At both battles, Van Dorn failed to conduct an adequate reconnaissance. Both featured impetuous, bloody, and unsuccessful charges, and both were Confederate defeats. Likewise, John Hood's tenure at army command featured fighting ferocity and little else.

AT THE BASE of the leadership pyramid is the most numerous class, officers who will obey orders, executing them without any particular flair or genius. Above them are the rarer men who can intelligently orchestrate more complex maneuvers as long as a superior officer provides operational orders. Only a handful of generals prove capable of exhibiting subordinate initiative, the ability to understand their orders and, if need be, adapt them to the unexpected. Such officers are the most valuable of subordinates. Rarest of all are the men capable of independent command—men possessing the moral courage to accept the consequences of issuing orders that might determine the fate of the nation.

While promotion in the Civil War was far from a strict meritocracy—the number of dim-bulb generals on both sides who achieved their rank because of political considerations is legion—eventually an essential relationship between ability and rank emerged. So the men in the Second Cavalry who were merely capable of obeying orders served as regimental officers. They are the less distinguished—the marksman Bradfute, who had killed one of his own men, became a Confederate cavalry colonel; the abolitionist Whiting commanded a cavalry regiment during 1862 and 1863 before being dismissed for speaking disrespectful words about Abraham Lincoln—men whose names appear on the unit's rosters in 1855 as lieutenants and captains and who achieve no special prominence in the Civil War.

Far more displayed real ability, whether in the Union or Confederate Army. The martial arts teacher George Cosby, Travis's antagonist Robert Wood, and the man who saved Sul Ross's life when he killed the Comanche Mohee, James Major, were among those who distinguished themselves at brigade command. Hard-drinking Shanks Evans, fun-loving Fitz Lee, handsome Charlie Field ascended to divisional command at the rank of major general. Some climbed to command corps: drillmaster William Hardee; Robert Lee's bulwark at Fort Mason, Richard Johnson. Most tellingly, the Second Cavalry contributed four of the Confederacy's eight full generals as well as Union army commander George Thomas. A tour of the horizon in the fall of 1864 sees General Lee holding the line in the east, Lieutenant General Hood and Major General Thomas squaring off in the center in Tennessee, and Lieutenant General Kirby Smith holding the Trans-Mississippi.

Jefferson Davis later recalled his anxious wait for Albert Sidney Johnston to appear in the Confederate capital during the war's early months: "I hoped and expected that I had others who would prove generals, but I knew I had *one*, and that was Sidney Johnston."[22] Had he merely looked into the ranks of the Second Cavalry, he would have seen that of the forty-three officers who served in Texas, an astounding sixteen became generals. No other regiment in the American army, before or since, produced so many general officers in such a short time. Jeff Davis's pet regiment was second to none, an unsurpassed cradle of leadership.

Appendix

Band of Brothers, Divided

——— The Regiment ———

After the Civil War, some northerners grumbled that Jefferson Davis must have anticipated that civil war would come. He filled the ranks of his pet regiment with prominent southerners and sent them to Texas for what amounted to a leadership laboratory. For additional evidence, they contrasted the Second Cavalry with its sister regiment. However, this notion does not withstand scrutiny. Massachusetts native Colonel Edwin V. Sumner originally commanded the First Cavalry. Lieutenant Colonel Joseph E. Johnston of Virginia served as his executive officer. Majors John Sedgwick and William H. Emory were majors. Among the other notable officers were Captain George B. McClellan and Lieutenant James Stuart. All would rise far during the Civil War, although as a group they could not compare to the officers in the Second Cavalry. Thirteen of the men originally appointed to the First Cavalry resigned their commissions to serve the South. Seventeen remained loyal to the Union. In the Second Cavalry thirteen of the original officers joined the Confederacy, while twelve fought for the Union.

The Second Cavalry contributed a mounted tradition that spanned the years from the Civil War through Operation Desert Storm. It distinguished itself in the post–Civil War Indian campaigns, where it again fought the Comanches as well as almost every other western tribe. It served in the Philippine insurrection. During 1916–17 it returned to the Mexican border to confront Pancho Villa. The regiment faced the same daunting physical environment that had plagued the Second Cavalry. The march into Mexico killed thirty horses. Thereafter, an average of one horse a day died. World War II found the regiment back in the Pacific, where it was assigned to the First Cavalry Division. It helped clear New Guinea and the Philippines. The division entered Korea three weeks after war broke out and remained for the duration. Known as the Black Knights, the Fifth Cavalry provided the reconnaissance force for the Ninth Infantry Division and contributed some of the 150,000 men who served in the First Cavalry Division (Airmobile) during the Vietnam War.

Vietnam featured a guerrilla-style warfare that would have been familiar to the troopers who served under Sidney Johnston, Robert Lee, Earl Van Dorn, and John Hood. However, the Second Cavalry in Texas never suffered the terrible attrition of Vietnam. The Comanches sought to steal horses, not to kill cavalrymen. In eight years of service in Texas, Kirby Smith recalled only two officers killed. He noted that this was a loss rate lower than the rate of accidents in the South. In contrast, so ferocious was combat in Vietnam that the First Cavalry Division lost more than thirty thousand killed or wounded, a casualty rate five times that suffered in World War II and twice that of the Korean War.

—— The Men ——

*The rank listed in parentheses is the rank
upon entering the Second Cavalry.*

Abraham K. Arnold (second lieutenant, Co. C): After conducting the regiment's last patrol in Texas, Arnold served as the

Fifth's regimental adjutant. Weary of staff duty, he resigned in order to lead a combat company in the Peninsular Campaign. Severely wounded at Gaines' Mill, he recovered to lead the Fifth Cavalry for a very active year in 1863 and 1864. Thereafter he taught cavalry tactics at West Point and returned to Texas in 1870. He commanded field operations against the Apaches in New Mexico throughout the decade and was promoted to brigadier general during the Spanish-American War.

Albert G. Brackett (captain, Co. I): Served as colonel of the Ninth Illinois Cavalry during the Civil War and fought Indians in the west afterward. He wrote a history of the U.S. Cavalry, which was published in 1865.

William R. Bradfute (captain, Co. G): Resigned from the army without being brought to trial for shooting a trooper and became a colonel of cavalry in the Confederate service.

George B. Cosby (second lieutenant, Co. A): He was again under Van Dorn's command in northern Mississippi in the autumn of 1862, this time as a brigadier general commanding a Mississippi cavalry brigade.

Nathan G. Evans (first lieutenant, Co. F): Prominent on the battlefield of First Manassas, where an orderly followed him carrying a "barralito" of whiskey. Posted his brigade of Louisiana and South Carolina Infantry at the Stone Bridge and performed well. His conduct at Ball's Bluff earned him a congressional vote of thanks but his drinking prevented further promotion until late in the war. Tried and acquitted for drunkenness and disobedience. As major general he commanded a division at Hatcher's Run in 1865.

Charles W. Field (first lieutenant, Co. I): Advanced from colonel of the Sixth Virginia Cavalry to infantry brigadier in A. P. Hill's vaunted Light Division. His performance impressed his superiors, including Lee. A severe wound at Second Manassas nearly killed him and he was unready to return to active duty until the spring of 1864. Thereafter he commanded Hood's old division through to war's end. Field surrendered the only thoroughly organized and effective division at Appomattox. After his insurance company failed in 1873, he served as inspector general in the khedive of Egypt's army before returning to the United States. He secured a position as doorkeeper of the House of Representatives, became a civil engineer, and even managed the Indian reservation at Hot Springs, Arkansas, before his death, in 1892.

Kenner Garrard (first lieutenant, Co. K): At the Battle of Gettysburg, Garrard commanded the 146th New York. He led it to Little Round Top, where it contributed to the defense of that key height. When Confederate sharpshooters, possibly Texans firing from Devil's Den, mortally wounded Brigadier General Weed, Garrard assumed brigade command. Promoted to brigadier general, thereafter he commanded a cavalry division in Sherman's army.

William J. Hardee (major): Rapidly rose to lieutenant general in Confederate service and was prominent in almost all of the major battles in the West. Known in the Army of Tennessee as Old Reliable.

James E. Harrison (second lieutenant, Co. H): Although Virginia-born, the former revenue service officer remained with his regiment during the Civil War. Active during the First Bull Run Campaign and in the Peninsula, he won a special commendation from McClellan for gallant conduct at Hanover Court-

House. He commanded the Fifth Cavalry during parts of 1862 and 1863. Because the chief of cavalry wanted this valuable officer to remain with the regiment, he had to decline opportunities for promotion with volunteer regiments. He again distinguished himself during Stoneman's raid toward Richmond. Poor health from exposure, possibly induced during his time in Texas, and sunstroke received just after another gallant performance at Beverly Ford compelled his departure from active service. He died of consumption in 1867.

Edward "Jack" Hayes (bugler, Co. B): The boy who had helped nurse Fitzhugh Lee, Hayes slipped through the lines to join Fitz Lee's Virginia Cavalry. Lee made him return to avoid the label of deserter. Thereafter he served as a Union cavalry officer and received a second lieutenant's commission in the Fifth Cavalry in 1866. He fought in numerous Indian campaigns, rising to brigadier general on the eve of his retirement in 1903.

John Bell Hood (second lieutenant, Co. G): One of the South's outstanding combat commanders, "the gallant Hood" was without peer as brigade and divisional commander. Received a crippling arm wound at Gettysburg and lost most of his right leg at Chickamauga. Promoted beyond his capacity to full general. With Sul Ross's Brigade of Texas Cavalry leading the way, Hood's Army of Tennessee marched north to confront George Thomas's forces in Tennessee in 1864.

Walter H. Jenifer (first lieutenant, Co. B): Received a patent for his saddle in June 1860. Some U.S. officers and many Confederate cavalrymen used it during the Civil War. A major at First Manassas, colonel of the Eighth Virginia Cavalry at Ball's Bluff. Promoted to brigadier general near the end of the war but never served in that grade.

Richard W. Johnson (first lieutenant, Co. G): Began the war as a Union brigadier general serving in the Army of the Ohio. A divisional commander from Stone's River through to the Atlanta Campaign, he received a severe wound at New Hope Church. Briefly served as corps commander and received promotion to major general. A solid subordinate without any particular flair.

Albert Sidney Johnston (colonel): Jefferson Davis appointed his friend full general and sent him to command the huge Department of the West. Driven out of Kentucky, he massed his forces for a counterstroke at Shiloh. Here he was hit in the leg and bled to death before anyone realized that the wound was serious. Whether he would have lived up to Davis's high esteem is an open question.

Manning M. Kimmel (second lieutenant, Co. G): Fought at Bull Run as company commander in the Second Cavalry. Resigned to enter Confederate service as a major, serving as Ben McCulloch's adjutant general. While serving as Van Dorn's chief of staff, Kimmel ushered Dr. Peters into Van Dorn's room and then withdrew, since it appeared to be a personal matter between gentlemen. Unknown to Kimmel, the cuckold Dr. Peters had come to kill his rival. Promoted to brigadier general, Manning continued in staff positions. Among his children was Admiral Husband Kimmel, the naval commander at Pearl Harbor on December 7, 1941.

Fitzhugh Lee (second lieutenant, Co. B): Received a plum posting to West Point as cavalry instructor in December 1860. Resigned on May 3, 1861, rising to major general in command of a cavalry division before he was twenty-eight. At Winchester in 1864 had three horses shot out from under him and received a serious wound. Elected governor of Virginia in 1885, he was consul general in Havana in 1896–98, where he displayed outstanding firmness and tact. A major general of U.S. Volunteers during the Spanish-American War, purportedly in the excitement of battle he urged his men on with exhortations to "charge the Yankees!"

Robert Lee (lieutenant colonel): After conducting a bungled campaign in western Virginia, grew to become the South's outstanding general.

William W. Lowe (second lieutenant, Co. K): Commended for his leadership of a company of Second Cavalry at Bull Run. He received appointment to colonel of the Fifth Iowa Cavalry. Active in the West, he distinguished himself sufficiently to be recommended for promotion to general. State politics interfered even though George Thomas was among his supporters. Thereafter he commanded a cavalry brigade with distinction but never received another step.

James P. Major (second lieutenant, Co. K): Entered Confederate service as an engineer major and served on Van Dorn's staff. Advanced to brigadier general in command of a brigade in the Trans-Mississippi.

Joseph H. McArthur (first lieutenant, Co. H): Helped raise the Sixth Pennsylvania Cavalry (Rush's Lancers) and became a lieutenant colonel of that regiment until mustered out of the volunteer service in order to return to the Fifth Cavalry as a captain. He fell ill on the voyage to Yorktown but returned to duty in June 1862. He was the senior surviving officer after Gaines' Mill and commanded the regiment until a relapse of typhoid fever compelled him to decline further active service.

James Oakes (captain, Co. C): Promoted to major in the regiment in April 1861, he subsequently declined an appointment as brigadier general because of ill health caused by his wounds. As he recovered he accepted a lieutenant colonelcy of the Fourth Cavalry. In this role he saw action at Shiloh and Corinth. Thereafter, poor health again sent him to rear-area duty.

Innis N. Palmer (captain, Co. D.): Commanded the regular cavalry during the First Bull Run Campaign. Appointed a brigadier general in the fall of 1861, he led a brigade in the Peninsular Campaign. Transferred to North Carolina, he commanded a division of the Eighteenth Corps.

Charles W. Phifer (second lieutenant, Co. F): Entered Confederate service as a major. In Corinth in 1862 he worked with "untiring energy" to drill and make soldiers "out of wild Texas boys." As a brigadier general in charge of a brigade, he commanded the Sixth Texas, led by Colonel Sul Ross.

Chief Placedo: The advent of the Civil War and the departure of federal troops left the relocated Texas Indians without protection. Seeking revenge for the skilled assistance that the Tonkawas had given to both the cavalry and the Texas Rangers, the Comanches attacked Placedo's Tonkawas on their new reservation in the Indian Territory and killed Placedo and many of his tribe. Five surviving Tonkawas avenged Placedo by guiding the U.S. Cavalry against the Comanches during the postwar years.

Lawrence Sullivan "Sul" Ross: Had an active Civil War career, rising first to command the Sixth Texas Cavalry Regiment in northern Mississippi and then an entire brigade of Texas troopers during the Atlanta Campaign and Hood's ill-fated invasion of Tennessee. A description of his men in 1863 reveals his troopers still looked very much like Texas Rangers back on the frontier: "What singular looking customers those Texans are, with their large brimmed hats, dark features, shaggy Mexican mustangs, and a lariet . . . around the pummel of their saddles. They are said to be unmerciful to prisoners, but are a tower of strength when there is a fight on hand." Ross returned to Texas after the war, serving as sheriff, state legislator, governor, and president of Texas A&M College.

William B. Royall (first lieutenant, Co. C): The wounds he suffered outside of Richmond disabled him from further field service. He had to decline the proffered command of the Twenty-seventh New Jersey although it was generally understood that he would thereafter be promoted to brigadier general. After performing rear-area assignments for the remainder of the Civil War, he conducted field operations against the Indians, including Crook's 1876 campaign against the Sioux.

Edmund Kirby Smith (captain, Co. B): Appointed brigadier general in June 1861, he commanded an infantry brigade at First Manassas and was severely wounded. Promoted to major general, he transferred west to command the Department of East Tennessee. He led the invasion of Kentucky. Disgusted with Braxton Bragg's leadership, he received a transfer to the Trans-Mississippi Department. He rose to full general. Because he was cut off from Richmond, he had to perform as virtual dictator. His department became known as Kirby Smithdom. He overcame civil-military challenges in ways he never could have dreamed possible back during his lonely days at Camp Cooper. He signed his name Kirby to distinguish himself from other Smiths but neither his family nor friends ever called him that.

John W. Spangler (first sergeant, Co. H): His fighting fame earned him a second lieutenant's commission in the Sixth U.S. Cavalry in May 1861. Full lieutenant on October 24, 1861, and breveted captain July 3, 1863, for gallant and meritorious service in the Gettysburg Campaign. Died when a yellow fever epidemic swept the Gulf coast in 1867.

George Stoneman Jr. (captain, Co. E): Promoted to major, Stoneman served on McClellan's staff during the West Virginia Campaign. He impressed McClellan, who took him to Washington and installed him as commander of the cavalry. After a brief interlude leading infantry, Stoneman became a major general and then Hooker's chief of cavalry for the newly created Cavalry Corps during the Chancellorsville Campaign. At the head of some ten thousand troopers, he conducted an abortive raid into Lee's rear; his failure caused him to be replaced. Out of favor in the Army of the Potomac, he was kicked upstairs to become chief of the Cavalry Bureau until he joined Sherman's command as a cavalry division commander for the 1864 campaign in Georgia. His poor judgment while conducting a raid to liberate the prisoners at Andersonville caused the loss of seven hundred men and his own capture. He was the highest-ranking Union officer to surrender during the entire war. He blamed the disaster on Sherman's interference with a cavalry division commanded by his old Second Cavalry comrade Kennar Garrard. After his exchange he led one more giant cavalry raid against southwestern Virginia that destroyed the Confederate saltworks and lead mines. In sum, Stoneman commanded some of the largest Union cavalry raids of the war. He retired in 1871 to California, where he lived on a magnificent estate near Los Angeles. The state elected him Democratic governor in 1883.

George H. Thomas (major): Appointed brigadier general in August 1861, the "Virginia renegade" did not encounter Kirby Smith during his service in the East. Transferred to Kentucky, he served as divisional commander and then second in command of the Army of the Ohio. He declined a chance at army command and was promoted to major general in April 1862. Thereafter, he served as corps commander until his great day at Chickamauga, where his stubborn defense earned him the nom de guerre the Rock of Chickamauga. Promoted to army command, he served under Grant and Sherman until detached to defend Tennessee against Hood's invasion. His subsequent victories earned him the thanks of Congress, one of only fifteen officers so honored. He was one of the Union's best commanders, and to this day some Virginians think his southern birth was the only thing holding him back from even greater wartime responsibility.

David E. Twiggs (brigadier general, Department of Texas): Three weeks after Lincoln dismissed him for treachery, Twiggs ascended to major general in command of the District of Louisiana. In broken health, he died in mid-July 1862.

Earl Van Dorn (captain, Co. A): Van Dorn rapidly rose to major general and returned east to command a division in Virginia in 1861. In January 1862, he took command of the Trans-Mississippi Department and led his army to defeat at Elkhorn Tavern (Pea Ridge). Thereafter he operated east of the Mississippi River. His bungled battle of Corinth prompted an investigation but he was acquitted of all charges. He transferred to a cavalry command in northern Mississippi. This was a level more appropriate to his gifts. He led successful raids against Grant's line of communication at Holly Springs. An inveterate womanizer, he fulfilled the prophecy he uttered to Lee when he was assassinated by an aggrieved husband on May 7, 1863, after having one carriage ride too many with his assailant's pretty wife.

Charles J. Whiting (captain, Co. K): Exchanged after Gaines' Mill, he returned to command the Fifth Cavalry until promoted to major and transferred to the Second Cavalry. He commanded either his regiment or the Reserve Cavalry Brigade during the Army of the Potomac's battles until he was transferred to command the Portland, Maine, draft station. He was dismissed for using contemptuous and disrespectful words against the president, but Andrew Johnson reinstated him in 1866.

Robert C. Wood Jr. (second lieutenant, Co. B): Following his dispute with Travis, Wood received a wound on the Concho River in 1857. He resigned the army and was in civilian pursuits when the Civil War broke out. Although northern-born, Wood joined the Confederacy and served as a captain on Bragg's staff. Promoted to lieutenant colonel, he served in Kentucky. He distinguished himself as John Morgan's second in command during some of that general's notable raids. Captured and exchanged, he served as a combat colonel in Nathan Forrest's cavalry.

Notes

——— 1. "Jeff Davis's Own" ———

1. Teresa Griffin Viele, *"Following the Drum": A Glimpse of Frontier Life* (New York: Rudd & Carleton, 1858), 171.

2. For a full understanding of the convoluted brevet system, see Percival G. Lowe, *Five Years a Dragoon* (Norman: University of Oklahoma Press, 1965), xvi–xxiii.

3. John B. Hood, *Advance and Retreat: Personal Experiences in the United States and Confederate States Armies* (New Orleans, 1880), 6.

4. Ibid., 7.

5. Rupert N. Richardson in Harold B. Simpson, ed., *Frontier Forts of Texas* (Waco: Texian Press, 1966), xvii.

6. Rupert N. Richardson, *The Comanche Barrier to South Plains Settlement* (Glendale, Calif.: Arthur H. Clark, 1933), 204.

7. Lena Clara Koch, "The Federal Indian Policy in Texas, 1845–1860," *Southwestern Historical Quarterly* 29, no. 1 (July 1925): 20–21.

8. W. C. Holden, "Frontier Defense, 1846–1860," *West Texas State Historical Association Yearbook* 6 (June 1930): 55.

9. Bexar County Committee to E. M. Pease, September 1, 1855, in Dorman H. Winfrey and James M. Day, eds., *The Indian Papers of Texas and the Southwest: 1825–1916*, vol. 3 (Austin: Pemberton Press, 1966), 233.

10. George F. Price, *Across the Continent with the Fifth Cavalry* (New York: Antiquarian Press, 1959), 16.

11. Frederick Law Olmsted, *A Journey through Texas* (New York: Dix, Edward & Co., 1857), 298.

12. Fitzhugh Lee, *General Lee* (Wilmington, N.C.: Broadfoot Publishing Company, 1989), 53.

13. See General Orders, No. 2, Adjutant General's Office, March 12, 1855, in Eben Swift, *The History of the Fifth U.S. Cavalry from March 3, 1855, to December 31,*

1905, 23, in Oversized Document File, 1805–1917, Box 123, Records of the Adjutant General's Office, 1780s–1917, Record Group 94, National Archives.

14. It is undoubtedly Davis's language: "The two regiments of cavalry will be regarded as a distinct army, and promotions therein be regulated accordingly." See General Orders, No. 4, Adjutant General's Office, March 26, 1855, in Eben Swift, *History*, 24 (see note 13).

15. For full details, see the revealing "Subjects by Semester," Appendix Two in James L. Morrison Jr., *"The Best School in the World": West Point, the Pre–Civil War Years 1833–1866* (Kent, Ohio: Kent State University Press, 1986), 161–63.

16. Richard W. Johnson, *Memoirs of Major General George H. Thomas* (Philadelphia: J.B. Lippincott, 1881), 29. Johnson, who served as a divisional commander under Thomas, doubtless heard this story from the general's lips.

17. Fitzhugh Lee, *General Lee*, 54.

18. Charles C. Roland, *Albert Sidney Johnston, Soldier of Three Republics* (Austin: University of Texas Press, 1964), 169.

—— 2. To the Staked Plain ——

1. Richard W. Johnson, *A Soldier's Reminiscences in Peace and War* (Philadelphia: J.B. Lippincott, 1886), 91.

2. Edmund Kirby Smith to his mother, October 20, 1855, Papers of Edmund Kirby Smith, Southern Historical Collection, Manuscripts Department, Wilson Library, University of North Carolina, Chapel Hill.

3. Teresa Griffin Viele, *"Following the Drum": A Glimpse of Frontier Life* (New York: Rudd & Carleton, 1858), 31. Viele relates a winter spent with her husband in Vermont at a recruiting post for the First Infantry, then serving in Texas.

4. Percival G. Lowe, *Five Years a Dragoon* (Norman: University of Oklahoma Press, 1965), 4.

5. Nathaniel C. Hughes Jr., *General William J. Hardee* (Baton Rouge: Louisiana State University Press, 1965), 21.

6. Edmund Kirby Smith to his mother, October 20, 1855, Papers of Edmund Kirby Smith.

7. Albert G. Brackett, *History of the United States Cavalry* (New York: Argonaut Press, 1965), 160–61.

8. Douglas C. McChristian, *The U.S. Army in the West 1870–1880* (Norman: University of Oklahoma Press, 1995), 21.

9. When Congress passed a bill on August 3, 1861, that organized all of the mounted troops into one branch, with all to be called cavalry, it authorized yellow as the color of the new corps.

10. The full details of the regiment's authorized uniform and equipment are in General Order No. 13, August 15, 1855, in Eben Swift, *The History of the Fifth U.S. Cavalry from March 3, 1855, to December 31, 1905*, 25–26, in Oversized Document File, 1805–1917, Box 123, Records of the Adjutant General's Office, 1780s–1917, Record Group 94, National Archives.

11. Robert E. Lee to his wife, July 1, 1855, in J. William Jones, *The Life and Letters of Robert E. Lee: Soldier and Man* (New York: Neale Publishing Company, 1906), 79.

12. William Preston Johnston, *The Life of Albert Sidney Johnston* (New York: D. Appleton & Co., 1878), 187.

13. Albert Sidney Johnston to W. Johnston, September 29, 1855, ibid., 186.

14. James R. Arnold and Roberta Wiener, *The American West: Living the Frontier Dream* (London: Blandford Press, 1996), 140.

15. Edmund Kirby Smith to his mother, November 30, 1855, Papers of Edmund Kirby Smith.

16. Richard C. Robbins and Charles P. Rolland, eds., "The Diary of Eliza (Mrs. Albert Sidney) Johnston," *Southwestern Historical Quarterly* 60, no. 4 (April 1957): 468.

17. Cited in John C. Waugh, *The Class of 1846* (New York: Warner Books, 1994), 142.

18. Robert E. Lee to W. H. F. Lee, May 30, 1858, in Jones, *Life and Letters*, 94.

19. Charles C. Roland, *Albert Sidney Johnston, Soldier of Three Republics* (Austin: University of Texas Press, 1964), 177.

20. Brackett, *History*, 169.

21. "Diary of Eliza Johnston," December 6, 1855, 480.

22. Travis to Ayers, March 3, 1836, in William C. Davis, *Three Roads to the Alamo* (New York: HarperCollins, 1998), 552–53.

23. Johnson, *Reminiscences*, 103.

24. George F. Price, *Across the Continent with the Fifth Cavalry* (New York: Antiquarian Press, 1959), 34.

25. Johnson, *Reminiscences*, 63.

26. "Diary of Eliza Johnston," 482.

27. Albert Sidney Johnston to W. Johnston, January 17, 1856, in Johnston, *Life*, 188.

28. Ibid., 188.

29. For a description of this land in its near-pristine state, a decade before the cavalry came, see United States Senate, 1846, "Message from the President of the United States Communicating a Report of an Expedition Led by Lieutenant Abert, on the Upper Arkansas and through the Country of the Camanche Indians, in the Fall of the Year 1845," 29th Congress, 1st Session, 61ff.

30. "Diary of Eliza Johnston," 487.

____ 3. War without Scruple ____

1. Rupert N. Richardson, *The Comanche Barrier to South Plains Settlement* (Glendale, Calif.: Arthur H. Clark, 1933), 81.

2. Journal of the Campaign of the Regiment of Dragoons, August 27, 1834, in 23rd Congress, 2nd Session, Senate Documents, 79.

3. Richardson, *Comanche Barrier*, 93.

4. Burnet to Neighbors, August 20, 1847, in 30th Congress, 1st Session, Reports of Committees, No. 171, 7.

5. William B. Parker, *Notes Taken through Unexplored Texas* (Austin: Texas State Historical Association, 1984), 235.

6. Randolph B. Marcy, *Thirty Years of Army Life on the Border* (New York, 1866), 156–57.

7. Neighbors to Henderson, December 10, 1847, in Senate Reports, 30th Congress, 1st Session, Reports of Committees, No. 171, 10–11.

8. Richardson, *Comanche Barrier*, 155.

9. W. C. Holden, "Frontier Defense, 1846–1860," *West Texas State Historical Association Yearbook* 6 (June 1930): 41.

10. Rupert N. Richardson in Harold B. Simpson, ed., *Frontier Forts of Texas* (Waco: Texian Press, 1966), xv.

11. Richardson, *Comanche Barrier*, 212.

12. "Negotiations between the United States and the Comanche, Lipan, and Mescalero Tribes of Indians," October 26, 1851, in Dorman H. Winfrey and James M. Day, eds., *The Indian Papers of Texas and the Southwest: 1825–1916*, vol. 3 (Austin: Pemberton Press, 1966), 143.

13. Parker, *Notes*, 241.

14. "Census of Tribes," March 14, 1855, in Winfrey and Day, *Indian Papers*, 217.

15. J. W. Wilbarger, *Indian Depredations in Texas* (Austin: Steck Company, 1935), 504.

16. Richard W. Johnson, *A Soldier's Reminiscences in Peace and War* (Philadelphia: J.B. Lippincott, 1886), 66.

17. Edmund Kirby Smith to his mother, November 1, 1859, Papers of Edmund Kirby Smith, Southern Historical Collection, Manuscripts Department, Wilson Library, University of North Carolina, Chapel Hill.

18. Radziminski to Emory, May 18, 1856, in Nathaniel C. Hughes Jr., *General William J. Hardee* (Baton Rouge: Louisiana State University Press, 1965), 54–55.

19. Support for this assertion comes from Fitzhugh Lee's melee, described in Chapter 7, and from the fact that the cavalry invariably did not take male Indian prisoners.

20. General Order No. 62, September 13, 1856, in Document Files, Adjutant General's Office, Record Group 94, National Archives. General Orders, No. 14, Army Headquarters, November 13, 1857, cited in Harold B. Simpson, *Cry Comanche: The 2nd U.S. Cavalry in Texas, 1855–1861* (Hillsboro, Tex.: Hill Junior College Press, 1979), 68. The expedition is summarized in Eben Swift, *The History of the Fifth U.S. Cavalry from March 3, 1855, to December 31, 1905*, 32, Oversized Document File, 1805–1917, Box 123, Records of the Adjutant General's Office, 1780s–1917, Record Group 94, National Archives. See also Richard C. Robbins and Charles P. Rolland, eds., "The Diary of Eliza (Mrs. Albert Sidney) Johnston," *Southwestern Historical Quarterly* 60, no. 4 (April 1957), 492.

21. Simpson, *Cry Comanche*, 69.

22. Frederick Law Olmsted, *A Journey through Texas* (New York: Dix, Edward & Co., 1857), 298.

23. "Diary of Eliza Johnston," 495.

24. Ibid., 493.

25. For an interesting view of Field before he joined the Second, see Percival G. Lowe, *Five Years a Dragoon* (Norman: University of Oklahoma Press, 1965), 14.

26. Johnson, *Reminiscences*, 107.

27. Albert Sidney Johnston to William Preston Johnston, July 28, 1850, in Charles C. Roland, *Albert Sidney Johnston, Soldier of Three Republics* (Austin: University of Texas Press, 1964), 178.

28. Albert G. Brackett, *History of the United States Cavalry* (New York: Argonaut Press, 1965), 147–48.

29. United States Senate, 1846, "Message from the President of the United States Communicating a Report of an Expedition Led by Lieutenant Abert, on the Upper Arkansas and through the Country of the Camanche Indians, in the Fall of the Year 1845," 29th Congress, 1st Session, 48–49.

30. Robert E. Lee to his wife, April 12, 1856, in Douglas S. Freeman, *R. E. Lee*, vol. 1. (New York: Charles Scribner's Sons, 1934), 364.

31. Buell to Lee, May 27, 1856, in Letters Sent 1800–1889, Document Files, Adjutant General's Office, Record Group 94, National Archives.

32. Parker, *Notes*, p. 214.

33. George F. Price, *Across the Continent with the Fifth Cavalry* (New York: Antiquarian Press, 1959), 45.

34. Robert E. Lee to his wife, August 4, 1856, in J. William Jones, *The Life and Letters of Robert E. Lee: Soldier and Man* (New York: Neale Publishing Company, 1906), 80.

35. Edmund Kirby Smith to his mother, July 31, 1856, Papers of Edmund Kirby Smith.

36. Scott to Secretary of War, May 8, 1857, in John William Jones, *Personal Reminiscences of General Robert E. Lee* (Richmond: United States Historical Society Press, 1989), 60.

37. Edmund Kirby Smith to his mother, September 1, 1856, Papers of Edmund Kirby Smith.

38. Ibid.

39. Order No. 3, San Antonio, September 19, 1856, in Orders and Circulars, 1797–1910, Document Files, Adjutant General's Office, Record Group 94, National Archives.

40. Albert Sidney Johnston to W. Johnston, December 24, 1856, in William Preston Johnston, *The Life of Albert Sidney Johnston* (New York: D. Appleton & Co., 1878), 193.

41. Johnston to William Preston Johnston, August 21, 1856, in Roland, *Johnston*, 183.

42. Smith says only "occasional straggling bands of Comanches from the Upper Red and Canadian Rivers depredate" upon the settlers. Edmund Kirby Smith to his mother, September 1, 1856, Papers of Edmund Kirby Smith.

43. Johnson, *Reminiscences*, 109.

44. General Order 14, Headquarters of the Army, November 13, 1857, describes this fight. See Eben Swift, *History*, 33 (note 20, above). For Johnson's account see Johnson, *Reminiscences*, 109–11. See also Price, *Across the Continent*, 54.

45. James Pike describes the Caddos finishing off the fallen Comanches in *Scout and Ranger: Being the Personal Adventures of James Pike of the Texas Rangers in 1859–60* (Princeton: Princeton University Press, 1932), 92.

4. "Tell Robert I Cannot Advise Him —— to Enter the Army" ——

1. See General Return, July 1, 1856, in Senate Executive Document 1856–1857, 34th Congress, 3rd Session, vol. I, pt. 2, 235. For the number of recruits who joined, see Adjutant General's Office Report of November 25, 1856, ibid., 249. For horses, see Martin L. Crimmins, ed., "Colonel J. K. F. Mansfield's Inspection Report of Texas," *Southwestern Historical Quarterly* 42, no. 2 (October 1938): 142.

2. Richard W. Johnson, *A Soldier's Reminiscences in Peace and War* (Philadelphia: J.B. Lippincott, 1886), 78.

3. Teresa Griffin Viele, *"Following the Drum": A Glimpse of Frontier Life* (New York: Rudd & Carleton, 1858), 106.

4. Johnston to Cooper, July 21, 1856, in Letters Received, 1805–1889, Document Files, Adjutant General's Office, Record Group 94, National Archives.

5. Heintzelman's diary, June 5, 1859, in Jerry Thompson, ed., *Fifty Miles and a Fight: Major Samuel Peter Heintzelman's Journal of Texas and the Cortina War* (Austin: Texas State Historical Association, 1998), 81.

6. Using the desertion figures provided in the Annual Returns and the April or May strengths, since this total represents the regiment's available manpower during the height of campaign season, yields 23 percent for 1857, 17 percent for 1858, 11 percent for 1859, and 15 percent for 1860. See Annual Returns 1855–1860 and Regimental Returns, 2nd U.S. Cavalry, Microfilm Copy No. M744, Roll 51, Record Group 94, National Archives.

7. The relevant documentation is Evans to Cooper, October 22, 1858; Witherell to Major, November 30, 1858; Lee to Major, November 17, 1858; in Letters Received, National Archives.

8. Douglas S. Freeman, *R. E. Lee*, vol. 1 (New York: Charles Scribner's Sons, 1934), 376.

9. Annual Returns 1855–1860 (see note 6, above). For the variety of sentences, see the comments in the regiment's Muster Rolls.

10. Robert Wooster, *Soldiers, Sutlers, and Settlers: Garrison Life on the Texas Frontier* (College Station: Texas A&M University Press, 1987), 84.

11. Crimmins, "Mansfield's Inspection Report" (note 1, above), *Southwestern Historical Quarterly* 42, no. 4 (April 1939): 371.

12. Smith to his mother, November 1, 1859, Papers of Edmund Kirby Smith, Southern Historical Collection, Manuscripts Department, Wilson Library, University of North Carolina, Chapel Hill.

13. This charming anecdote, provided by a widow of a soldier in Van Dorn's command, is cited in W. S. Nye, *Carbine and Lance: The Story of Old Fort Sill* (Norman: University of Oklahoma Press, 1969), 25.

14. Viele, *"Following the Drum,"* 138.

15. Smith to his mother, December 24, 1859, Papers of Edmund Kirby Smith.

16. Frederick Law Olmsted, *A Journey through Texas* (New York: Dix, Edward & Co., 1857), 497.

17. See "Pay of Officers," in Letter from the Secretary of War, February 4, 1856, Executive Documents, 34th Congress, 1st Session, 24–37.

18. Kenneth Franklin Neighbours, *Robert Simpson Neighbors and the Texas Frontier 1836–1859* (Waco: Texian Press, 1975), 210.

19. Lydia Spencer Lane, *I Married a Soldier* (Albuquerque: University of New Mexico Press, 1964), 30.

20. Olmsted, *Journey,* 317, relating a conversation with a barkeep at Eagle Pass.

21. Lee to W. H. F. Lee, May 30, 1858, in J. William Jones, *The Life and Letters of Robert E. Lee: Soldier and Man* (New York: Neale Publishing Company, 1906), 94.

22. Viele, *"Following the Drum,"* 106.

23. Lane, *I Married a Soldier,* 173.

24. Johnson, *Reminiscences,* 62.

25. Ibid., 69.

26. J. Evetts Haley, *Charles Goodnight: Cowman and Plainsman* (Norman: University of Oklahoma Press, 1949), 10.

27. Lane, *I Married a Soldier,* 86.

28. Ibid., 84.

29. James L. Nichols, *General Fitzhugh Lee: A Biography* (Lynchburg, Va.: H. E. Howard, 1989), 185 n. 61.

30. United States Senate, 1846, "Message from the President of the United States Communicating a Report of an Expedition Led by Lieutenant Abert, on the Upper Arkansas and through the Country of the Camanche Indians, in the Fall of the Year 1845," 29th Congress, 1st Session, 42ff.

31. William B. Parker, *Notes Taken through Unexplored Texas* (Austin: Texas State Historical Association, 1984), 111.

32. Olmsted, *Journey,* 288–89, 295–97.

33. Parker, *Notes,* 115.

34. Viele, *"Following the Drum,"* 121.

35. Van Dorn to his wife, May 1856, in E. V. Miller, ed., *A Soldier's Honor: With Reminiscences of Major-General Earl Van Dorn* (New York: Abbey Press, 1902), 339.

36. Morris W. Foster, *Being Comanche: A Social History of an American Indian Community* (Tucson: University of Arizona Press, 1991), 47.

37. Cited in Lena Clara Koch, "The Federal Indian Policy in Texas, 1845–1860," *Southwestern Historical Quarterly* 28, no. 4 (April 1925): 276.

38. Smith to his mother, September 28, 1852, Papers of Edmund Kirby Smith.

39. James K. Greer, ed., *Buck Barry: Texas Ranger and Frontiersman* (Lincoln: University of Nebraska Press, 1978), 100.

40. Cited in Thompson, *Fifty Miles*, 127 n. 31.

41. Nathaniel C. Hughes Jr., *General William J. Hardee* (Baton Rouge: Louisiana State University Press, 1965), 37.

42. J. W. Wilbarger, *Indian Depredations in Texas* (Austin: Steck Company, 1935), 598.

43. George Wythe Baylor, *Into the Far Wild Country* (El Paso: Texas Western Press, 1996), 159.

44. Parker, *Notes*, 217.

45. George F. Price, *Across the Continent with the Fifth Cavalry* (New York: Antiquarian Press, 1959), 38.

46. Smith to his mother, September 1, 1856, Papers of Edmund Kirby Smith.

47. Van Dorn to his wife, April 27, 1856, cited in Miller, *A Soldier's Honor*, 337.

48. Freeman, *R. E. Lee*, vol. 1, 365.

49. Cited in Fitzhugh Lee, *General Lee* (Wilmington, N.C.: Broadfoot Publishing Company, 1989), 84–85.

50. James Pike, *Scout and Ranger: Being the Personal Adventures of James Pike of the Texas Rangers in 1859–60* (Princeton: Princeton University Press, 1932), 58.

51. Lane, *I Married a Soldier*, 27.

52. Lee to his wife, October 3, 1856, in Jones, *Life*, 81.

53. Lee to his wife, December 27, 1856, ibid., 82–83.

54. Johnston to William Preston Johnston, August 21, 1856, in Charles C. Roland, *Albert Sidney Johnston, Soldier of Three Republics* (Austin: University of Texas Press, 1964), 181.

55. Price, *Across the Continent*, 38.

—— 5. Hood's Epic ——

1. Kenneth Franklin Neighbours, *Robert Simpson Neighbors and the Texas Frontier 1836–1859* (Waco: Texian Press, 1975), 153.

2. William B. Parker, *Notes Taken through Unexplored Texas* (Austin: Texas State Historical Association, 1984), 192.

3. George Wythe Baylor, *Into the Far Wild Country* (El Paso: Texas Western Press, 1996), 5.

4. Darius N. Couch, "George Stoneman," *Twenty-sixth Annual Reunion of the Association of the Graduates of the United States Military Academy . . . June 10, 1895* (Saginaw, Mich.: Seeman & Peters, 1895), 25.

5. See "Journey of the Leach Wagon Train across Texas, 1857," in Jesse Wallace Williams, *Old Texas Trails* (Burnet, Tex.: Eakin Press, 1979), 327–28.

6. Neighbours, *Neighbors*, 186.

7. Neighbors to Commissioner of Indian Affairs, September 16, 1857, in 35th Congress, 1st Session, 551.

8. Harold B. Simpson, *Cry Comanche: The 2nd U.S. Cavalry in Texas, 1855–1861* (Hillsboro, Tex.: Hill Junior College Press, 1979), 96.

9. Richard W. Johnson, *A Soldier's Reminiscences in Peace and War* (Philadelphia: J.B. Lippincott, 1886), 144.

10. For a good depiction of this, see Edwin Eastman, *Seven and Nine Years among the Camanches and Apaches* (Jersey City, N.J.: Clark Johnson, 1879).

11. James K. Greer, *Colonel Jack Hays: Texas Frontier Leader and California Builder* (College Station: Texas A&M University Press, 1987), 104.

12. Hays's testimony, included in the report of the Senate Military Committee, is reproduced in Charles T. Haven and Frank A. Belden, *A History of the Colt Revolver* (New York: William Morrow & Co., 1940), 304.

13. Ibid.

14. Harney's letter of November 8, 1850, ibid., 308.

15. Ibid., 309–10.

16. Neighbors to Twiggs, July 17, 1857, in Executive Documents, 35th Congress, 1st Session, 555.

17. John B. Hood, *Advance and Retreat: Personal Experiences in the United States and Confederate States Armies* (New Orleans, 1880), 8.

18. John P. Dyer, *The Gallant Hood* (New York: Bobbs-Merrill Company, 1950), 23.

19. Ibid., 26.

20. Hood, *Advance and Retreat*, 8.

21. United States Senate, 1846, "Message from the President of the United States Communicating a Report of an Expedition Led by Lieutenant Abert, on the Upper Arkansas and through the Country of the Camanche Indians, in the Fall of the Year 1845," 29th Congress, 1st Session, 55ff.

22. J. Evetts Haley, *Charles Goodnight: Cowman and Plainsman* (Norman: University of Oklahoma Press, 1949), 42.

23. Smith to his mother, September 1, 1857, Papers of Edmund Kirby Smith, Southern Historical Collection, Manuscripts Department, Wilson Library, University of North Carolina, Chapel Hill.

24. Simpson, *Cry Comanche*, 86.

25. Hood, *Advance and Retreat*, 11.

26. Herman Rost's account, in Simpson, *Cry Comanche*, 89.

27. Hood, *Advance and Retreat*, 13.

28. Ibid.

29. For a complete examination, see Eben Swift, "The Pistol, the Mellay and the Fight at Devil's River," *U.S. Cavalry Journal* 24, no. 99 (November 1913): 553–66. Swift does overstate his case a bit.

30. Sources for this battle are Hood, *Advance and Retreat*, 8–15; Hood's official report, "Hood to Phifer," July 27, 1857, T-189, 1857, Enclosure 1, Letters Sent 1800–1889, Document Files, Adjutant General's Office, Record Group 94, National Archives; Eben Swift, *The History of the Fifth U.S. Cavalry from March 3, 1855, to December 31, 1905*, 35, in Box 123, Oversized Document File, 1805–1917, Records of the Adjutant General's Office, 1780s–1917, Record Group 94, National Archives.

31. For a typical description of such a raid, see "Jones to Pease," September 22, 1855, in Dorman H. Winfrey and James M. Day, eds., *The Indian Papers of Texas and the Southwest: 1825–1916*, vol. 3 (Austin: Pemberton Press, 1966), 245.

32. James Pike, *Scout and Ranger: Being the Personal Adventures of James Pike of the Texas Rangers in 1859–60* (Princeton: Princeton University Press, 1932), 49.

33. Frederick Law Olmsted, *A Journey through Texas* (New York: Dix, Edward & Co., 1857), 298.

34. James K. Greer, ed., *Buck Barry: Texas Ranger and Frontiersman* (Lincoln: University of Nebraska Press, 1978), 131.

35. Lee to his wife, October 24, 1856, in Fitzhugh Lee, *General Lee* (Wilmington, N.C.: Broadfoot Publishing Company, 1989), 62.

36. Carl Coke Rister, *Robert E. Lee in Texas* (Norman: University of Oklahoma Press, 1946), 80.

37. Lee to his wife, April 26, 1857, in J. William Jones, *The Life and Letters of Robert E. Lee: Soldier and Man* (New York: Neale Publishing Company, 1906), 85–86.

38. Douglas S. Freeman, *R. E. Lee*, vol. 1 (New York: Charles Scribner's Sons, 1934), 375.

39. See General Returns of July 1, 1857, in Senate Executive Document, 35th Congress, 1st Session, 67.

40. Freeman, *R. E. Lee*, vol. 1, 378.

41. Hood, *Advance and Retreat*, 8.

42. The basis for this hypothesis comes from the compilation of cavalry engagements provided by Eben Swift. With increasing frequency, the results are "all their horses and camp equipage captured." See Eben Swift, *The History of the Fifth U.S. Cavalry from March 3, 1855, to December 31, 1905*, 32–46, in Box 123, Oversized Document File, 1805–1917, Records of the Adjutant General's Office, 1780s–1917, Record Group 94, National Archives.

—— 6. The Reputation of the Regiment ——

1. Frederick Law Olmsted, *A Journey through Texas* (New York: Dix, Edward & Co., 1857), 498.

2. William Preston Johnston, *The Life of Albert Sidney Johnston* (New York: D. Appleton & Co., 1878), 193.

3. Ibid., 194.

4. Johnston to Henrietta Johnston, March 27, 1857, in Charles C. Roland, *Albert Sidney Johnston, Soldier of Three Republics* (Austin: University of Texas Press, 1964), 184.

5. Johnson to Johnston, November 3, 1857, ibid.

6. "To the People of Utah," June 14, 1858, in Executive Documents, 35th Congress, 2nd Session, 121.

7. Johnston, *Life*, 725.

8. Roland, *Johnston*, 196.

9. Circular from Army Headquarters, January 11, 1858, in Executive Documents, 35th Congress, 2nd Session, 31.

10. McDowell to Johnston, April 2, 1858, in Executive Documents, 35th Congress, 2nd Session, 67.

11. Johnston to Henrietta Johnston, August 15, 1859, in Roland, *Johnston*, 236.

12. Wayne to Davis, May 14, 1856, in 34th Congress, 3rd Session, Senate Executive Document No. 62, 98.

13. "The Report of Edward Fitzgerald Beale to the Secretary of War," April 26, 1858, in Lewis B. Lesley, *Uncle Sam's Camels: The Journal of May Humphreys Stacey Supplemented by the Report of Edward Fitzgerald Beale* (Cambridge: Harvard University Press, 1929), 115.

14. DeLeon to Floyd, May 6, 1858, in Executive Documents, 35th Congress, 2nd Session, 456.

15. *Harper's Weekly*, January 24, 1857, 51, and September 12, 1857, 583.

16. Richard W. Johnson, *A Soldier's Reminiscences in Peace and War* (Philadelphia: J.B. Lippincott, 1886), 92.

17. General Orders, No. 19, August 16, 1859, in General Orders, Microfilm 1094, Roll 8, Record Group 94, National Archives.

18. Johnson, *Reminiscences*, 126.

19. Smith to his mother, September 1, 1856, Papers of Edmund Kirby Smith, Southern Historical Collection, Manuscripts Department, Wilson Library, University of North Carolina, Chapel Hill.

20. Olmsted, *Journey*, 308.

21. Journal of May Humphreys Stacey, June 30, 1857, in Lesley, *Uncle Sam's Camels*, 48.

22. Twiggs to Army Headquarters, January 13, 1858, in Executive Documents, 35th Congress, 2nd Session, 248.

23. Kenneth Franklin Neighbours, *Robert Simpson Neighbors and the Texas Frontier 1836–1859* (Waco: Texian Press, 1975), 199.

24. Some authorities assert that the Comanches rallied in their own defense because they feared that the soldiers had come to massacre them. This is what the Comanches themselves claimed the next day.

25. Withers to commanding officer at Fort Belknap, September 15, 1858, in Rupert N. Richardson, *The Comanche Barrier to South Plains Settlement* (Glendale, Calif.: Arthur H. Clark, 1933), 226.

26. *Dallas Herald*, August 21, 1858, in Judith Benner, *Sul Ross: Soldier, Statesman, Educator* (College Station: Texas A&M University Press, 1983), 24 n. 8.

27. Brooke to Scott, May 28, 1850, in Dorman H. Winfrey and James M. Day, eds., *The Indian Papers of Texas and the Southwest: 1825–1916*, vol. 3 (Austin: Pemberton Press, 1966), 119.

——— 7. Chastising the Indians ———

1. Cited in E. V. Miller, ed., *A Soldier's Honor: With Reminiscences of Major-General Earl Van Dorn* (New York: Abbey Press, 1902), 261.

2. Richard W. Johnson, *Memoirs of Major General George H. Thomas* (Philadelphia: J.B. Lippincott, 1881), 32–33.

3. For this warning, see Prince to Twiggs, August 9, 1858, in Report of the Secretary of War, Senate Executive Documents, 35th Congress, 2nd Session, 262.

4. For Van Dorn's orders, see Special Orders, No. 71, Headquarters Department of Texas, August 9, 1858, in Eben Swift, *The History of the Fifth U.S. Cavalry from March 3, 1855, to December 31, 1905*, 37, in Oversized Document File 1805–1917, Box 123, Records of the Adjutant General's Office 1780s–1917, Record Group 94, National Archives.

5. "Proceedings of a Board of Officers," February 18–19, 1858, in Charles T. Haven and Frank A. Belden, *A History of the Colt Revolver* (New York: William Morrow & Co., 1940), 372.

6. William B. Parker, *Notes Taken through Unexplored Texas* (Austin: Texas State Historical Association, 1984), 125–26.

7. Ferdinand Roemer's description, in Rupert N. Richardson, *The Comanche Barrier to South Plains Settlement* (Glendale, Calif.: Arthur H. Clark, 1933), 148.

8. William Y. Chalfant, *Without Quarter: The Wichita Expedition and the Fight on Crooked Creek* (Norman: University of Oklahoma Press, 1991), 42.

9. Van Dorn to his wife, October 12, 1858, in Robert G. Hartje, *Van Dorn: The Life and Times of a Confederate General* (Nashville: Vanderbilt University Press, 1967), 68.

10. Whiting to Prince, October 1, 1858, in Report of the Secretary of War, 35th Congress, 2nd Session, 271.

11. Van Dorn to Prince, October 5, 1858, Letters Received 1805–1889, Document Files, Adjutant General's Office, Microfilm 567, Record Group 94, National Archives.

12. Van Dorn to his wife, October 12, 1858, in Miller, *A Soldier's Honor*, 39.

13. Judith Benner, *Sul Ross: Soldier, Statesman, Educator* (College Station: Texas A&M University Press, 1983), 29.

14. Hardee to Van Dorn, November 4, 1858, in Hartje, *Van Dorn*, 69.

15. Twiggs to Thomas, October 22, 1858, Letters Received 1805–1889, Adjutant General's Office, Record Group 94, National Archives.

16. Twiggs to Army Headquarters, October 7 and 18, 1858, in Report of the Secretary of War, Senate Executive Documents, 35th Congress, 2nd Session, 267–68.

17. "The Recent Fight with the Comanches," *New York Weekly Times*, October 29, 1858, in Letters Received by the Office of the Adjutant General (Main Series) 1822–1860, Microfilm 567, Record Group 94, National Archives.

18. General Orders, No. 22, Headquarters of the Army, November 10, 1858, in Report of the Secretary of War, 35th Congress, 2nd Session, 26.

19. Twiggs to Thomas, December 18, 1858, Letters Received 1805–1889, Adjutant General's Office, Record Group 94, National Archives.

20. Twiggs to Lorenzo, November 18, 1858, Letters Received 1805–1889, Adjutant General's Office, Record Group 94, National Archives.

21. J. W. Wilbarger, *Indian Depredations in Texas* (Austin: Steck Company, 1935), 623.

22. *Clarksville Standard*, January 15, 1858, in Richardson, *Comanche Barrier*, 244.

23. Ryan to Runnels, November 13, 1858, in Dorman H. Winfrey and James M. Day, eds., *The Indian Papers of Texas and the Southwest: 1825–1916*, vol. 3 (Austin: Pemberton Press, 1966), 308.

24. Allen to Runnels, November 21, 1858, ibid., 309.

25. Kenneth Franklin Neighbours, *Robert Simpson Neighbors and the Texas Frontier 1836–1859* (Waco: Texian Press, 1975), 224.

26. Ibid., 227.

27. *Northern Standard*, June 12, 1859, in W. C. Holden, "Frontier Defense, 1846–1860," *West Texas State Historical Association Yearbook* 6 (June 1930): 62.

—— 8. "Near to Death's Door" ——

1. Van Dorn to Withers, December 28, 1858, Letters Received 1805–1889, Document Files, Adjutant General's Office, Record Group 94, National Archives.

2. Fitzhugh Lee to A. M. Fitzhugh, April 1, 1855, and September 15, 1858; Fitzhugh Lee to Maria Wheaton, September 1858, Papers of Fitzhugh Lee, Mss 8494, Special Collections, Alderman Library, University of Virginia, Charlottesville.

3. Van Dorn to Withers, December 28, 1858, Letters Received 1805–1889, Document Files, Adjutant General's Office, Record Group 94, National Archives.

4. William Burnett to his father, March 25, 1859, in Raymond Estep, ed., "Lieutenant Wm. E. Burnett: Notes on Removal of Indians from Texas to Indian Territory," *Chronicles of Oklahoma* 38, no. 3 (Autumn 1960): 291.

5. Edmund Kirby Smith to his mother, June 18 and July 31, 1858, Papers of Edmund Kirby Smith, Southern Historical Collection, Manuscripts Department, Wilson Library, University of North Carolina, Chapel Hill.

6. Edmund Kirby Smith to his mother, June 12, 1859, ibid.

7. For a vivid depiction of the campaign, see Edmund Kirby Smith's letters to his mother written during this time, beginning with his April 15, 1859, letter, written from Camp Radziminski.

8. Edmund Kirby Smith to his mother, June 2, 1859, Papers of Edmund Kirby Smith.

9. Van Dorn to Withers, May 31, 1859, Letters Received 1805–1889, Document Files, Adjutant General's Office, Record Group 94, National Archives.

10. Joseph B. Thoburn, "Indian Fight in Ford County," *Kansas Historical Collections* 12 (1911–12): 323.

11. Van Dorn to Withers, May 13, 1859, Letters Received 1805–1889, Document Files, Adjutant General's Office, Record Group 94, National Archives. Battle accounts are provided in Edmund Kirby Smith to Sidney Smith Lee, May 14, 1859, Papers of Edmund Kirby Smith; and Fitzhugh Lee to Mr. or Mrs. S. S. Lee, June 3, 1859, Papers of Fitzhugh Lee.

12. Thoburn, "Indian Fight," 325.

13. Fitzhugh Lee to Mr. or Mrs. S. S. Lee, June 3, 1859, Papers of Fitzhugh Lee.

14. Van Dorn to Withers, May 31, 1859, Letters Received 1805–1889, Document Files, Adjutant General's Office, Record Group 94, National Archives.

15. "Journey of the Leach Wagon Train across Texas, 1857," in Jesse Wallace Williams, *Old Texas Trails* (Burnet, Tex.: Eakin Press, 1979), 330.

16. Rupert N. Richardson, *The Comanche Barrier to South Plains Settlement* (Glendale, Calif.: Arthur H. Clark, 1933), 245.

17. J. W. Wilbarger, *Indian Depredations in Texas* (Austin: Steck Company, 1935), 441–42.

18. George Wythe Baylor, *Into the Far Wild Country* (El Paso: Texas Western Press, 1996), 149.

19. J. Evetts Haley, *Charles Goodnight: Cowman and Plainsman* (Norman: University of Oklahoma Press, 1949), 24.

20. James K. Greer, ed., *Buck Barry: Texas Ranger and Frontiersman* (Lincoln: University of Nebraska Press, 1978), 112.

21. Kenneth Franklin Neighbours, *Robert Simpson Neighbors and the Texas Frontier 1836–1859* (Waco: Texian Press, 1975), 239.

22. Haley, *Charles Goodnight*, 26.

23. Wilbarger, *Indian Depredations*, 442.

24. Burnett to his father, May 26, 1859, in Estep, "Burnett," 306. Burnett's letters provide a detailed, invaluable view of the conflict between Texans and the reserve Indians.

25. Thomas to Withers, May 26, 1859, Letters Received 1805–1889, Document Files, Adjutant General's Office, Record Group 94, National Archives.

26. Rupert N. Richardson, "The Comanche Reservation in Texas," *West Texas Historical Association Year Book* 5 (June 1929): 58.

27. Neighbours, *Neighbors*, 283.

28. W. W. Bent, in Report of October 5, 1859, Senate Executive Document No. 2, vol. I, 36th Congress, 1st Session, 506.

___ 9. Crisis on the Rio Grande ___

1. General Orders, No. 19, August 16, 1859, in General Orders, Microfilm 1094, Roll 8, Record Group 94, National Archives.

2. For examples, see Thomas to Assistant Adjutant General, December 15, 1859, Microfilm 3348, Record Group 94, National Archives.

3. Richard W. Johnson, *A Soldier's Reminiscences in Peace and War* (Philadelphia: J.B. Lippincott, 1886), 67.

4. "The Report of Edward Fitzgerald Beale to the Secretary of War," April 26, 1858, in Lewis B. Lesley, *Uncle Sam's Camels: The Journal of May Humphreys Stacey Supplemented by the Report of Edward Fitzgerald Beale* (Cambridge: Harvard University Press, 1929), 154–55.

5. *San Antonio Texan*, May 26, 1859, in Harold B. Simpson, *Cry Comanche: The 2nd U.S. Cavalry in Texas, 1855–1861* (Hillsboro, Tex.: Hill Junior College Press, 1979), 125.

6. Lucy A. Erath, "Memoirs of George Bernard Erath," *Southwestern Historical Quarterly* 27, no. 2 (October 1923): 155.

7. General Order No. 11, Headquarters of the Army, November 23, 1860, in George F. Price, *Across the Continent with the Fifth Cavalry* (New York: Antiquarian Press, 1959), 666.

8. The entire fascinating letter is provided in W. C. Holden, "Frontier Defense, 1846–1860," *West Texas State Historical Association Yearbook* 6 (June 1930): 65–66.

9. Twiggs to Secretary of War, November 12, 1859, in Clarence C. Clendenen, *Blood on the Border: The United States Army and the Mexican Irregulars* (Toronto: Macmillan Co., 1969), 24.

10. Diary entry, November 15, 1859, in Jerry Thompson, ed., *Fifty Miles and a Fight: Major Samuel Peter Heintzelman's Journal of Texas and the Cortina War* (Austin: Texas State Historical Association, 1998), 119.

11. Frederick Law Olmsted, *A Journey through Texas* (New York: Dix, Edward & Co., 1857), 318.

12. James Pike, *Scout and Ranger: Being the Personal Adventures of James Pike of the Texas Rangers in 1859–60* (Princeton: Princeton University Press, 1932), 21–22.

13. Heintzelman diary, December 31, 1859, in Thompson, *Fifty Miles*, 162.

14. Houston to Floyd, April 24, 1860, ibid., 208 n.4.

15. Stoneman to Heintzelman, December 29, 1859, ibid., 157 n.54.

16. Carl Coke Rister, *Robert E. Lee in Texas* (Norman: University of Oklahoma Press, 1946), 113.

17. Lee to Cooper, March 12, 1860, Letters Received 1805–1889, Document Files, Adjutant General's Office, Record Group 94, National Archives.

18. Lee to G. W. Custis Lee, March 13, 1860, in John William Jones, *The Life and Letters of Robert E. Lee: Soldier and Man* (New York: Neale Publishing Co., 1906), 110.

19. Rister, *Lee in Texas*, 120.

20. Lee to Treviño, April 2, 1860, in Jones, *Life and Letters*, 111.

21. Lee to Garcia, April 12, 1860, and Lee to Custis Lee, April 16, 1860, ibid., 111–14.

22. Fitzhugh Lee to A. M. Fitzhugh, September 1, 1859, Papers of Fitzhugh Lee, Mss 8494, Special Collections, Alderman Library, University of Virginia, Charlottesville.

23. Edmund Kirby Smith to his mother, November 1, 1859, Papers of Edmund Kirby Smith, Southern Historical Collection, Manuscripts Department, Wilson Library, University of North Carolina, Chapel Hill.

24. Edmund Kirby Smith to his mother, December 24, 1859, ibid.

25. Edmund Kirby Smith to his mother, December 24, 1859, and January 15, 1860, ibid.

26. Lee's extended account appeared in the *National Intelligencer* as "a letter of a young lieutenant of cavalry to a lady relative," dated September 22, 1859, from Camp Colorado. It is in microfilm M 1829 P, Special Collections, Alderman Library, University of Virginia, Charlottesville. Hayes's account, provided by M. L. Crimmins, is reproduced in Simpson, *Cry Comanche*, 146–47. Where Simpson's and my accounts differ, I have relied upon Lee. Smith's account is in Edmund Kirby Smith to his mother, January 15, 1860, Papers of Edmund Kirby Smith.

—— 10. Twiggs's Treachery ——

1. Mrs. Frances K. Smith to Edmund K. Smith, January 11, 1860, and Smith to his mother, January 28, 1860, Papers of Edmund Kirby Smith, Southern Historical Collection, Manuscripts Department, Wilson Library, University of North Carolina, Chapel Hill.

2. Burleson to Houston, March 4, 1860, in Dorman H. Winfrey and James M. Day, eds., *The Indian Papers of Texas and the Southwest: 1825–1916*, vol. 4 (Austin: Pemberton Press, 1966), 22.

3. Edmund Kirby Smith to his mother, October 2, 1860, Papers of Edmund Kirby Smith.

4. Richard W. Johnson, *Memoirs of Major General George H. Thomas* (Philadelphia: J.B. Lippincott, 1881), 34. For Thomas's report, see Thomas to Lee, August 31, 1860, in R. C. Crane, "Major George H. Thomas on the Trail of Indians in 1860," *West Texas Historical Association Year Book* 20 (October 1944): 80–83. For Lee's report, see Martin L. Crimmins, "Colonel Robert E. Lee's Report on Indian Combats in Texas," *Southwestern Historical Quarterly* 39, no. 3 (July 1935): 31.

5. Judith Benner, *Sul Ross: Soldier, Statesman, Educator* (College Station: Texas A&M University Press, 1983), 49.

6. Ibid., 44.

7. J. Evetts Haley, *Charles Goodnight: Cowman and Plainsman* (Norman: University of Oklahoma Press, 1949), 55.

8. J. W. Wilbarger, *Indian Depredations in Texas* (Austin: Steck Co., 1935), 337.

9. Benner, *Sul Ross*, 57.

10. Wilbarger, *Indian Depredations*, 339.

11. Ford to Runnels, June 2, 1858, in Winfrey and Day, *Indian Papers*, vol. 5, 242–43.

12. Charles Anderson, *Texas before and on the Eve of the Rebellion* (Cincinnati: Peter G. Thomson, 1884), 5.

13. Lea to Houston, February 24, 1859, in Roy Syvan Dunn, "The KGC in Texas 1860–1861," *Southwestern Historical Quarterly* 70 (April 1967): 549.

14. Heintzelman diary, December 19, 1860, in Jerry Thompson, ed., *Fifty Miles and a Fight: Major Samuel Peter Heintzelman's Journal of Texas and the Cortina War* (Austin: Texas State Historical Association, 1998), 303.

15. Anderson, *Texas*, 42.

16. Edmund Kirby Smith to his mother, November 10, 1860, Papers of Edmund Kirby Smith.

17. General Orders, No. 5, Adjutant General's Office, March 1, 1861, in *War of the Rebellion: Official Records of the Union and Confederate Armies*, ser. 1, vol. 1 (Washington, D.C.: Government Printing Office, 1880), 597.

18. Richard W. Johnson, *A Soldier's Reminiscences in Peace and War* (Philadelphia: J.B. Lippincott, 1886), 133.

19. Caroline Baldwin Darrow, "Recollections of the Twiggs Surrender," in *Battles and Leaders of the Civil War*, vol. 1. (Edison, N.J.: Castle, n.d.), 36.

20. Anderson, *Texas*, 24.

21. Return of February 26, 1861, Returns from Regular Army Cavalry Regiments 1833–1916, M744, 5th Cavalry, March 1855–December 1863, Microfilm Roll 51, Adjutant General's Office, Record Group 94, National Archives.

22. Commissioners' Circular, February 18, 1861, in *Official Records* (see note 17, above), vol. 1, 516.

23. Report of Captain E. Kirby Smith, March 1, 1861, in ibid., 559.

24. Edmund Kirby Smith to his mother, March 25, 1861, Papers of Edmund Kirby Smith.

25. Burleson to Johnson, February 24, 1861, in *Official Records*, vol. 1, 595.

26. Waul to Davis, March 26, 1861, in ibid., 615.

27. For Van Dorn's orders, see Cooper to Van Dorn, April 11, 1861, in ibid., 623.

28. Van Dorn to his wife, April 14, 1861, in E. V. Miller, ed., *A Soldier's Honor: With Reminiscences of Major-General Earl Van Dorn* (New York: Abbey Press, 1902), 47.

29. Mrs. Samuel Posey, "Capture of the *Star of the West*," *Confederate Veteran* 32 (May 1924): 174.

30. Anderson, *Texas*, 51.

31. George Wythe Baylor, *Into the Far Wild Country* (El Paso: Texas Western Press, 1996), 191.

32. Johnson, *Reminiscences*, 156.

33. Ibid., 159.

⎯⎯ 11. Cradle of Leadership ⎯⎯

1. Lee to Scott, April 20, 1861, in Fitzhugh Lee, *General Lee* (Wilmington, N.C.: Broadfoot Publishing Company, 1989), 88.

2. Richard W. Johnson, *A Soldier's Reminiscences in Peace and War* (Philadelphia: J.B. Lippincott, 1886), 161.

3. Joseph H. Parks, *General Edmund Kirby Smith C.S.A.* (Baton Rouge: Louisiana State University Press, 1954), 128.

4. J. Evetts Haley, *Charles Goodnight: Cowman and Plainsman* (Norman: University of Oklahoma Press, 1949), 64.

5. Lucy A. Erath, "Memoirs of George Bernard Erath," *Southwestern Historical Quarterly* 27, no. 2 (October 1923): 157.

6. Kenneth Franklin Neighbours, *Robert Simpson Neighbors and the Texas Frontier 1836–1859* (Waco: Texian Press, 1975), 291.

7. The First Dragoons, organized in 1833, became the First Cavalry; the Second Dragoons, organized in 1836, the Second Cavalry; the Mounted Rifles, organized in 1846, the Third Cavalry; the First Cavalry, organized, like the Second, in 1855, became the Fourth Cavalry. A newly raised regiment, organized in 1861, became the Sixth Cavalry. These six regular regiments made up only a small percentage of cavalry total, which rose to about eighty thousand by war's end.

8. John Esten Cooke, *Wearing the Gray* (New York: E.B. Treat & Co., 1867), 177.

9. Harry M. Henderson, *Texas in the Confederacy* (San Antonio: Naylor Co., 1955), 12.

10. W. H. Hitchcock, "Recollections of a Participant in the Charge," in *Battles and Leaders of the Civil War*, vol. 2 (New York: Thomas Yoseloff, 1956), 346.

11. Merritt's statement is in John K. Herr and Edward S. Wallace, *The Story of the U.S. Cavalry 1775–1942* (Boston: Little, Brown, and Co., 1953), 124. Also see Merritt to Headquarters, February 28, 1864, in *War of the Rebellion: Official Records of the Union and Confederate Armies*, ser. I, vol. 11, part 2 (Washington, D.C.: Government Printing Office, 1884), 43. For the Porter-Cooke controversy, see Fitz John Porter, "Hanover Court House and Gaines's Mill," *Battles and Leaders of the Civil War*, vol. 2, 319–43, and Philip St. George Cooke, "The Charge of Cooke's Cavalry at Gaines's Mill," ibid., 344–46.

12. James K. Greer, ed., *Buck Barry: Texas Ranger and Frontiersman* (Lincoln: University of Nebraska Press, 1978), 132.

13. Wells to Houston, February 16, 1860, in Dorman H. Winfrey and James M. Day, eds., *The Indian Papers of Texas and the Southwest: 1825–1916*, vol. 4 (Austin: Pemberton Press, 1966), 11.

14. Greer, *Buck Barry*, 103.

15. Rupert N. Richardson, "The Comanche Reservation in Texas," *West Texas Historical Association Year Book* 5 (June 1929): 58.

16. Jacob D. Cox, *Military Reminiscences of the Civil War*, vol. 1 (New York: Charles Scribner's Sons, 1900), 174–75.

17. Edmund Kirby Smith to his mother, October 2, 1860, Papers of Edmund Kirby Smith, Southern Historical Collection, Manuscripts Department, Wilson Library, University of North Carolina, Chapel Hill.

18. John B. Hood, *Advance and Retreat: Personal Experiences in the United States and Confederate States Armies* (New Orleans, 1880), 8.

19. Johnson, *Reminiscences*, 280.

20. Johnson to Couch, December 7, 1894, in Darius N. Couch, "George Stoneman," in *Twenty-sixth Annual Reunion of the Association of the Graduates of the United States Military Academy . . . June 10, 1895* (Saginaw, Mich.: Seeman & Peters, 1895), 27.

21. Martin L. Crimmins, ed., "Colonel J. K. F. Mansfield's Inspection Report of Texas," *Southwestern Historical Quarterly* 42, no. 4 (April 1939): 373.

22. William Preston Johnston, *The Life of Albert Sidney Johnston* (New York: D. Appleton & Co., 1878), 291.

Bibliography

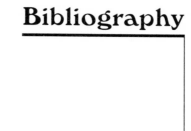

—— Manuscript Sources ——

National Archives—Adjutant General's Office, Document Files, Record Group 94
Letters Sent, 1800–1889.
Letters Received, 1805–1889.
Muster Rolls of Regular Army Organizations 1784–1912, Second Cavalry 1856–60.
Orders and Circulars, 1797–1910.
Record of Regulations and Orders Received from the Secretary of War, May 31, 1821–July 17, 1829.
Returns from Regular Army Cavalry Regiments 1833–1916, M 744, Fifth Cavalry, March 1855–December 1863, Microfilm Roll 51.
Swift, Eben. *The History of the Fifth U.S. Cavalry from March 3, 1855, to December 31, 1905.* Oversized Document File, 1805–1917, Box 123, Records of the Adjutant General's Office, 1780s–1917.
Southern Historical Collection, Manuscripts Department, Wilson Library, University of North Carolina, Chapel Hill
Papers of Edmund Kirby Smith.
Special Collections, Alderman Library, University of Virginia, Charlottesville.
Typescript of the Roster from Register of the United States Army for 1860 (Second Regiment of Cavalry) and 1861 (Fifth Regiment of Cavalry), Mss 38–269 (boxed with 38–252).
Letters of Robert E. Lee, Mss 990-b 1085.
Papers of Fitzhugh Lee, Mss 8494.
Papers of William Gordon McCabe, Mss 38–269.

—— Published Sources ——

Anderson, Charles. *Texas before and on the Eve of the Rebellion.* Cincinnati: Peter G. Thomson, 1884.
Arnold, James R. *Presidents under Fire: Commanders in Chief in Victory and Defeat.* New York: Crown Publishers, 1994.

Arnold, James R., and Roberta Wiener. *The American West: Living the Frontier Dream.* London: Blandford Press, 1996.

Ballenger, T. L. "Colonel Albert Sidney Johnston's March through Indian Territory in 1855." *Chronicles of Oklahoma* 47 (Summer 1969): 132–37.

Barrett, Arrie. "Transportation, Supplies, and Quarters for the West Texas Frontier under the Federal Military System 1848–1861." *West Texas Historical Association Year Book* 5 (June 1929): 95–108.

Baylor, George Wythe. *Into the Far Wild Country.* El Paso: Texas Western Press, 1996.

Beall, John B. *In Barracks and Field.* Dallas: Smith & Lamar, 1906.

Benner, Judith. *Sul Ross: Soldier, Statesman, Educator.* College Station: Texas A&M University Press, 1983. Well-researched, entertaining read about a fascinating figure.

Bollaert, William. *William Bollaert's Texas.* Edited by W. Eugene Hollon and Ruth Lapham Butler. Norman: University of Oklahoma Press, 1956.

Boniface, John J. *The Cavalry Horse and His Pack.* Kansas City, Mo.: Hudson-Kimberly Publishing Co., 1903.

Brackett, Albert G. *History of the United States Cavalry.* New York: Argonaut Press, 1965.

Braman, D. E. E. *Information about Texas.* Philadelphia: J.B. Lippincott & Co., 1857.

Buenger, Walter L. *Secession and the Union in Texas.* Austin: University of Texas Press, 1984.

Canales, Jose T., and Charles W. Goldfinch. *Juan N. Cortina: Two Interpretations.* New York: Arno Press, 1974.

Chalfant, William Y. *Without Quarter: The Wichita Expedition and the Fight on Crooked Creek.* Norman: University of Oklahoma Press, 1991.

Clendenen, Clarence C. *Blood on the Border: The United States Army and the Mexican Irregulars.* Toronto: Macmillan Co., 1969.

Cooke, John Esten. *Wearing the Gray.* New York: E. B. Treat & Co., 1867.

Cooke, Philip St. George. "The Charge of Cooke's Cavalry at Gaines's Mill." In *Battles and Leaders of the Civil War.* vol. 2. New York: Thomas Yoseloff, 1956.

Couch, Darius N. "George Stoneman." In *Twenty-sixth Annual Reunion of the Association of the Graduates of the United States Military Academy . . . June 10, 1895.* Saginaw, Mich.: Seeman & Peters, 1895.

Cox, Jacob D. *Military Reminiscences of the Civil War.* 2 vols. New York: Charles Scribner's Sons, 1900.

Crane, R. C. "Major George H. Thomas on the Trail of Indians in 1860." *West Texas Historical Association Year Book* 20 (October 1944): 77–85.

Crimmins, Martin L. "Colonel Robert E. Lee's Report on Indian Combats in Texas." *Southwestern Historical Quarterly* 39, no. 3 (July 1935): 21–33.

———. "First Sergeant John W. Spangler, Company H, Second United States Cavalry." *West Texas Historical Association Year Book* 26 (October 1950): 68–75.

———. "Major Van Dorn in Texas." *Southwestern Historical Quarterly* 16 (October 1940): 121–29.

———. "The Military History of Camp Colorado." *West Texas Historical Association Year Book* 28 (October 1952): 71–80.

———, ed. "Colonel J. K. F. Mansfield's Inspection Report of Texas." *Southwestern Historical Quarterly* 42, no. 2 (October 1938): 122–48; no. 4 (April 1939): 351–87.

Current, Richard N., ed. *Encyclopedia of the Confederacy.* New York: Simon & Schuster, 1993.

Darrow, Caroline Baldwin. "Recollections of the Twiggs Surrender." In *Battles and Leaders of the Civil War.* vol. 1. Edison, N.J.: Castle, n.d.

Davis, Jefferson. *The Rise and Fall of the Confederate Government.* 2 vols. New York: Da Capo Press, 1990. Reprint of the 1881 original.

Davis, William C. *Three Roads to the Alamo.* New York: HarperCollins, 1998.

———, ed. *The Confederate General.* Harrisburg, Pa.: National Historical Society, 1991.

De Bruhl, Marshall. *Sword of San Jacinto: A Life of Sam Houston.* New York: Random House, 1993.

De Shields, James T. *Cynthia Ann Parker: The Story of Her Capture.* St. Louis: Chas. B. Woodward Printing, 1886.

Dolbeare, Benjamin. *A Narrative of the Captivity and Suffering of Dolly Webster among the Camanche Indians in Texas.* New Haven: Yale University Press, 1986.

Dunn, Roy Syvan. "The KGC in Texas 1860–1861." *Southwestern Historical Quarterly* 70 (April 1967): 543–73.

Dyer, John P. *The Gallant Hood.* New York: Bobbs-Merrill Co., 1950.

Eastman, Edwin. *Seven and Nine Years among the Camanches and Apaches.* Jersey City, N.J.: Clark Johnson, 1879.

Erath, Lucy A. "Memoirs of George Bernard Erath." *Southwestern Historical Quarterly* 27, no. 2 (October 1923): 140–63.

Estep, Raymond, ed. "Lieutenant Wm. E. Burnett: Notes on Removal of Indians from Texas to Indian Territory." Parts 1–3. *Chronicles of Oklahoma* 38, no. 3 (Autumn 1960): 274–309; no. 4 (Winter 1960): 369–96; 39, no. 1 (Spring 1961): 15–41.

Fallwell, Gene. *The Comanche Trail of Thunder and the Massacre at Parker's Fort.* Booklet published by the author, 1960.

Foreman, Grant, ed. *Adventure on Red River: Report on the Exploration of the Headwaters of the Red River by Captain Randolph B. Marcy and Captain G. B. McClellan.* Norman: University of Oklahoma Press, 1937.

Foster, Morris W. *Being Comanche: A Social History of an American Indian Community.* Tucson: University of Arizona Press, 1991.

Frazer, Robert Walter. *Forts of the West: Military Posts and Presidios and Posts Commonly Called Forts West of the Mississippi River to 1898.* Norman: University of Oklahoma Press, 1972.

Freeman, Douglas S. *R. E. Lee.* vol. 1. New York: Charles Scribner's Sons, 1934.

Greer, James. K. *Colonel Jack Hays: Texas Frontier Leader and California Builder.* College Station: Texas A&M University Press, 1987.

————, ed. *Buck Barry: Texas Ranger and Frontiersman*. Lincoln: University of Nebraska Press, 1978. A candid account of frontier brutality.

Haley, J. Evetts. *Charles Goodnight: Cowman and Plainsman*. Norman: University of Oklahoma Press, 1949.

Hartje, Robert G. *Van Dorn: The Life and Times of a Confederate General*. Nashville: Vanderbilt University Press, 1967.

Haven, Charles T., and Frank A. Belden. *A History of the Colt Revolver*. New York: William Morrow & Co. 1940.

Havins, Thomas R. *Beyond the Cimarron*. Brownwood, Tex.: Moore Printing Co., 1968.

Henderson, Harry M. *Texas in the Confederacy*. San Antonio: Naylor Co., 1955.

Herr, John K., and Edward S. Wallace. *The Story of the U.S. Cavalry 1775–1942*. Boston: Little, Brown, and Co., 1953.

Hitchcock, W. H. "Recollections of a Participant in the Charge." In *Battles and Leaders of the Civil War*. vol. 2. New York: Thomas Yoseloff, 1956.

Holden, W. C. "Frontier Defense, 1846–1860." *West Texas State Historical Association Yearbook* 6 (June 1930): 39–71.

Hood, John B. *Advance and Retreat: Personal Experiences in the United States and Confederate States Armies*. New Orleans: n.p., 1880.

Hughes, Nathaniel C., Jr. *General William J. Hardee*. Baton Rouge: Louisiana State University Press, 1965.

Johnson, Richard W. *Memoirs of Major General George H. Thomas*. Philadelphia: J.B. Lippincott, 1881.

————. *A Soldier's Reminiscences in Peace and War*. Philadelphia: J.B. Lippincott, 1886.

Johnston, William Preston. *The Life of Albert Sidney Johnston*. New York: D. Appleton & Co., 1878.

Jones, John William. *The Life and Letters of Robert E. Lee: Soldier and Man*. New York: Neale Publishing Co., 1906.

————. *Personal Reminiscences of General Robert E. Lee*. Richmond: United States Historical Society Press, 1989.

"Journal of the Campaign of the Regiment of Dragoons for the Summer of 1834." In *United States Senate Documents*, 23rd Congress, 2nd Session (1834), 73–93.

Kavanagh, Thomas W. *Comanche Political History: An Ethnohistorical Perspective*. Lincoln: University of Nebraska Press, 1996.

Koch, Lena Clara. "The Federal Indian Policy in Texas, 1845–1860." Parts 1–3. *Southwestern Historical Quarterly* 28, no. 4 (April 1925): 259–86; 29, no. 1 (July 1925): 19–35; 29, no. 2 (October 1925): 101–27.

Lambert, Joseph I. *One Hundred Years with the Second Cavalry: By the Commanding Officer, Second Cavalry*. Fort Riley, Kans.: Capper Printing Co., 1939. The history of the Second Dragoons.

Lane, Lydia Spencer. *I Married a Soldier*. Albuquerque: University of New Mexico Press, 1964. Lane's husband served in the Mounted Rifles. Her evident pleasure with frontier army life makes this a fun read.

Lee, Fitzhugh. *General Lee.* Wilmington, N.C.: Broadfoot Publishing Company, 1989. Reprint of the 1894 original.

Lesley, Lewis B. *Uncle Sam's Camels: The Journal of May Humphreys Stacey Supplemented by the Report of Edward Fitzgerald Beale.* Cambridge: Harvard University Press, 1929.

Lowe, Percival G. *Five Years a Dragoon.* Norman: University of Oklahoma Press, 1965.

Lowe, Richard, ed. *A Texas Cavalry Officer's Civil War.* Baton Rouge: Louisiana State University Press, 1999.

Marcy, Randolph B. *Thirty Years of Army Life on the Border.* New York, 1866. He surveyed the Indian reservations in Texas.

Matthews, Jay A., Jr. "The Second U.S. Cavalry in Texas, 1855–1861." *Military History of Texas and the Southwest* 11 (1973): 229–31.

McChristian, Douglas C. *The U.S. Army in the West 1870–1880.* Norman: University of Oklahoma Press, 1995.

Merrill, James M. *Spurs to Glory: The Story of the United States Cavalry.* Chicago: Rand McNally & Co., 1966.

"Message from the President of the United States Communicating a Report of an Expedition Led by Lieutenant Abert, on the Upper Arkansas and through the Country of the Camanche Indians, in the Fall of the Year 1845." In *United States Senate Documents,* 29th Congress, 1st session (1846): 438–513.

Miller, E. V., ed. *A Soldier's Honor: With Reminiscences of Major-General Earl Van Dorn.* New York: Abbey Press, 1902.

Morrison, James L., Jr. *"The Best School in the World": West Point, the Pre–Civil War Years 1833–1866.* Kent, Ohio: Kent State University Press, 1986.

Neighbours, Kenneth Franklin. *Robert Simpson Neighbors and the Texas Frontier 1836–1859.* Waco: Texian Press, 1975.

Newcombe, W. W. *The Indians of Texas.* Austin: University of Texas Press, 1961.

Nichols, James L. *General Fitzhugh Lee: A Biography.* Lynchburg, Va.: H.E. Howard, 1989.

Nye, W. S. *Carbine and Lance: The Story of Old Fort Sill.* Norman: University of Oklahoma Press, 1969.

Olmsted, Frederick Law. *A Journey through Texas.* New York: Dix, Edward & Co., 1857.

Paris, Compte de. *History of the Civil War in America.* vol. 1. Philadelphia: Porter & Coates, 1875.

Parker, William B. *Notes Taken through Unexplored Texas.* Austin: Texas State Historical Association, 1984.

Parks, Joseph H. *General Edmund Kirby Smith C.S.A.* Baton Rouge: Louisiana State University Press, 1954.

Pike, James. *Scout and Ranger: Being the Personal Adventures of James Pike of the Texas Rangers in 1859–60.* Princeton: Princeton University Press, 1932. A reprint of the 1865 account of a rarity, a northern-born Texas Ranger who went north when the war began.

Posey, Mrs. Samuel. "Capture of the *Star of the West.*" *Confederate Veteran* 32 (May 1924): 174.

Price, George F. *Across the Continent with the Fifth Cavalry.* New York: Antiquarian Press, 1959.

Radzyminski, Stanley F. "Charles Radziminski: Patriot, Exile, Pioneer." *Chronicles of Oklahoma* 38, no. 4 (Winter 1960): 354–68.

Richardson, Rupert N. *The Comanche Barrier to South Plains Settlement.* Glendale, Calif., Arthur H. Clark, 1933.

———. "The Comanche Reservation in Texas." *West Texas Historical Association Year Book* 5 (June 1929): 47–71.

———. "Some Details of the Southern Overland Mail." *Southwestern Historical Quarterly* 29, no. 1 (July 1925): 1–18.

Rippy, J. Fred. "Border Trouble along the Rio Grande 1848–1860." *Southwestern Historical Quarterly* 23, no. 2 (October 1919): 104.

Rister, Carl Coke. *Robert E. Lee in Texas.* Norman: University of Oklahoma Press, 1946.

Robbins, Richard C., and Charles P. Rolland, eds. "The Diary of Eliza (Mrs. Albert Sidney) Johnston." *Southwestern Historical Quarterly* 60, no. 4 (April 1957): 463–500.

Roland, Charles C. *Albert Sidney Johnston, Soldier of Three Republics.* Austin: University of Texas Press, 1964.

Rowland, Dunbar, ed. *Jefferson Davis, Constitutionalist: His Letters, Papers, and Speeches.* vol. 2. Jackson: Mississippi Department of Archives and History, 1923.

Sawicki, James A. *Cavalry Regiments of the U.S. Army.* Dumfries, Va.: Wyvern Publications, 1985.

Sherman, William Tecumseh. *Memoirs of General W. T. Sherman.* New York: Library of America, 1990.

Simpson, Harold B. *Cry Comanche: The 2nd U.S. Cavalry in Texas, 1855–1861.* Hillsboro, Tex.: Hill Junior College Press, 1979.

———, ed. *Frontier Forts of Texas.* Waco: Texian Press, 1966.

Steffen, Randy. *The Horse Soldier.* vol. 2. Norman: University of Oklahoma Press, 1978.

Strode, Hudson. *Jefferson Davis: American Patriot, 1808–1861.* 3 vols. New York: Harcourt, Brace & Co., 1955–64.

Swift, Eben. "The Pistol, the Mellay and the Fight at Devil's River." *U.S. Cavalry Journal* 24, no. 99 (November 1913): 553–66.

Thoburn, Joseph B. "Indian Fight in Ford County." *Kansas Historical Collections* 12 (1911–12): 312–29.

Thomas, Wilbur. *General George H. Thomas: The Indomitable Warrior.* New York: Exposition Books, 1964.

Thompson, Jerry. *Sabers on the Rio Grande.* Austin: Presidial Press, 1974.

———, ed. *Fifty Miles and a Fight: Major Samuel Peter Heintzelman's Journal of Texas and the Cortina War.* Austin: Texas State Historical Association, 1998.

United States Senate. Executive Documents, 34th Congress, 3rd session, and 35th Congress, 1st Session, 1856–57.

United States War Department. *War of the Rebellion: Official Records of the Union and Confederate Armies.* Washington, D.C.: Government Printing Office, 1880.

Utley, Robert M. *The Indian Frontier of the American West 1846–1890.* Albuquerque: University of New Mexico Press, 1984.

Van Horne, Thomas B. *The Life of Major-General George H. Thomas.* New York: Charles Scribner's Sons, 1882.

Viele, Teresa Griffin. *"Following the Drum": A Glimpse of Frontier Life.* New York: Rudd & Carleton, 1858.

Waugh, John C. *The Class of 1846.* New York: Warner Books, 1994.

Wilbarger, J. W. *Indian Depredations in Texas.* Austin: Steck Co., 1935. Reprint of the 1889 original.

Williams, Jesse Wallace. *Old Texas Trails.* Burnet, Tex.: Eakin Press, 1979.

Wilson, R. L. *Colt: An American Legend.* New York: Abbeville Press, 1985.

Winfrey, Dorman H., and James M. Day, eds. *The Indian Papers of Texas and the Southwest: 1825–1916.* vols. 3–5. Austin: Pemberton Press, 1966.

Wooster, Robert. *Soldiers, Sutlers, and Settlers: Garrison Life on the Texas Frontier.* College Station: Texas A&M University Press, 1987.

Wormser, Richard. *The Yellowlegs: The Story of the United States Cavalry.* Garden City, N.Y.: Doubleday & Co., 1966.

Index